London Religious Tract Society

Mexico

The Country, History and People

London Religious Tract Society

Mexico
The Country, History and People

ISBN/EAN: 9783337227425

Printed in Europe, USA, Canada, Australia, Japan

Cover: Foto ©Andreas Hilbeck / pixelio.de

More available books at **www.hansebooks.com**

PREFACE.

There is very much in Central America to claim our attention, and excite our interest. First, perhaps, in importance may be placed its commanding geographical position. The rapid extension of commercial enterprise, the opening up of China and Japan to European intercourse, and the discovery of the goldfields of California, Australia, and British Columbia, combine to make the Isthmus of Panama, with the adjacent territories, a great highway for commerce, the value of which it would be difficult to exaggerate. The communications between Europe and the eastern shores of America on the one hand, and the densely-peopled empires, and rapidly-growing settlements of the Pacific on the other, must be carried on either across some part of Central America, or by the tedious and perilous circumnavigation of Cape Horn, or the Cape of Good Hope.* Hitherto the anarchy which

---

* For reasons upon which we need not enter here, the Suez route is left out of account as being, probably, visionary and impracticable.

has prevailed in these Central American Republics has prevented the full development of the immense facilities afforded by the Panama route. But even in spite of the political and social confusion which have proved so disastrous, that route is rapidly rising in importance; and the whole civilised world is too deeply interested in securing a safe and speedy communication between the Atlantic and Pacific to allow such obstructions to block up the way much longer. It was the dream of Columbus, when he set sail for America, that he should discover a new and easy passage to the far-off regions of the East. The establishment of order in Mexico, and the adjacent republics, will fulfil that dream, and make the Isthmus of Panama the gateway of the Pacific.

But Mexico has other claims besides that afforded by its commanding geographical position. Its extraordinary geological conformation, and the strange convulsions and upheavings of its mountain-chains, continuing down to the present day, rivet the attention of the geologist. The student of natural history reads with wonder of the richness, strangeness, and variety of its fauna and flora. The antiquarian seeks to penetrate the mystery which hangs over the Cyclopean ruins which encumber the soil—the sole relics of Aztec or Toltec civilisation, or which, perchance, bear witness to the existence of yet earlier races, of which the very names are forgotten. The merchant, too, thinks of Mexico not only as his future highway to regions which lie beyond, but anticipates the time when the mineral wealth of its mountain ranges, and the exuberant fertility of its sunny plains, and well-watered valleys, shall be laid under tribute to increase the wealth of the world.

Nor can the Christian think of those vast regions, now "sitting in darkness and the shadow of death," without a sad and mournful interest. We claim them as forming part of the domains of the world's true King, and long for the time when Satan, who now reigns there with a scarcely questioned supremacy, shall be dethroned and cast out. Nor shall our hopes be vain. The mighty fabrics of imposture and superstition, which so long have dominated over that unhappy land, shall be demolished, and the kingdom of righteousness and peace shall be established on their riuins. The traveller in the depths of Mexican forests comes ever and anon to ruined temples, where the hdeous idol has fallen from its shrine, the blood-stained altar is overthrown, and the massive walls, which once witnessed the foul and murderous orgies of Aztec worship, are rent asunder by some mighty and irresistible agency. What is the power which has triumphed over edifices, the colossal grandeur of which might vie with those of Ancient Egypt? It has not been by the throes of the earthquake, or the fires of the volcano, or the more destructive assaults of man, that the ruin has been wrought. A tiny seed borne by the passing breeze, or dropped by some wandering bird has fallen into a crevice of the Titanic masonry; there it has germinated, and by its living, expansive force has torn to fragments the edifice which seemed to set at defiance the ravages of time. So shall "the seed of the word" fall upon these strongholds of sin, and in its living might and energy shall overthrow them.

It is to a condensed and popular description of this country that the following pages are devoted. It is hoped that the brief account here given of its history, its scenery, its natural productions, and its social condition will be found to contain much interesting and valuable information.

CHAPTER I.

THE COUNTRY.

The Gulf Stream—Boundaries, Natural and Political—Physical Geography—Table-Lands—Volcanoes—Geology--General Scenery—Rivers—Sea Board—Climate—Dry and Rainy Seasons—Descriptive Sketch of the States—Las Chiapas, Tabasco, Tamaulipas, Vera Cruz, Oaxaca, Puebla, Mexico—The Capital —Guerrero—Mechoacan—Jorullo—Colima, Jalisco, Sinaloa, Sonora, Queretaro, Guanaxuato, San Luis Potosi, Zacatecas, New Leon, Cohahuila, Durango, Chihuahua, Lower California.

THE voyager across the Atlantic Ocean as he looks down upon its troubled waters, with their ceaseless ebb and flow, might readily imagine that they tossed their foaming crests without any definite direction, as they are driven hither and thither by the capricious impulses of the winds. But really the mass is moved onward by a mighty and uniform influence, and travels over thousands of miles in the same direction. There are rivers in the ocean, the courses of which are almost as regular and as well defined as those which flow through the land. Strange as this statement may seem, it is not the less true, having been ascertained by patient and accurate inquiry. Drift-wood is found to float uniformly in certain given directions, and bottles thrown out from vessels, for this purpose, in differents parts of the ocean, are almost invariably picked up or cast ashore in the line of these marine rivers. Two of these ocean currents, flowing in a westerly direction from the coast of Africa, meet in the Caribbean Sea, and are turned northward by the American Continent, where they form the Gulf Stream.* This stream, as it flows out from its torrid bed, sweeps past the coasts of Newfoundland, and is then turned eastward toward our own shores. Its waters still retain much of the heat they had received in the tropical regions whence they flow, and this confers upon us the blessings of a warm and genial climate. Every westerly wind that blows to us bears with it a portion of this heat to temper our winters' cold. But for this strange, yet most merciful provision, our climate would be as inclement as that of Labrador, which lies nearly in the same latitude with the British Isles. How wondrous is the wisdom thus displayed in the arrangement of the earth, and all that is therein! He who calleth for the waters of the sea, and poureth them out upon the earth, has so guided them that they rule the climate of a people thousands of miles from the place whence they flow!

It is of Mexico, the land which forms the cradle of this mighty ocean-stream, and which determines its course, that we are to speak in the following pages. The Pacific and the Atlantic Oceans wash its eastern and western shores. It rises between them as a vast table-land, bounded on the north by California, New Mexico and Texas, on the east by the Gulf of Mexico and the Caribbean Sea, on the south-east by British Honduras and Guatemala, on the west and south-west by the Pacific Ocean. From the want of accurate

* It has been conjectured that the force of current, as it sweeps round from west to east on the shores of Central America, has, in the course of ages, hollowed out the Gulf of Mexico, leaving the hard and rocky fragments, which have resisted its power, to form the Islands of the West Indies.

surveys its area is somewhat uncertain, but it may be roughly stated at 830,000 English square miles, though some estimates make it much more extensive.

Few countries have so often removed their borders as Mexico. When Cortez landed at San Juan, and conquered the country for Charles V., his master's claims to territorial authority were only limited by his power to enforce them. All North America was supposed to be the property of the pope, and to be given by him to the Spanish king. The title deeds of the Romish bishop were never subjected to a legal inquiry. They were the consequence of his claim to universal empire. Wherever the swords of Castille prevailed, there was a sufficient title for Charles. Cortez won for him Mexico, so called from the Aztec god of war. Alvarado added Guatemala to his possessions. The Jesuits and their monkish brethren acquired California and New Mexico for his successors. There were no defined boundaries in those days, save where the waves shut in the continent.

The physical geography of the country is very extraordinary. Perhaps no other region of the globe presents such varieties of surface or climate within the same extent of territory. Along the coast there lies a narrow fringe of lowland. Advancing into the interior, the ground rises rapidly, sometimes mountain ranges stretch precipitously like a mighty wall for leagues, sometimes the ascent is more gradual and slopes upward at a scarcely perceptible angle. But whatever may be the gradient the ascent is continuous till an elevation of from 5,000 to 7,500 feet above the level of the sea is attained. The traveller having reached this altitude comes to vast plateaux of tableland which extend for many hundreds of miles. These broad sweeps of level plains on the tops of the mountain chains occupy almost the entire area of Mexico, and form the platform from which the volcanic and other mountains rise into the region of perpetual snow.

These table-lands rise to different heights, and enjoy a varied climate. Their surface is much broken up by lesser mountain ranges, but the plateau of Anahuac, in which the city of Mexico stands, stretches away in an almost unbroken level for 1,600 miles together; a distance as great as from the North of Scotland to the Straits of Gibraltar. This plain is widest at the latitude of the capital where it spreads out to 360 miles in breadth. Its eastern or Atlantic side is 7,500 feet above the level of the sea, and it gradually decreases to a height of about 4,000 feet as it approaches the shore of the Pacific. Of course so enormous a space does not literally present an unbroken surface; but this is actually the case for many leagues together, and carriages may roll down from Mexico to Santa Fè, a distance of fifteen hundred miles, without any serious interruption of the gradual decline. The mountains which enclose the plain of Anahuac on the eastern side are called the Sierra Madre. They are broken up by the ridges of the Sierra Altamira, and the group that contains the silver mines of Fresnillo and Zacatecas. In some places they rise to the height of 17,000 feet above the level of the sea.

In describing the mountains of Mexico, we must not omit to notice its volcanoes. There is a remarkable line of these about 16 miles south of the capital. In regular order their tapering cones rise one after another, the most eastern, called Tuxtla, being in the 95th degree of west longitude: then comes the snowy peak of Orizaba, followed by Popocateptl, which is 2,000 feet higher than the loftiest of our European mountains, whilst Iztaccihuatl and Toluca bear away to the east. These mightier monarchs are connected by a chain of smaller attendant volcanoes, and stand like huge sentinels to guard the city and plain of Mexico. A rival to these ancient mountains, however, very unexpectedly appeared. On the night of September 29, 1759, after a succession of violent earthquakes, there suddenly sprung from the earth a new cone, which has been named Jorullo. This giant youngster rose in one night to the height of 1,600 feet. Like it in solitary grandeur, but nearer to the Pacific, towers the peak of Colima, the last of the volcanic series.

These volcanoes contribute some of its most striking features to Mexican scenery. The eye wanders for miles over slopes of marvellous beauty, bathed in a light the brilliancy of which we in these northern climes can scarcely conceive. The transparency of the atmosphere enables the eye to penetrate to an almost incredible distance. The horizon is bounded by hills that are gradually lost in shadow. In the midst of such scenes, the regular and snow-clad forms of the volcanoes break upon the eye with astonishing effect. The purity of their untrodden snows, the dark masses of scoria and lava, or the deep fringes of pine trees that skirt their bases, and by night the fiery vapour emitted from their summits combine to form a picture of surpassing loveliness. The native Mexicans deemed volcanoes to be the abodes of the departed spirits of wicked rulers—the fable, repeated in another form, of the Titans sent to suffer under Ætna—and saw in the convulsions of an eruption the evidence of their fiery agonies. The Christian sees in them only one of the many wonders of God, who, "by His strength, setteth fast the mountains, being girded with power."

The geological formation of Mexico is peculiar. The surface of the Cordilleras presents masses of porphyry, greenstone, amygdaloid, basalt, obsidian, and other similar rocks, overlying the granite which forms the foundation of the geological system throughout the country. As the land declines to the Pacific Ocean, the upper strata are wanting, and the port of Acapulco is a natural excavation in granitic rocks, which here rise to the surface. The granite crops out at intervals as we ascend from the western coast to the table-land, and appears for the last time through the porphyry between Zumpango and Zopilote. The great central plateau of Anahuac, between the 14th and 21st degrees of latitude, is an enormous mass of porphyritic rocks, which differ from those of Europe by the constant presence of hornblend, and by the absence of quartz. The primary and secondary strata occur in the same order as in the eastern hemisphere, but hitherto neither rock-salt nor coal has been discovered in any quantity in the table-land of Mexico. The porphyry in some places assumes fantastic shapes, which bear a resemblance to ruined walls and towers. The most remarkable of these is the Coffre de Perote, whose summit presents the appearance of a gigantic sarcophagus, surmounted by a pyramid at one end; others again, as the mountains of Jacal and Oyamel, terminate in basaltic columns, crowned with forests. In some regions, the surface of the land is rent by deep fissures, termed barrancas, which occasionally furnish serious obstacles to the formation of roads. It is amongst the rocks of porphyry that the veins of gold and silver are found, from whence such immense supplies of those precious metals have been drawn.

The country is singularly deficient in large rivers; the mountains border so closely on the sea that the streams which pour down their sides are little more than torrents, and the table-land is so encircled by mountains that its waters are gathered into lakes. The Rio Grande del Norte, which forms the northern boundary of the country, is the most important river. It takes its rise amidst the mountains of New Mexico, and, after a course of 1,800 miles, runs into the Gulf of Mexico at the 20th degree of north latitude, the northern point of Tamaulipas. The Santander, the Tampico, and the Panuco or Moctezuma, all flow through the same state to the eastern coast, and, in the state of Tabasco, the rivers Tabasco and Usumasinta contribute their united waters to the same sea.

Still less noticeable are the rivers which empty themselves into the Pacific Ocean. The Rio Balsas in Mechoacan, the Santiago in Jalisco, the Del Fuerte in Sinaloa, and the Yagui in Sonora, are the principal drains by which the western states are relieved of their superfluous waters.

But if the rivers of Mexico are inferior in size and capabilities for navigation, they are unsurpassed for the beauty of their scenery, and the prodigal luxuriance of their banks. Their special features are due to the peculiar character of the soil and the tropical heat of the country through which they pass. At times the streams collecting their waters in some concealed basin break through a rent in the hills of porphyry which hang with precipitous sides over the deep gorges through which the current flows. In other spots, the quiet tide rolls on languidly through forests, which seem to spring out from its bosom; bamboos bending gracefully before the breeze; tall cabbage palms, their crown the food and their straight trunks the canoe of the wild Indian; the banana, laden with its useful fruit: these, and many others, grow spontaneously by thousands on its banks; whilst the most characteristic feature of the scene is furnished by the parasitical plants which wave in bright festoons from the branches of the trees. The foliage thus blended forms a wall of living green, whence long tendrils dip into the water, as if to drink and carry life to those that bear them.

The lakes with which Mexico abounds, are merely the remains of immense basins of water which once covered a large portion of the plain of the Cordilleras. Lake Chapala, in Jalisco, has an area of 1,300 square miles, double the size of the lake of Constance. The lakes Pascuaro, in Mechoacan; Cayman and Parras, in Cohahuila, are also considerable. The valley of Mexico contains five lakes, of which further mention will presently be made.

The commercial importance of the sea-board of any country can hardly be exaggerated, and in this respect Mexico labours under considerable disadvantages. The mighty influence which has uplifted the Cordilleras has been fatal to the mercantile prosperity of the Pacific shore. Acapulco, by far the finest natural harbour on the western coast, is now almost deserted, although at one time very prosperous. Nor is the Atlantic coast much more highly favoured. Long lagunes and shallows extend for leagues together on the eastern shore of Mexico, whilst violent winds sweep over the gulf and render navigation perilous during their continuance.

To the configuration of the country are due its extraordinary inequalities of climate, as, in consequence of its height above the level of the sea, a large portion of the country which lies within the tropics enjoys a cool and temperate atmosphere. The whole country may be divided into three zones:—The cold lands, *tierras frias*, comprehend those table-lands which are elevated more than 7,200 feet above the sea, yet even here the thermometer rarely falls to freezing point, except on the mountain tops, and the mean temperature is 62° Fahrenheit. The temperate region, *tierras templadas*, lies on the slope of the Cordilleras, at a height of from 4,000 to 5,000 feet, and enjoys a perpetual spring. Most European fruits flourish in this genial climate, and the frequent presence of fogs from the sea appears but to quicken the beauty and strength of its vegetable productions. The *tierras calientes*, or torrid district, includes the low lands on either coast, and all the ground which is less than 2,000 feet above the sea. There all the products of the tropics are to be met with in great luxuriance, and their rank growth in the hot damp atmosphere begets the terrible vomito (yellow fever), which desolates the coast. An English traveller, on a visit to Vera Cruz, remarked a dull yellowish haze that hung over the town, and asked a boatman what it was. " Senor," he answered, quite seriously, "it is the fever." From the virulence of this disease, Vera Cruz has been aptly named, " the city of death."

The climate of the district lying north of the capital, the Provincias Internas, is marked by much greater variation of temperature, the winters being cold, and the summers oppressively hot. This region suffers exceedingly from want of water; there are but few natural springs, and the rains flow away through the vast fissures with which the volcanic regions abound. The improvidence of the Spaniards has aggravated these physical disadvantages, inasmuch as they have levelled vast forests to provide timber for the mines, without taking the trouble to supply their place by young plantations. In this way tracts of country once fertile have been rendered desolate and barren.

The year in Mexico is commonly divided into the dry and the rainy seasons; the former lasting from October to May, the latter extending over the remaining four months. The clouds begin to gather on the coast of Vera Cruz, and there the first showers descend fifteen or twenty days before the weather breaks on the central table-land. Violent storms generally accompany the earliest rains. Fierce gusts sweep along the shore. Wherever moisture abounds in Mexico, there is found side by side great unhealthiness and extraordinary fertility of the soil. Still, with the exception of a few sea-ports and deep valleys, Mexico must be considered as a healthy country. Even in the region of the vomito, the natives and strangers, acclimatized by several years' residence, rarely fall victims to this deadly malady.

After this general outline of its physical geography we must describe the political divisions of the country; we shall then be better able to trace its history and the condition of its inhabitants. The territory of Mexico is divided into states, which we shall group together according to their geographical positions. The eastern states comprise Las Chiapas, Tabasco, Vera Cruz, and Tamaulipas. The first two and the last of these hardly call for any remarks. Chiapas is almost wholly unexplored. It lies upon the northern incline of the Cordilleras, and among the fertile valleys enclosed within the spurs of that great mountain chain. Its area is, however, almost unknown, and its fertility has never yet been fairly tested. In Tabasco the haciendas, or farms, are more numerous. Large forests of oaks, cedars, mahogany and iron-wood; crops of coffee, cocoa, pepper, sugar, and tobacco; woods rich in game, and rivers teeming with fish, might suffice to support a dense population. But it contains no more than 70,000 inhabitants, and those chiefly native Indians. Tamaulipas is separated from Tabasco by Vera Cruz. Stretching along the sea coast, with a mild and healthy climate, a soil well watered and fertile, and with the attraction of magnificent scenery in the broken ground that fills up most of its superfices, this state, which is almost as large as England, can only boast a population of 110,000 souls.

Vera Cruz is worthy of a more extended notice. It includes within its limits the ports of Vera Cruz and Tampico, as well as the beautiful district of Jalapa. Vera Cruz is the most important port of Mexico, and through it there passes by far the greatest portion of its foreign trade. Yet its harbour is shallow and exposed, it is swept from October to April by dangerous winds, called "nortes," and during their continuance all communication between the shipping and the town is at an end; this is the case even with vessels moored immediately under the castle walls or secured to the shore. The air is filled with sand, the sky is dark with clouds, and the whole coast line is one unbroken sheet of foam. Moreover, the pedestrian at such times can scarcely keep his feet in the streets of the city. Vera Cruz itself is a desolate and dreary looking place, and is so unhealthy during the season of the vomito, from May to November, that the merchants and their families retire to Jalapa. On

this latter district the God of nature has bestowed
his gifts with unsparing bounty. The climate is genial
and salubrious; the grain, the trees, the fruits, the
flowers of both the temperate and tropical regions are
disseminated in rich profusion. The beauty and
fragrance of a thousand flowers, the rich foliage of
trees of every tint, and the waving corn or green pastures, combine to form a picture of surpassing splendour. This district maintains 405,587 animals, but
only 270,000 human beings.*

The western and central states are Oaxaca, Puebla,
Mexico, Mechoacan, Jalisco, Colima, Sinaloa, Sonora,
Guerrero, and Lower California.

The beautiful state of Oaxaca lies on the shores of
the Pacific Ocean, and covers an area of more than
5,000 square leagues, with a population of 700,000
persons. Blessed with a salubrious climate and a fertile
soil, it would be hard to find a more agreeable place of
residence, if the efforts of man had but turned to good
account the manifold gifts of God. Between the
ridge of the Cordilleras that skirt the Pacific and a
range that runs through the middle of the country,
there lies embossomed the fruitful valley from which
Cortez took his title of Marquis del Valle de Oaxaca.
At the period of the revolution, the family estates
extended over 49 villages, containing a population of
17,700 souls. Huge haciendas, vast farms and sugar

---

* The following list may serve to illustrate the variety of the products
of Jalapa:—Tobacco, coffee, sugar, cotton, corn, barley, wheat, jalap,
sarsaparilla, vanilla, mamies, papayas, pine-apples, oranges, citrons, lemons,
pomegranates, zapotes, bananas, chirimoyas, tunas, pears, water-melons,
peaches, apricots, guavas, grapes: mahogany, ebony, cedar, oak, dragon-blood, tamarinds, palms, dye-wood, and a thousand other plants, trees,
shrubs, cereals, and parasites, spring almost spontaneously from the soil
and render the necessary labour of man insignificant.—MAYER, vol. II.,
pp. 195—6.

mills, are scattered over its surface. Nothing but the fatal wars which have desolated it could arrest the prosperity of so highly favoured a region.

The same encomium may be passed upon the natural advantages of Puebla, which lies to the north of Oaxaca. It contains an area of 2,700 square leagues, and a population of about 700,000 souls. The country is beautiful and fertile, being broken up by mountains, amidst which there lie valleys of extraordinary productiveness. Cotton, rice, coffee, sugar, Indian corn, wheat, barley, maguey, and other plants are cultivated. Nearly three-fourths of the soil belongs to the church and to hospitals: and the wealth of the clergy contrasts very sadly with the miserable condition of the lower classes.

When Gage visited Mexico, in 1625, Puebla was already a flourishing town, celebrated for its manufactures. Cloth, felt, and glass, were among its most noted productions; but the early efforts of the Mexicans in this direction were discountenanced by Spain. The city is now the Manchester of Mexico, and amidst the numerous churches with which it is adorned, and the convents which vie with one another in elegance and comfort, there rise the dreary prison-looking buildings in which the cotton manufacture is carried on. Two articles of dress are in special demand; the reboso and the serape. The first is a long shawl worn by the women. The second a blanket, with a hole in the centre for the head and falling in folds down from the shoulders. Everybody wears them—the smart cavalier riding in the park at Mexico, as well as the lepero in its filthy courts. They vary in cost from twenty-five to five hundred dollars. Nearly one-third of the whole native manufactures are made in Puebla.

Cholula, a flourishing city at the period of the Spanish conquest, is situated in this state. Close to the town is the great pyramid, an extraordinary structure, perhaps the oldest and most remarkable ruin in Mexico. This huge monument is nine miles from Puebla, and appears to have been built in four terraces, traces of which may still be distinguished. Upon the summit once stood the temple of Quetzalcoatl, the site of which is now occupied by the chapel of Our Lady de los Remedios. The present appearance is that of a tree-grown hill about 200 feet in height, with a base of more than 1,000 feet. "Cholula in the days of Cortez, contained 40,000 householders, and the whole plain was studded with populous villages. The plain is now comparatively a desert, and two or three thousand miserable leperos build their mud huts, and practice their thievish propensities upon the site of the holy city."*

The metropolitan state, lying to the west of La Puebla, is the most populous division of the Republic, and contains nearly a million of inhabitants, scattered over an area of 19,535 square miles. Its most striking physical feature is the great valley of Mexico, in the midst of which the capital is situated, and which is shut in by irregular mountains, those to the north and north-east embracing the silver mines of Real del Monte. The valley itself is extraordinarily fertile; its general figure is an oval of about 200 miles in circumference, over which the eye ranges from the summit of any of the mountains by which it is enclosed.

The most interesting feature of the valley of Mexico is the vast system of drainage, by which the capital

---

* MAYER, vol. II., p. 230.

is protected against the inundations of the lake of Tezcuco, which, during the first two centuries after the conquest, repeatedly threatened it with destruction. The valley of Mexico serves as a receptacle for all the waters that pour down from the mountains which surround it on every side, and which have only one natural outlet, the river Arrago. This stream is insufficient to carry them off, and they consequently spread into fine lakes, two of which, Chalco and Xochimilco, lie to the south of the capital, Tezcuco which immediately adjoins it, and San Christoval and Zumpango to the north. The level of the waters of Tezcuco is not much more than a foot below the site of the capital; when therefore the lakes of San Christoval and Zumpango, which are at a greater elevation, are swollen by an unusually rainy season, they burst their barriers, and pouring into the lake of Tezcuco cause it to rise in turn and inundate the streets of the city. Various occurrences of this kind, attended of course with much disaster, forced the government to adopt measures that might avert the danger.

Immense works were found to be necessary. A vast *desague*, or canal, was cut to carry off the waters of the lake of Zumpango. This artificial drain is 12 miles in length, 300 feet in breadth, and 150 feet in depth, and for upwards of a 1,000 yards is pierced through the solid rock. It directs the waters of the lake in a north-eastern direction, right through the mountain barrier which shuts them in, and empties them into the river Tula, which flows into the Atlantic Ocean. This stupendous work is said to have been accomplished in eleven months. The workmen were some thousands of the natives, who were compelled to complete it at the sacrifice of a vast amount of human life. By this contrivance the capital is secure against inundations from the northern lakes; but no such precautions have been taken against the swelling of the lakes of Chalco and Xochimilco, by which it may at any time be overwhelmed.

It is hard to picture a fairer scene than that presented by the Mexican capital, lying as it does near to the waters of the Tezcucan lake, in the heart of this fertile valley. On whichever side you turn, there rise the serrated ridges of the Cordilleras, encompassing the city with a gigantic azure belt. The streets run in long and unbroken straight lines, bisecting one another at right angles; and in the clear atmosphere of the table-land the varied colour of the houses is beautifully toned down by the back ground of purple hills. To the south, the two volcanoes which overtop the other peaks of the sierra, raise their majestic summits covered with eternal snow, which in the light of the evening sun put on a pale purple tint, here and there flecked with delicate ruby. At the foot of the mountains are two sparkling lakes, where the wild swans sport in large flocks, disturbing the calm surface which at other times reflects the floating clouds. Dusty roads intersect the verdant pastures like gold stripes on a green ground. A tree, peculiar to these regions, somewhat like the weeping willow, bends its long interlaced branches, loaded with odoriferous leaves and red berries, and a solitary palm-tree rises here and there above clumps of olives with their pale-green foliage.

In the city itself the stranger will commonly first direct his steps to the Plaza Mayor or Great Square. On its north side the cathedral towers majestically aloft, standing on the alleged site of the *teocalli* of Mexitli, the Aztec god of war. The east side of the square is entirely occupied by the president's palace, a huge and cumbrous pile without any architectural pretension. The building is quadrangular, with four interior courts and has room enough for all the public offices, the senate house, the two chambers of deputies, the mint, two barracks, two prisons and a botanic garden. Two immense markets fill up the remaining sides of the square, into which there constantly pours a flood of human beings belonging to every grade of Mexican society.

Save the school of mines and the academy of arts, churches and convents are the only public buildings in the capital, in addition to those in the Plaza Mayor. Some of the churches are magnificent. But the pleasing impression which Mexico produces upon strangers seems to be due more to the purity of the atmosphere, the variety of costumes that throng the streets, and the luxuriant flowers and fruits that are carried to its markets, than to any architectural effects. There is a charming public park, the Alameda, whither the upper classes of the city resort on horseback or in carriages, and several promenades or public walks, the most beautiful of which, the Paseo de la Viga, skirts the lake Chalco canal. Hundreds of canoes, too, of various sizes, filled with native Indians, may be seen passing along the canals in every direction. On the borders of the lake are a number of *chinampas*, or floating gardens, as they are termed. These are artificial islands, some of them 60 yards long and four or five wide, on which the choicest fruits and flowers are cultivated for the markets of the capital.

With great natural advantages, Mexico has made

but little progress—social, commercial, or political. Science, education, and the arts are sadly neglected. It numbers about 170,000 inhabitants, and shows only a very slight increase since the days of the conquest, while the population in the immediate neighbourhood of the capital has declined very materially, Indeed, so much is this the case that few of the cities of Mexico require any special description. Tezcuco, Tumba, and other cities on the lakes, have now degenerated into petty villages. Tacubaya, the residence of the Archbishop and San Augustin, the seat of the great festival to which all Mexico resorts, alone call for a passing mention in our rapid sketch of this state.

To the south of the districts of Mexico and La Puebla lies the state of Guerrero. This state was created by the constitution of 1847, and is composed of certain districts which formerly belonged to Mexico, Puebla, and Mechoacan. It contains 270,000 inhabitants and an area of 32,000 square miles.

The state of Mechoacan, lying to the north-west of Mexico, on the western slope of the Cordilleras, presents one feature of extraordinary interest (to which a passing allusion has been already made), in the volcanic cone of Jorullo. The appearance of this mountain is without parallel in the annals of the world's physical history. Humboldt, who on all such questions is our great authority, gives the following narrative of this extraordinary event:—" Geology gives us no example of the formation, from the centre of a thousand burning cones, of a mountain of scoriæ and ashes, 1,695 feet in height, comparing it only with the level of the adjoining plains, in the interior of a continent, thirty-six leagues distant from the coast, and more than forty-two leagues from every other active volcano.

THE COUNTRY.

"Till the middle of the last century, fields, covered with sugar-cane and indigo, occupied the extent of ground between the two brooks called Cuitimba and San Pedro. They were bounded by basaltic mountains, the structure of which seems to indicate that all this country, at a very remote period, had been already several times convulsed by volcanoes. These fields, watered by artificial means, belonged to the farm of Don Pedro di Jorullo, and were among the most fertile in the country.

"In the month of June, 1759, hollow sounds of the most alarming nature were heard, accompanied by frequent earthquakes, which succeeded each other for from fifty to sixty days, to the great consternation of the inhabitants of the farm. From the beginning of September everything seemed to announce the complete re-establishment of tranquillity, when, in the night of the 28th and 29th, the horrible subterraneous noises recommenced. The affrighted Indians fled to the mountains of Aguasarco. *A tract of ground from three to four square miles in extent rose up in the shape of a bladder.* The bounds of this convulsion may still be distinguished by the fractured strata.

" Those who witnessed this great catastrophe from the top of Aguasarco, assert that the flames were seen to issue forth for an extent of more than half a square league, that fragments of burning rocks were thrown to prodigious heights, and that through a thick cloud of ashes, illumined by volcanic fire, the softened surface of the earth was seen to swell up like an agitated sea. The rivers of Cuitimba and San Pedro precipitated themselves into the burning chasms. The decomposition of the water contributed to invigorate the flames, which were visible at the city of Pascuaro. Eruptions of mud, and especially of strata of clay, enveloping balls of decomposed basalt in concentrical layers, appear to indicate that subterraneous water had no small share in producing this extraordinary revolution. Thousands of small cones, from six to ten feet in height, called by the natives *ovens* (hornitos), issued forth from the plain. Although, according to the testimony of the Indians, the heat of these volcanic ovens has suffered a great diminution during the last fifteen years, I have seen the thermometer rise to 212° on being plunged into fissures which exhale an aqueous vapour. Each small cone is a chimney, from which a thick vapour ascends to the height of from twenty-two to thirty-two feet.

"In the midst of the ovens six large masses, elevated from 300 to 1,600 feet each above the level of the old plains, sprung up from a chasm. The most elevated of these is the great volcano of Jorullo. It is continually burning, and has thrown up from its north side an immense quantity of scorified and basaltic lavas, containing fragments of primitive rocks. These great eruptions of the central volcano continued till the month of February, 1760. In the following years, they became gradually less frequent.

"The Indians, frightened at the horrible noises of the new volcano, abandoned at first all the villages situated within seven or eight leagues distance of the plain of Jorullo. They became gradually, however, accustomed to this terrific spectacle; and having returned to their cottages, they advanced towards the mountains of Aguasarco and Santa Inĕs, to wonder at the streams of fire discharged from an infinity of small volcanic apertures of various sizes. The roofs of the houses at Queretaro, at a distance of more than forty-eight leagues in a straight line from the scene of the explosion, were at that time covered with ashes.

"Although the subterraneous fires now appear far from violent, and the plain and the great volcano begin to be covered with vegetation, we nevertheless found the ambient air heated to such a degree, by the action of the ovens, that the thermometer at a great distance above the ground, and in the shade, rose to 109° of Fahrenheit. This fact proves that there is no exaggeration in the accounts of several Indians, who affirm that for many years, after the first eruption, the plains of Jorullo, even at a great distance from the ground which had been thrown up, were uninhabitable from their excessive heat.

"The traveller is still shown, near the Carro de Santa Inĕs, the rivers of Cuitimba and San Pedro, whose limpid streams formerly watered the sugar cane plantations. These streams disappeared on the night of September 29, 1759; but, at a distance of 6,500 feet farther west, in the tract which was the theatre of the convulsion, two rivers are now seen bursting through the argillaceous vault of the ovens."*

Since Humboldt's visit, the ovens have almost entirely subsided; very few of them any longer emit a vapour or indicate a higher temperature than the surrounding atmosphere. Soon luxuriant crops of sugarcane and indigo will again cover the whole region which was the scene of so amazing a convulsion.

Morelia, the capital of the state of Mechoacan, contains about 25,000 inhabitants, and consists chiefly of one long street—broad, and well paved. The great square has broad piazzas on three of its sides, the fourth being exclusively occupied by the cathedral.

* Nouvelle Espagne, p. 248.

Its centre is the site of a crowded market, where the dealers display their goods, according to the custom common throughout Mexico, under the shade of umbrellas made of matting. The houses have flat roofs, and long projecting waterspouts which occasionally deluge the unwary traveller.

Colima, with a capital and volcano of the same name, lies on the Pacific, to the north of Mechoacan, embracing an area of 3,000 square miles, and a population of nearly 62,000 souls. The climate is warm, but not unhealthy; the vegetation is luxuriant: cotton, sugar, tobacco, and cocoa are its chief productions; and rich iron ore has been recently discovered.

Jalisco stretches on the Pacific shore to the north of Colima, along the western slope of the Cordilleras, and is in parts much broken up by mountain ranges, composed of rugged hills interspersed with fertile valleys. It has an area of 48,590 square miles, and a population of 774,000 souls. The city of Guadalaxara, its capital, stands on a wide plain at the distance of 450 miles from Mexico. The town is well built, its streets running at right angles to one another, the houses are good, and the roads well paved. It boasts no less than fourteen squares, twelve public fountains, and a number of churches and convents. The Alameda is prettily laid out, and the shops within the Portales de Commercio are unusually well supplied with goods. Altogether Guadalaxara is one of the most flourishing places in Mexico. The condition and capacity of Jalisco has been pithily stated by Mr. Ruxton—"It is a land where all tropical productions *might* be cultivated, and *are not.*"

The two states of Sinaloa and Sonora rise one above the other to the northern boundary of the country;

they have a united area of 157,000 square miles, and not much more than 200,000 inhabitants. Parts of the coast are almost uninhabitable, through excessive heat, and large districts in the interior are arid and barren, but much fertile land remains uncultivated, and it would be hard to tell what agricultural wealth might not be derived from these regions in the hands of an industrious and intelligent population. Through a part of the country there flow some considerable rivers, the Mayo, the Yagui, and others; and wherever irrigation is practised considerable crops have been raised. Rich mineral products also abound; and should these resources ever be fully developed, they will doubtless greatly enhance the value of these now almost desert regions.

We must now turn to the central provinces, which are eight in number. The most southern of these is the small state of Queretaro, to the north-west of Mexico. Its chief city is a place of some trade, with nearly 50,000 inhabitants, and contains many handsome ecclesiastical buildings, especially the convent of Santa Clara, which is itself a miniature town, laid out in streets and squares. There are cloth manufactories here, but in a rather depressed condition. The most flourishing branch of commerce is the manufacture and sale of cigars.

Between Queretaro and the adjoining state of Guanaxuato, the geological features of the country undergo a change, limestone taking the place of primary and volcanic rocks. The climate is warmer and more tropical. The plains are exceedingly beautiful, well cultivated, and teeming with fertility. " The gardens and maize patches of the small Indian villages are enclosed with hedges, or rather walls of organo, a species of single, square-stemmed cactus, which grows to the height of from 40 to 50 feet. It is called *organo* on account of its resemblance to the pipes of an organ. Planted close together the walls of organo are impervious to pigs and poultry, and form admirable enclosures to the Indian huts. Here the houses are built of uncemented limestones, piled loosely on one another, and are sometimes roofed with talc." *

The town of Guanaxuato owes its existence to the Veta Madre, or Mother Vein of Silver, close to which it is built. This prolific seam has yielded 225,935,736 dollars since the year 1766. The city contains 50,000 inhabitants, and is very irregularly built; its houses and streets being distributed according to the vacancies left by the surrounding mountains, and interspersed with works for the reduction of the ores. It presents, also, those striking contrasts with which Mexico abounds. Some of its mansions and churches are magnificent, but the entrance to the town is along the bed of a torrent, which flows impetuously in the rainy season, and causes numerous accidents, but which it has never been attempted to improve.

San Luis Potosi lies to the west of Tamaulipas, and north of Mexico; it covers an area of 29,000 square miles. This state enjoys a variable climate, mild on the table-lands, warm and unhealthy on the eastern slopes. There are manufactures of wool and cotton fabrics, glass, leather, pottery and hardware; but its prosperity is mainly dependent on the mines of Catorce. The soil is fertile, and abundant produce might be raised in the haciendas, but there is no market for it. Three hundred pounds of maize will not always find purchasers at the price of a single dollar.

Nothing can be more dreary than the region in which

* Ruxton, p. 71.

THE COUNTRY.

Catorce is situate. A few narrow mules' paths, or the bed of a torrent, alone break the monotonous dark colour of the Cordillera : not a tree, not a blade of grass, is to be seen, although fifty years ago it was covered with waving forests. As you approach it from below, the town is entirely hidden by a brow of the mountain, and it takes more than an hour's good riding from the bottom to come within sight of it. Then a curious scene is presented: the place lies in a hollow, the houses following the course of the Veta Madre; the ground is cut up by ravines, which wind about so intricately that many of the houses have one story on one side of a ravine, and two or three on the other.

West of San Luis Potosi is the state of Zacatecas; area, 30,000 square miles ; population, 356,000. Almost the whole of this state is occupied by the spurs of the Cordilleras, so that it possesses no rivers, and almost all irrigation is carried on by the aid of tanks and reservoirs. The capital of the same name contains a population of nearly 40,000, and the whole region abounds in silver mines, amongst which those of Fresnillo and Sombrerete were once in high repute. The people bear a very indifferent character, and the state is rendered extremely insecure by the Indians.

"Fresnillo is a paltry, dirty town, with the neighbouring sierra honeycombed with mines, which are rich, and yield considerable profits. A share which the government had in their mines gave an annual profit of nearly half a million of dollars; but that shortsighted vampyre, which sucks the blood of poor Mexico, eager to possess all the golden eggs at once, sold its interest for less than one year's income." *

The state of Nuevo Leon requires but a brief passing

* Ruxton, p. 87.

notice. It was colonized by the Viceroy Monterey, after whom its chief city is named. The grazing of cattle is the chief occupation of the people. There are no manufactures, and hardly any mines, although lead and silver are said to be abundant.

The large states of Cohahuila, Durango, and Chihuahua, occupy all the northern territory of Mexico. Cohahuila lies to the west of Nuevo Leon, and Durango still further in the same direction, Chihuahua to the north of the latter. Their united area extends over upwards of 200,000 square miles, but cannot boast of more than some 385,000 inhabitants. They possess natural advantages of the most varied character. A cool and healthy climate, a fertile soil, and vast mineral resources, might have been expected to tempt a numerous body of colonists; but these inducements are rendered powerless through the horrible insecurity of the country.

The city of Durango is the *ultima Thule* of Mexican civilization, and Chihuahua merely a sort of advanced out-post in the desert land. Beyond the former town lie vast unpeopled and uncultivated plains, in which tribes of fierce Indians, the Apaches and Camanches, have their dwelling places, from which they sweep down upon the farms and settlements of the Mexicans, driving off their herds, murdering the unarmed males, and carrrying the women and children into slavery. Every hacienda has its mournful story of such acts of bloodshed and pillage, and travellers express their astonishment that the whole country has not long since been abandoned. Yet a body of resolute colonists of the Anglo-Saxon race would speedily ensure security and peace throughout the land.

It only remains that we should notice the territory

of Lower California, a long peninsular strip of land, bounded on the east by the Gulf of Mexico, and on the west by the Pacific. The district is about 700 miles in length, and varies from 30 to 100 miles in breadth. The country is generally barren, dreary and desert. Throughout its surface there runs a chain of irregular rocks, in which valuable ores of gold, silver, copper and lead are known to exist, but have hardly been disturbed. The pearl fishery in the Gulf of Mexico, formerly so valuable, has dwindled into insignificance. The shores are irregular and sandy, but the port of Magdalena affords a safe and commodious anchorage, and is much resorted to by whalers during the winter season.

With this rapid glance of the country itself, we shall now proceed to treat of the history and character of its inhabitants.

CHAPTER II.

EARLY HISTORY.

Obscurity of Early Annals—The Toltecs—Chichemecs—Acolhuans—Xolotl the Wise—His Burial—Tezcucan Civilization—Romantic Adventures of Nezahualcoyotl—Tezcucan Fidelity—Nezahualcoyotl King—His wisdom, poetry, splendour—His humility, justice, and kindness to his subjects—He falls into sin—Reluctantly induced to allow human sacrifices—His Death—Nezahualpilli—The Tlascalans—Emigration to Tlascala—The Aztecs—Origin of Mexico—Aztec Government—Laws—Tenure of Land—Taxes—Posts—Army—Literature—Picture-writing—Calendar—Agriculture—Arts—Domestic Life and Manners—Montezuma's Mode of Life—Superstition—Human Sacrifices—The True Atonement.

THE origin of a savage nation is almost always hopelessly obscure. The people themselves in their infancy are commonly ignorant of the arts by which to preserve any record of their history, and at the same time are generally indifferent to all remembrance of the past. Then, as time rolls on, the memory of some gallant warrior or some just ruler is carefully cherished, and all the benefits they long for or enjoy are attributed by the nation to this favourite ancestor. Thus truth and fiction become intermingled, until it is impossible in after years to assign to each their proper place: and a few facts alone stand out clearly in the midst of a surrounding mass of fable.

The early history of the Mexican nation is no exception to this general principle. The inhabitants of the country, when the Spaniards reached it, were evidently composed of many separate races, and a variety of reasons were assigned to account for their origin and intermixture. It would be quite useless to record the uncouth names given by chroniclers to the original population of the great table-land. The Toltecs are the most ancient people of whom we have any coherent account. They are said to have migrated from the north about the middle of the seventh century, and to have built a city called Tula, about 50 miles east of the capital of Mexico. A curious law prevailed among them, that each of their kings should reign for 52 years and no more. If the monarch died within this period, the government was continued by a regency in his name; if he survived it, he was obliged to abdicate his throne. For four centuries the Toltecs increased in numbers and influence: they spread over the country and built many cities, but suddenly in the very height of their prosperity, they were almost annihilated by a terrible pestilence, succeeded by a drought which swept away nearly the whole nation. The miserable remnant abandoned Tula about 1051, A.D.

Although the Toltecs were lost as a nation, they appear to have been the real founders of Mexican civilization. They were acquainted with agriculture and the art of working in metals; they invented the intricate calendar used by the Aztecs; they executed many useful mechanical arts; above all they raised buildings of such importance that, "their name passed into a synonyme for architecture." * A peculiar interest attaches to this early race, which has left behind it

* Prescott's Mexico, vol. I. p. 9.

such deep traces, whilst the people itself has passed away.

Different tribes, probably akin to the Toltecs, succeeded to their deserted lands. Of these the Chichemecs were the most considerable. They were a barbarous and migratory horde, amounting in number to some thousands, who wandered about from place to place under the rule of a chief named Xolotl. Their persons were almost entirely naked, and their only object of worship was the sun. Establishing themselves in the valley of Mexico, they intermarried with the inhabitants, and learned from them to cultivate cotton and to build permanent dwellings. At the news of their prosperity seven other tribes set out to join them. Though called by different names, taken from the localities in which they settled, they were all allied to one another, all spoke the same language, and all had the same habits of life. They arrived at intervals, and being gladly welcomed by Xolotl and the Chichemecs they formed a number of independent states. Xochimilco, Chalco, Colhuacan, Tlascala, and Mexico, were the names of their towns; whilst the whole people were called Nahuatlacs (dwellers by the waters), for all their early settlements were near the lake of Tezcuco.

Another nation, the Acolhuans, now appear upon the scene. Their origin is unknown, though it is probable they came from the north. Under the guidance of three young chieftains, beautiful of countenance and persuasive of speech, they advanced across the plateau of Anahuac until they reached the territory of the Chichemecs. Xolotl received them with open arms, bestowed his two daughters on two of the chieftains, and found a fair maiden of Chalco for the third.

Their subjects imitated the example of the royal house, and the united peoples pursued with success the arts of peace. Some warlike spirits that could not endure so regular a life left them to join the Otomies, a barbarous tribe on the northern boundary, which maintains to this day its ancient enmity to civilization. The remainder, under the fourth king after Xolotl, built the city of Tezcuco, and held it until the period immediately preceding the Spanish conquest.

Great was the lamentation of his subjects at the death of the wise Xolotl. They looked on him as the founder of their prosperity, they cherished the memory of his courage, his energy, and his justice. At his burial the royal corpse, covered with curiously wrought figures in gold and silver, was placed upon a couch made of aromatic substances: there it rested five days, until the nobles could arrive who were invited to the funeral; it was then solemnly burned, according to the custom of the Chichemecs. The ashes were collected into a vast urn of stone, which was exposed for forty days in one of the halls of the palace, and each day the nobles came to mourn the father of their country and to pay him the tribute of their tears. It was afterwards borne in grand procession to the place of royal sepulchre, and stored up within one of the pyramidal structures which are so common throughout Mexico, where it was consigned to the guardianship of the god of death. The account of this burial bears witness both to the advanced state of civilization of the people, and to the conviction that has so firm a hold upon the mind of man, namely, that there is a life beyond the grave. It is the priceless blessing of the Gospel that it at once confirms and satisfies this conviction, in revealing to us the Saviour who said,

"I am the Resurrection and the Life; he that believeth on me, though he were dead, yet shall he live."

Under the care of Xolotl's successors, Tezcuco became the Athens of Anahuac. It was the seat of its poetry and art, the chosen home of its learned men. The dominion of the Tezcucans spread over the surrounding country, but a sad reverse was in store for them. About the year 1418, A.D., they were invaded by the Tepanecs; a terrible struggle ensued, the city was taken, the king slain, and Nezahualcoyotl,* his heir, after seeing his father murdered before his eyes, only escaped by concealing himself in the branches of a tree. The subsequent history of this prince is full of romantic interest. He fell into the enemy's hands, and was confined in a dungeon; but an old servant of his father's succeeded in effecting the young king's escape, though his own life was the penalty of his loyalty. At length the royal family of Mexico interceded for the fugitive prince, and he was permitted to return to Tezcuco, and even to inhabit the regal palace. Eight years were spent in unmolested study, but the death of the Tepanec usurper, and the jealousy of his son, Maxtla, were the source of new troubles. Nezahualcoyotl hastened to pay his homage, but Maxtla spurned his offering of flowers, and showed such manifest disfavour that the Tezcucan prince hurried back to his home. Baffled in a scheme to assassinate him at a banquet, Maxtla next had recourse to open violence; but his intended victim courteously received his soldiers, and whilst they were refreshing themselves at his invitation, he effected his escape by a subterranean passage, and found an asylum in the cottage of one of his subjects.

* i.e., the hungry fox.

For some time, the proscribed prince led a wretched wandering life. A price was set upon his head, and the strictest search was instituted to discover him. Hunted from place to place—at one time concealed in the dense forests that fringed the territory of Tlascala, at another hidden in the cot of some humble Tezcucan—Nezahualcoyotl owed his preservation to the love and fidelity of his people. Once he took refuge within a large drum, around which a party of soldiers were dancing; on another occasion, when hard pressed, a maiden covered him with the stalks of *chian* she was reaping in the open field, and then pointed his pursuers to a false direction as that which he had selected. A large grant of land, and a bride of noble birth, were offered to any one who should capture him, dead or alive: but no bribe could tempt the poorest Tezcucan to betray their king. At length, the oppression of the Tepanecs became intolerable. The neighbouring states lent their aid to throw off the yoke, and after a bloody engagement, the Tezcucan prince recovered his rightful dominion. The territory of the Tepanecs was laid waste, and reserved as the great slave market of Anahuac: and a formal league, offensive and defensive, was arranged between Tezcuco, Mexico, and Tlacopan.

Restored to the throne of his fathers, Nezahualcoyotl reigned with wisdom and magnificence. He established councils of his wisest nobles to regulate the finances of his kingdom, and to decide all questions of war and justice. From the ordinary tribunals of the country an appeal lay to the supreme courts, and there was none of the delay so much complained of in our modern courts, as every four months a report was forwarded of all cases. Learning was encouraged and schools were established, whilst a rigid censorship was maintained over the productions of authors. On stated days, historical compositions and poems were recited, as at the Olympic games. The monarch himself turned poet, and some of his poems are still extant. They breathe the spirit of one who has drank the cup of pleasure, and is half tempted to cry, with Solomon, "all is vanity!" But knowing no better alternative, he returns to it again, saying, "let us eat and drink, for to-morrow we die."

Here is a specimen of his muse. "Banish care; if there are bounds to pleasure, the saddest life must also have an end. Then weave the chaplet of flowers, and sing thy songs in praise of the all-powerful God, for the glory of this world soon fadeth away. Rejoice in the green freshness of thy spring, for the day will come when thou shalt sigh for these joys in vain; when the sceptre shall pass from thy hands, thy servants shall wander desolate in thy courts, thy sons and the sons of thy nobles shall drink the dregs of distress, and all the pomp of thy victories and triumphs shall live only in their recollection. Yet the remembrance of the just shall not pass away from the nations, and the good thou hast done shall ever be held in honour. The goods of this life, its glories and its riches, are but lent to us, its substance is but an illusory shadow, and the things of to-day, shall change on the coming of the morrow."* How mournful is the chord thus struck by the Indian king in the height of his prosperity. How different from the firm faith of the apostle in the midst of his sufferings, "our light affliction, which is but for a moment,

* Prescott, vol. I. p. 148. It ought to be added that these reports of early Mexican civilization have been suspected of exaggeration.

worketh for us a far more exceeding and eternal weight of glory!"

It was no mean share of the world's wealth which had fallen to Nezahualcoyotl. The royal palace rose in the midst of the capital, extending for nearly three quarters of a mile in length, by more than half a mile in depth. It comprised two vast courts, the outer one served as the market-place of the city, whilst the inner one contained halls for the despatch of public business, for the reception and entertainment of foreign embassies, and for the retreat of men of science and learning. Here, too, were gathered the literature and archives of the past, and authors assembled to pursue their studies, or to recite their compositions. Hard by were the royal apartments, and the saloons of the king's numerous concubines: their walls bright with alabaster or gorgeous with hangings of feather work. These rooms opened into gardens laid out with much intricacy and beauty, dotted with fountains and baths of clear water, and enlivened by the varied plumage of tropical birds: whilst animals and birds that could not be brought there alive, were skilfully modelled in gold and silver. Upwards of 400,000,000 of pounds of maize, nearly 300,000,000 of pounds of cocoa, 8,000 turkeys, 1,300 baskets of salt, with game, vegetables, and condiments innumerable, were yearly supplied for the royal table. Nor is it at all incredible that the pile contained three hundred apartments, some of them fifty yards square, when we read the accounts of the vast ruins that still attest the magnificence of the palace, or when we recall to mind that its remains have furnished the materials for all the churches and other buildings since erected at Tezcuco by the Spaniards.

In the midst of so much pomp and splendour Nezahualcoyotl, formerly the proscribed fugitive, ruled supreme. Once in each four months, perhaps much oftener, his mind reverted to his former fortunes; for then the whole court, dressed in robes of the coarsest linen, were assembled to hear an address on the Tezcucan code of morality and on the uncertainty of human things. The preacher boldly rebuked any one who had been guilty of notorious crime, not even excepting the monarch himself; and it is said that the audience were often moved to tears. But beneath all this magnificence of the court there must have been abject terror in the minds of the people, as the smallest offence was punished with death: in one instance, indeed, this severity was relaxed, as will be seen from the following anecdote:

The king was fond of stripping off the robes of state and mixing in disguise with his people. One day he fell in with a boy gathering sticks for fuel. "Why do you not go into the woods and get as many as you want?" asked the monarch. "Because the wood belongs to the king, and it is death to be caught trespassing there." "What sort of a man is your king?" replied the questioner. "A very hard man, who denies the people what God gave them," was the answer. The king pressed the boy to disregard so harsh a law, but the lad stoutly refused, and at last turned upon him with the accusation that he wished to betray him. Nezahualcoyotl went home, and sending for the boy and his parents, dismissed them with a liberal present, and relaxed the severity of his forest laws.

Another anecdote is far less favourable to the monarch's character. On a visit to an aged noble, the latter, out of compliment to his sovereign, bade his young and beautiful wife wait on them at the banquet. The king conceived a violent passion for her; but, dissembling his feelings, he returned home, and then adopted the stratagem of David against Uriah. He ordered the nobleman to take the field against the enemy, and commanded two of his attendants to lead him into the thickest of the fight. The old man saw through the design, and foretold its issue. After a decent interval, and with every effort to avoid suspicion, the widow was then summoned to court, and became the legitimate wife of the monarch.

Our space forbids us to linger over the life of Nezahualcoyotl, but one more circumstance must be recorded ere we pass on. The marriage which had been so iniquitously contrived was not blessed with offspring, and the monarch in his difficulty consulted the priests. They made answer that the gods withheld the boon because they were not honoured by human sacrifices, and that nothing else would avail. To such offerings the king had been always most averse; for the simple religious rites of the Tezcucans were not marked by the blood we shall presently find so freely shed by the Aztecs. At length he reluctantly consented. The sacrifices were offered, but the Queen was yet childless. He then withdrew to his rural palace, where he remained for forty days, fasting at fixed intervals and making no other offerings than sweet incense and aromatic herbs. At length his desire was accomplished. In his joy he raised a huge pyramid, surmounted by a lofty tower, which he dedicated to " the unknown God, the Cause of causes." No image was to be allowed to be reared in his temple, and no blood to stain his altars.

From this time the monarch lived much in retirement, dwelling upon the shadowy speculations as to human nature and its destiny, which are all that man, unaided by the Bible, can grasp. He could say " Let us aspire to that heaven where all is eternal, and corruption cannot come ;" but he knew not how to reach it through faith in Him who came down from heaven to raise his people thither. He died full of years and honours, commending his infant son to his most trusty councillors, and maintaining in the agonies of death an unbroken spirit of endurance, which was only melted on bidding farewell to those most dear to him. When they had said their adieus, the brave old man ordered that no one else should be admitted to his presence, and died in the solitary dignity which was supposed to become his station.

Nezahualpilli (the prince for whom one has fasted), was but eight years old at the time of his father's death. When he grew up, he in many respects resembled his father, but his character was cast in a sterner mould. With greater self-restraint, he had less compassion for the erring. When his favourite son was detected in a criminal intrigue, the king caused the youth to be tried by the ordinary tribunal, and allowed the sentence of death passed by it to be put into execution. This event embittered the monarch's heart, and he spent some time in seclusion, mourning in solitude over his sorrow. Perhaps it was to drown the memory of this grief that he afterwards abandoned himself to a life of luxurious ease. At any rate his early vigour and warlike spirit were lost, and the Mexican Montezuma, his rival, encroached upon the Tezcucan territories and assumed the title of supremacy which the Tezcucan monarch had hitherto borne. Under the pressure of these calamities, Nezahualpilli sickened and died in the year 1515, and when the Spaniards arrived, a few years later, they found the empire in the power of Montezuma.

Tlascala has been mentioned as one of the Nahuatlac cities built among the Chichemecs, on the borders of the lake of Tezcuco. For some unexplained reason the Tlascalans incurred the enmity of the neighbouring states, who combined against them, and a bloody battle ensued, in which the Tlascalans were victorious. They determined, however, to leave a country which was encircled on all sides by their foes, and selected the region between the sierra of Tlascala and the mountains that shut in the valley of Mexico. Here they found a district strongly fortified by nature, abounding in fertile valleys running up into the hills, and sweeping downwards towards the east, in which direction alone an open plain, some six miles in width, seemed to invite the attacks of their enemies. They raised a strong wall across the mouth of this valley, and entrusted its custody to a body of the Otomies, a wild race who made common cause with them.

Entrenched in such a territory, the Tlascalans passed a free and simple life. The name of their country (Tlascala, meaning "the land of bread,") signified the abundance with which they were blessed. Their state was divided into four republics, united into a federation, but each of which was ruled by its own aristocracy. The people were divided into an order of hereditary nobility and a mass of plebeians. Trained from their childhood to endurance and other habits which might make them good soldiers, the Tlascalans enjoyed a high reputation for bravery in war, and for wisdom and honour in peace. Amongst other evidences of civilization, the Spaniards found an order of knighthood existing among them, entrance to which was much coveted by the young Tlascalan nobles.

The Tlascalans seem to have incurred the enmity of their neighbours very soon after their settlement in their new country. The adjoining state of Cholula was the first to attack them; but met with such a repulse as deterred the Cholulans from repeating the attempt. At a later period, when the empire of Montezuma was extended over the whole surrounding country, he was especially indignant that his power should be defied by so small a state, in the very heart of his territory. His rage was yet more inflamed when a force he sent against them was defeated, and his son, who commanded the expedition, was slain. Immense preparations were then made to subjugate the Tlascalans, but the hardy mountaineers dashed down the sides of their native hills, or inveigled their enemies into the narrow passes; and, although unceasing hostilities were carried on for some years, and their country was so completely blockaded that for more than half a century they had neither cotton, cocoa, nor salt, yet the little republic still remained unsubdued. These efforts naturally engendered that bitter hatred of Montezuma and his Aztec subjects which Cortez turned to his own advantage in the conquest of the country.

The Aztecs were the most important of all the Mexican races when the Spaniards arrived in the country. Descending from the north, at the close of the twelfth century of our era, they wandered for upwards of a hundred years and endured incredible hardships: nor was it until the year 1325 that they founded the city of Mexico. As they halted on the south-western side of the principal lake (so runs the legend), they beheld a royal eagle of vast size perched upon the stem of a prickly pear, his broad wings spread out to the sun, and a serpent in his talons. Its appearance was regarded as an auspicious omen, and on this spot they accordingly commenced their city, which they themselves called Tenochtitlan, but which is better known as Mexico, from Mexitli, the Aztec god of war.

At its origin Mexico was a miserable village of huts, built upon piles thrust into the lake, and its inhabitants lived mainly by fishing. By what means they gradually advanced we are unable to record. They allied themselves with the people of Tezcuco and Tlacopan, and the three states flourished during the season of security which their combined strength secured. The prosperity of the Aztecs reached its height under Montezuma. Through his diplomatic skill and courage the allied peoples of Tezcuco and Tlacopan were reduced to tributaries. Far and wide was the monarch's power extended, until across the valley of Mexico and over the mountains to the coasts of the Gulf his supremacy was universally acknowledged, with the single exception of the Tlascalans; and when Cortez landed he found the whole country under the rule of this powerful king.

The Aztec government was despotic. The monarch was elected to his office by the four chief nobles, whose choice was confined to the royal family. After him came the great caciques or chieftains, the heads of the native tribes. There was an order of hereditary nobility, a large sacerdotal class, and then a mass of plebeians and slaves. These members made up the body of the Aztec people. The great chieftains possessed immense territories, and their power and wealth made them so formidable to the emperor, that he insisted on their presence in the capital during a part of each year, and required hostages for their good behaviour in their absence. Of the priesthood we shall speak more particularly when we advert to the religion of the Aztecs. Slavery existed, though in a very modified form. Slaves could hold property, could not be required to render more than a certain amount of service, and their lives were protected by law. Intermarriages between slaves and their masters were not uncommon, and no one could be born to slavery; even the children of slaves being free from their birth.

The laws of the country were enacted by the emperor, but their administration was confided to judges, who held their office for life, and could not be removed by the monarch except on conviction of injustice. Death was the penalty of almost all offences: adultery, theft, drunkenness in young persons, removal of a neighbour's boundary, or peculation in acting as the guardian of an orphan, were all capital crimes. There was no appeal from the judge to the sovereign, and with the contempt for human life so frightfully evinced in their sacrifices, execution followed immediately upon the sentence. The same punishment awaited any judge who received a bribe, and was even inflicted upon one who had heard causes in his own house instead of the public courts.

The tenure of land was somewhat singular. Each tribe possessed its own lands, and these were divided amongst its members by officers appointed for that purpose. If a family became extinct, or removed to another region, the lands it had held could not be alienated by sale, but reverted to the common stock of the tribe, and were again distributed. There were vast crown lands, which were cultivated for the benefit of the royal treasury; and a part of the agricultural produce of the whole country was assigned for the support of the immense household which was gathered around the person of the monarch. Besides this tribute, particular taxes were imposed upon certain districts, which had to supply materials or artificers for building, or to furnish provisions and fuel.

These exactions might seem trifling in most primitive countries, but the valley of Mexico was thickly populated, and the inhabitants were often hard pressed to feed the court of Montezuma. But the revenue officers did not confine their demands to these requirements, there were heavy taxes upon all the manufactures of the country. Here is a list compiled from the Mexican records which will amuse those who are curious in such matters—the items were those furnished by different cities for the imperial use.

"Twenty chests of ground chocolate, 40 pieces of armour of a particular device; 2,400 loads of large mantles of twisted cloth; 800 loads of small mantles or rich wearing apparel; 5 pieces of armour of rich feathers; 60 pieces of armour of common feathers; a chest of beans; a chest of *chian ;* a chest of maize; 8,000 reams of paper; 2,000 loaves of very white salt, for the consumption only of the lords of Mexico; 8,000 lumps of unrefined copal; 400 small baskets of refined copal; 100 copper axes; 80 loads of red chocolate; 800 *xcicaras*, out of which they drank chocolate; a little vessel of small turquoise stones; 4 chests full of maize; 4,000 loads of lime; tiles of gold, of the size of an oyster and as thick as the finger; 40 bags of cochineal; 20 bags of gold-dust, of the finest quality; a diadem of gold of a specified pattern; 20 lips jewels of clear amber, ornamented with gold; 200 loads of chocolate; 100 pots or jars of liquid amber; 8,000 handfuls of rich scarlet feathers; 40 tigers' skins; 1,600 bundles of cotton, &c., &c."* Such a catalogue, although without any pretension to be an accurate and exhaustive account of the revenues paid in this form, may serve as a guide to the splendour of the Aztec monarch. Just before the arrival of the Spaniards, some of these imposts became so burdensome as to create much dissatisfaction among the subjects of Montezuma. Thus the way was largely opened for the conquest of the country.

In an extensive empire, which is the fruit of conquest and is held by force, it is necessary to have a system of communication between the capital and the most distant regions, that any attempt at insurrection may be promptly met and crushed. Such a line of posts was established in Mexico. Couriers were trained from childhood to run at great speed from city to city. By this means Montezuma was immediately acquainted with the entrance of the fleet of Cortez into the harbour of St. Juan de Ulua. The same agency ministered to the luxury of the palace. Fish caught in the Gulf of Mexico, two hundred miles distant, was served up in twenty-four hours upon the royal table.

The army of the Aztecs was carefully organized. Each district provided its assigned number of men, under the command of their native chieftains. The companies were massed in divisions eight thousand strong, the whole army being usually led by the king in person. Much of the agency now common in Europe was employed to animate and strengthen the troops. Orders of military knighthood were esta-

* Prescott's Mexico, vol. I. p. 3².

blished. The right of wearing armorial devices was only to be won by some gallant deed. Strict discipline was maintained. And the standard of the empire was the rallying point of its defenders. The host made a brave show as it marched forth with the gold and silver cuirasses of the chieftains, or their brilliant mantles of feather work. The Spaniards were excited to admiration by the light skirmishing and combined movements of the Mexican host. United action must, however, have been greatly interfered with by their anxiety to take prisoners in battle. To secure a prisoner for the sacrifice, not to slay him on the field, was their first object. No amount of ransom could purchase the freedom of a captive.

Nor were the Mexicans altogether ignorant of the politer walks of literature. They invented a species of picture-writing, and thus past history was transmitted by a method far more reliable than oral tradition. Their system, of course, lacked the accuracy of letters, and it needed special instruction in the secret meaning of the symbols to enable any one to interpret their manuscripts. Many things were expressed by rude representations; where this was impossible emblems were used. Thus a tongue, denoted speaking; a foot-print, travelling; a man sitting on the ground, an earthquake; and so on.* The priests had also a peculiar system of sacred hieroglyphics, in which their religious mysteries were preserved and recorded.

This picture-writing was of a very primitive character, very inferior to the Egyptian hieroglyphics. The colours of the figures also conveyed some further information as to the meaning of the writing. They had a much more simple method of representing num-

* Prescott, vol. I. p. 79.

bers. The first twenty numbers were expressed by as many dots; certain combinations of which were employed to represent higher figures. Their writings were delineated on cloth, or skins, or more commonly on a kind of paper manufactured from the leaves of the Mexican aloe. This latter formed a beautiful soft material, and was often painted in brilliant colours, amongst which the red of the cochineal (first obtained from Mexico) was conspicuous. The manuscripts were either done up into rolls or shut up in the shape of folding-screens, and divided into volumes of moderate size.

But there is no more striking proof of the high state of Aztec civilization than the elaboration of their calendar. The year was divided into eighteen months of twenty days. Each month was divided into four weeks of five days, and on the fifth day a market was held for the sale of goods. As this plan only embraced 360, out of the 365 days of the solar year, they added five days which belonged to no month, and were esteemed as of ill omen. On the yearly recurrence of these days, the Mexicans broke their household images, destroyed their domestic utensils, rent their clothes, and waited in much apprehension for the dawn of new year's morning, when fresh things were brought out, amidst general rejoicings, to replace those which had been destroyed.

A still more remarkable proof of the accuracy of their observation is afforded by the fact that they intercalated twenty-five days every 104 years, or rather twelve days and a half every cycle of fifty-two years. Thus they corrected the error which would have gradually crept into their computation from the absence of a day corresponding to the 29th of February, or leap year, with ourselves. The cycle of fifty-two years was divided into four periods of thirteen years each, and by a very ingenious system of hieroglyphics, comprising only four symbols, but so arranged that the same symbol did not express the same year in any one of the four periods, they represented with ease every year in the cycle. These careful schemes indicate an acuteness and accuracy of thought which are most astonishing in a half barbarous people.

Agriculture was pursued with much success, and the large numbers of the population gave considerable importance to this branch of industry. We shall speak elsewhere of the natural products of Mexico, with which the grateful soil made abundant return for the care bestowed on its cultivation. Maize, the aloe, and the banana, were the most important crops. Large public granaries stored up the surplus produce, and provided a remedy against years of scarcity, which proved so disastrous under Spanish rule.

Mexico is pre-eminently the land of flowers, and the natives fostered them with much care. They trained them about their huts, wove them into garlands, or strewed them as a thick carpet on their feast days; and as their canoes shot across the lake of Tezcuco to the capital, the coarsest freight was beautified with a plentiful covering of blossoms.

The Mexicans were clever workmen in the precious metals. Considering how much silver was afterwards found in the country, it seems strange that we hear so little of it at the period of the conquest; probably the attention of the Spaniards was engrossed by the gold of which Montezuma had such vast store. Figures, in imitation of birds and animals, beautifully wrought, some with alternate feathers of gold and silver, extorted the marked approval of Cortez. They were ignorant of the use of iron, but had a kind of bronze composed of tin and copper, of which they made their tools. They used also obsidian for knives and axes. It is marvellous how they managed with such implements, and without any beasts of burden to transport huge masses of stone to the capital, or even to cut them from the quarry. The celebrated calendar stone was a block of dark porphyry, weighing some fifty tons, and this had been brought a distance of many leagues across lakes and over bridges. There were *guilds* or companies of trades, and the dignity of labour was comprehended by the Aztecs. "Apply thyself, my son," said an aged chief, "to agriculture, or to feather-work, or some other honourable calling; thus did your ancestors before you, else how would they have provided for themselves and their families? Never was it heard that nobility alone was able to maintain its possessors."* The merchants seem frequently to have travelled in caravans, like the company of Ishmaelites to whom Joseph was sold, and like them too, they held slave-dealing to be an honourable pursuit. On their journeys they were often employed as ambassadors, and some of their number were always near the person of the Aztec monarch.

Let us try to get a glimpse of the Mexicans at home. The estimation in which woman is held is a very decisive test of the condition of a people. Amongst the North American Indians women are slaves, and perform all the severe labour, war or hunting being the only pursuit of the men. With the civilized Hindoos they held no higher place. But amongst the Mexicans the gentler sex was treated with almost European

* Prescott, vol. I. p. 124.

courtesy and kindness. The most elaborate politeness (a marked feature in the natives to this day,) was observed, and visits of etiquette were paid on all the more important occasions of daily life. Banquets were given to which friends were summoned, and all the luxury of precious metals and elaborate cookery was employed to render them agreeable. Game in abundance smoked upon the board; pastry and fruits were served up; chocolate, beaten up into a thick paste, was handed round and eaten cold. The old people drank pulque (too much of it sometimes), whilst the young folks danced before them. They smoked tobacco, and sometimes swallowed its fumes; they even took snuff, so that many of our own bad habits could find a parallel in Mexican native customs. To all this refinement there was often a horribly revolting adjunct; the flesh of a slave, very carefully prepared, was eaten upon great occasions.

The children were taken from home at an early age and educated by the priests, the girls under teachers of their own sex. They were treated with much severity, and early experienced the truth that there is no royal road to knowledge. Their education finished, they returned home and met with a kindness much in contrast with their school days, and which must have endeared the parents' roof to them. When a daughter was married she was addressed by her parents on her duty as a wife. She was told to be simple and modest in manner, to be obedient to her husband, to be cleanly in her person. The latter duty appears unhappily to be no longer recognised in Mexico.

Bernal Diaz, who accompanied Cortez, has given us the following account of Montezuma's mode of life. " His cooks had upwards of thirty different ways of cooking meats, and they had earthen vessels so contrived as to keep them constantly hot. For the table of Montezuma himself above three hundred dishes were dressed, and for his guards above one thousand. Before dinner, Montezuma would sometimes go out and inspect the preparations, and his officers would point out to him which were the best, and explain of what birds and flesh they were composed, and of these he would eat. But this was more for amusement than anything else.

"It is said that at times the flesh of young children was dressed for him; but the ordinary meats were domestic fowls, pheasants, geese, partridges, quails, venison, Indian hogs, pigeons, hares, and rabbits, with many other animals and birds peculiar to the country. At his meals, in cold weather, a number of torches, of the bark of a tree which makes no smoke and has an aromatic smell, were lighted, and that they should not throw too much heat, screens, ornamented with gold and painted with figures of idols, were placed before them.

"Montezuma was seated on a low throne, or chair, at a table proportioned to the height of his seat. The table was covered with white cloths and napkins, and four beautiful women presented him with water for his hands in vessels with plates under them to catch the water. They also presented him with towels.

"Then two other women brought small cakes of bread; and when the king began to eat, a large screen of wood was placed before him, so that during that period people should not behold him. The women having retired to a little distance, four ancient lords stood by the throne, to whom Montezuma from time to time addressed questions, and, as a mark of peculiar favour, gave to each of them a plate of that which he was eating. I was told that these old lords, who were his near relations, were also councillors and judges. The plates which Montezuma presented to them they received with high respect, eating what was on them without taking their eyes off the ground. He was served in earthenware of Cholula, red and black. While the king was at the table, none of his guards in the vicinity of his apartment dared for their lives to make any noise. Fruit of all kinds produced in the country was laid before him; he ate very little, but from time to time a liquor, prepared from cocoa and of a stimulative quality, was presented to him in golden cups.

"At different intervals during the dinner, there entered certain Indians, humpbacked, very deformed and ugly, who played tricks of buffoonery, and others who were jesters. There was also a company of singers and dancers, who afforded Montezuma much entertainment. To these he ordered the vases of chocolate to be distributed. The four female attendants then took away the cloths, and again with much respect presented him with water to wash his hands, during which time Montezuma conferred with the four old noblemen formerly mentioned, after which they took their leave with many ceremonies.

"One thing I forgot to mention in its place, and that is, during the time Montezuma was at dinner, two very beautiful women were busily employed making small cakes, with eggs and other things mixed therein. These were delicately white, and, when made, were presented to him on plates covered with napkins. Also another kind of bread was brought to him in long loaves, and plates of cakes resembling wafers.

"After he had dined, they presented to him three little canes, highly ornamented, containing liquid amber mixed with a herb which they call tobacco; and when he had sufficiently viewed and heard the singers, dancers, and buffoons, he took a little of the smoke of one of these canes, and then laid himself down to sleep."

We have thus far noticed the favourable features of Aztec civilization, and it is difficult to determine with accuracy, how far they extended amongst the mass of the population, or whether they were mainly confined to the higher orders. Nor can we discriminate between the actual condition of Mexican society and the bright or dark medium through which it has been regarded by the chroniclers, to whom we are indebted for information concerning it. This much at any rate is certain. A high standard of material comfort and elegance had been reached by the Aztecs. Many branches of art were successfully pursued, and their social condition was not altogether deficient in those humanizing influences which exert a beneficial power over the mind of man. But side by side with these there were sterner elements which gave quite an opposite character to the public ceremonies of the Mexicans. These were connected with their religious ceremonies, with some account of which we shall conclude this notice of the early history of the country.

The religious system of the Aztecs combined two strangely diverse elements. The one breathed a gentle spirit, the other was stern and cruel. It would seem that the people had once been possessed of a milder faith, upon which the sanguinary rites were afterwards engrafted which the Spaniards found to be prevalent on their arrival.

The Aztecs had certain expressions which spoke of a supreme Creator, the Lord of the Universe. They spoke of him as "the god by whom we live, that knoweth all thoughts and giveth all gifts, without whom man is as nothing, and under whose wings he finds repose and a sure defence." This confession was, however, merely speculative, and did not lead to any practical result. Their creed embraced thirteen principal, and more than two hundred inferior deities.

The most pleasing of these was Quetzalcoatl, the god of the air, the benignant deity of Aztec mythology. In an early age, according to their legends, he had come to reside amongst men. He had taught them the arts of agriculture, manufacture, and government. He had blessed their fields with abundant produce. In short he had inaugurated a golden age. Did the superior gods envy man the blessings which he conferred? We know not, but at any rate they drove him from Mexico. On his departure he promised to return and renew the season of prosperity. This tradition was cherished by the people, and when the Spaniards landed on their shores they believed that the appointed era was come. The image of the god represented a man tall of stature, with a fair skin, dark hair, and a flowing beard.

Huitzilopotchli, the god of war, was a terrible contrast to Quetzalcoatl. He rejoiced in the blood of human sacrifices, and captives taken in the field were offered as victims on his altars. His temples, like those of the other Aztec deities, were large mounds of earth, pyramidal in shape, and cased with brick or stone. They were divided into terraces, access to which was gained by flights of steps. All the ceremonial of worship was performed in the open air.

Long lines of procession were formed. After mounting the first flight of steps they wound round the terrace to the second flight, then round the second terrace, and so on to the flat summit. Here stood the altars on which the sacrifices were immolated, beneath the vault of heaven. Two tall towers contained the images of the deity to whom the teocalli or temple was dedicated.

There was a numerous sacerdotal order, headed by two high priests, who ranked next in dignity to the emperor. They were allowed to marry, but during the period of their ministrations they lived apart from their families in a kind of monastery. Like the priests of Baal, they practised great austerities, and cut themselves with knives and lancets. They were intrusted with the education of the Aztec youth. Thrice each day, and once at night, they were summoned to prayers.

Many rites were observed which have their counterpart in the Romish creed. Confession was practised, its secrets were held inviolable, and absolution gave a legal acquittal in case of arrest. The same offence, however, was not forgiven twice; and confession was therefore often put off till death drew near, a proceeding which may find a parallel in Romish practice. Children were baptized with water. Penance was exacted and performed. Humility, morality, and charity to the poor, were enjoined. Yet the priests, who inculcated these maxims, purchased the children of their poorer countrymen to offer them in sacrifice to their gods.

Human sacrifices are said to have been adopted about two centuries before the conquest. They were intended to enforce with greater solemnity the lessons of life, or the nature of the gods. We select a single example. A year before the feast of Tezcatlepoca, "the soul of the world," a captive of great personal beauty was selected for the sacrifice. For twelve months he was treated with regal magnificence. The most abject homage, the most splendid dress, the most gorgeous banquets, the most beauteous concubines were provided for him: and he was worshipped as a god. The fatal day came. He was led away to the temple, was bidden to throw away his garlands, as he mounted to its summit, and on reaching the altar was quickly despatched by the priests. His heart was plucked out, and the warm and quivering body was hurled down the sides of the teocalli to be torn in pieces and devoured by the multitude below. In this horrible tragedy the Aztecs read the drama of human life: fair in its outset and gloomy at its close.

As the empire advanced, human sacrifice prevailed more largely. Thousands of victims perished at the shrines. The temples were multiplied, and the capital was lighted up at night with the undying flames upon 600 altars. How terrible the system finally became may be estimated from two facts. In one temple alone, the Spaniards counted the skulls of one hundred and thirty-six thousand victims. The lowest computation estimates that twenty thousand human beings were annually sacrificed.

How may we solve the strange enigma which such a creed as that of Mexico presents? How can we reconcile these startling contradictions—the existence of so horrible a practice of cannibalism and human slaughter, side by side with the exalted maxims we have quoted? We know no other answer to this inquiry than that which is supplied to us by the

Inspired Word of God. The corruption of human nature since Adam's fall explains the evil; the purity in which man was first created, some feeble and powerless relics of which still survive, accounts for the better elements in the character of mankind. Deeply underlying all this horrible human bloodshed, lay the consciousness that man was alienated from God, and needed through some means of suffering and sacrifice to be reconciled to him. In his blindness the poor Aztec sought by such a mode of worship to appease the Deity whom he felt he had offended, and of whose wrath he was afraid. If St. Paul had stood within the Aztec capital he might have seized upon these witnesses for the gospel which he preached, and have declared at once the true character of man's sin, and the only remedy by which that sin can be removed.

As we dwell upon such a history as this of Mexico before its conquest by Hernando Cortez, it seems to afford us an almost startling insight into human nature. In the depth of degradation to which the nation sank despite all the civilization it could boast of, what a strong confirmation there is of the deceitfulness of sin, and of the desperate wickedness of the heart of fallen man. In the utter inability of all their noblest maxims to exert any powerful or practical influence upon the life and conduct of the people, what an illustration is afforded us of man's need of some aid from without, which may enable him not only to perceive and know what he ought to do, but may also give him grace and power faithfully to fulfil it. And even in the horrible sacrifice of so many thousands of their fellow creatures, what an evidence is vouchsafed us of the almost universal conviction of mankind, that " without shedding of blood there can be no remission of sin." Whilst such thoughts are suggested to us by the narrative we have been reading, they surely ought to lead us to self-examination, that we may "make our own calling and election sure." We live in a country blessed with the light of gospel truth, as well as highly favoured with an advanced civilization; but no merely outward influence which these may have exerted on our minds and our lives, will avail us in the day of judgment. We must be changed in heart, we must be born again, must be converted and receive a new nature; only those who in Christ Jesus have become new creatures, with changed tastes, habits, and affections, can enter into the kingdom of heaven. Reader —have you experienced such a change? Are you a possessor, are you at least a searcher for the aid from without, of which we have spoken, even of the guidance of the Holy Spirit which God has promised to give to them that seek it in prayer? In the consciousness of your weakness, are you asking to be "strengthened with might by his Spirit in your inner man"? In the consciousness of your sinfulness, are you asking to be cleansed from all guilt by the application of Christ's redeeming blood? These are the precious, the inestimable blessings, which are offered to us freely in the gospel, and they alone can satisfy all the yearnings of our hearts on earth, or make us meet to be partakers of eternal happiness in heaven.

NOTE TO CHAPTER II.

The following versified specimen of Nezahualcoyotl's poetry is taken from the appendix to Prescott's "Conquest of Mexico." The entire poem is too long for insertion, and its burden is the same throughout. *

> When sorrows shall my truth attest,
> And this thy throne decline,
> The birds of thy ancestral nest,
>   The princes of thy line,
> The mighty of thy race, shall see
> The bitter ills of poverty:
> And then shall memory recall
> Thy envied greatness, and on all
>   Thy brilliant triumphs dwell;
> And as they think on bygone years,
> Compared with present shame, their tears
>   Shall to an ocean swell.
>
> Then Nezahualcoyotl, now,
>   In what thou *hast*, delight
> And wreathe around thy regal brow
>   Life's garden blossoms bright;
> List to my lyre and to my lay,
> Which aim to please thee, and obey
> The pleasures, which our lives present,
> Earth's sceptres, and its wealth, are lent,
>   Our shadows fleeting by;
> Appearance colours all our bliss;
> A truth so great, that now to this
>   One question, make reply.
>
> What has become of Cihuapan
>   Quantzintecomtzin brave,
> And Conahuatzin, mighty man?
>   Where are they? In the grave!
> Their names remain, but they are fled,
> For ever numbered with the dead;
> Would that those now in friendship bound,
> We whom Love's thread encircles round,
>   Death's cruel edge, might see,
> Since good on earth is insecure,
> And all things must a change endure
>   In dark futurity.

* The poet is supposed to be addressing the monarch.

CHAPTER III.

THE STORY OF THE CONQUEST.

Spain in the 16th Century—Discovery of Cuba—Hernando Cortez—His early history—Sails to San Domingo—Discovery of Yucatan—Cortez appointed by Velasquez over the Expedition to Mexico—Suspicions of Velasquez—Armament sets sail—Character of Cortez - Cozumel reached— Aguilar—Yucatan—Conversion of the Tabascans—Landing at Vera Cruz—Embassy from Montezuma—Negotiations— Refusal of Montezuma—Determination to proceed—Dissensions in the Camp—A Colony formed—Cortez re-appointed Leader—Cunning Policy of Cortez—March to Cempoalla— Beautiful Scenery—Joy of the Spaniards—Civilization of the Indians—Character of Spanish Religion—Preaching at Cempoalla—Further Dissensions—March to Tlascala—Fierce Battles—Enter Tlascala—Embassy from Montezuma—Cortez goes to Cholula—Conspiracy against the Spaniards—Massacre at Cholula—Reflections—March to Mexico—First View of the Capital—Montezuma's Fears—Hospitable Reception— Imprisonment and Unworthy Treatment of Montezuma— Fresh Troops arrive from Velasquez—Narvaez Conquered— Insurrection of the Mexicans—Death of Montezuma— Perilous Position of Cortez—The Sad Night—Retreat from Mexico—Tactics of Cortez—Towns on the Lake of Tezcuco —Siege and Fall of Iztapalapan—A New Fleet built— Battle of Xaltocan—Launch of the Fleet—Naval Battle— Sufferings of the Spaniards—Mexico Invested—Rash Assault —Losses of the Spaniards—Aztec Obstinacy—Horrors of the Siege—Mexico taken—Capture of Guatemozin—Reflections on the Conquest—False and True Greatness.

THERE were few countries that could vie with Spain in the early part of the 16th century. Its different divisions had been united under one government by the marriage of Ferdinand of Aragon with Isabella of Castille, from whom the country descended entire into the hands of Charles V. The states thus combined retained their own representative bodies, and so large a measure of freedom as to occasion much disgust to their haughty sovereign. The people were a bold and manly race, possessed of considerable energy of character, the fruit of many years contest with the Moors for the freedom of their native land; and now that there was peace at home, they were looking eagerly abroad for new scenes of fame and wealth, either on the fields of Italy, or in the yet unknown country across the sea which had just been revealed to them by Columbus.

Before the period of which we are about to treat, the West India Islands were already known, and among them Cuba and Hispaniola had been made the seats of Spanish settlements. From these islands several expeditions had set out to explore the new country. Vasco Nunez, of Balboa, had landed at Darien, and had there met with a civilization superior to anything that had been seen upon the islands. The western point of Cuba approaches so nearly to Yucatan, that we are quite prepared to learn that this portion of the mainland was soon visited: this was done by Hernandez, of Cordova, in 1517. The following year, Velasquez, the governor of Cuba, despatched a fleet under the command of Grijalva, which, after sighting Cozumel, entered the river of Tabasco that falls into the Gulf of Mexico. On this occasion, the name of New Spain was first applied to the surrounding country. Grijalva was severely blamed on his return for having made no settlement in the new territory;

a circumstance which should be remembered in the course of the following narrative. Before his arrival, Velasquez had fitted out a larger armament with a view to prosecute further researches, and over this he placed Hernando Cortez, the future conqueror of Mexico.

Hernando Cortez was born at Medellin, in Estremadura, A.D., 1485. He came of a poor but noble family. His continued sickness in infancy, his idle habits at school, and profligacy at the University of Salamanca, were a source of constant anxiety to his parents : and when the youth came home from Salamanca, wearied with law and a poor student's life, his irregularities broke in upon the order and destroyed the peace of his father's hearth. To such a lad the only refuge was a soldier's career, and adopting this, Cortez, being then only sixteen years old, determined to sail with Ovando, who had just been appointed governor of Hispaniola. But in pursuing some intrigue he fell from the wall of a court-yard, and the fever which followed detained him in bed whilst the expedition started. He next proposed to join the Italian army, and went to Valencia with that object; but here he again fell ill and passed a year in poverty and sickness. This discipline seems for a time to have steadied his wild recklessness ; for, before finally setting out for the Indies, he went home to receive his parents' blessing. The vessel that bore him reached St. Domingo after a stormy voyage, which, as well as Cortez's behaviour in the hour of peril, was an emblem of his future career.

Ovando, the governor of Hispaniola, was absent when Cortez arrived at St. Domingo. But his secretary assured the young adventurer that he would, no doubt, obtain a liberal grant of land on which to settle. " I came to get gold," was the reply, " not to till the soil like a peasant." The handsome lad of seventeen, however, soon ingratiated himself into the governor's favour and received substantial tokens of his regard; and when Diego Velasquez was despatched to subdue the Island of Cuba, Cortez accompanied him as one of his secretaries.

At Cuba, we find Cortez involved in trouble from his old habits of profligacy and intrigue. He had some dispute with Velasquez, who required him to marry a certain Catalina Xuarez, to whom Cortez is said to have pledged himself, although he was now unwilling to fulfil his promise. The accounts of his subsequent conduct are not very clear. For some time he was in bitter hostility to Velasquez, and stories are told of his behaviour that well accord with his audacity and libertine habits. At length he was reconciled to the governor, and after his marriage with Catalina, their friendship was confirmed by his appointment to be alcalde of Santiago, the new Cuban capital. As, according to one of his biographers, he threw great diligence into everything he did, Cortez now became a prosperous man, was master of a valuable estate, and with a number of Indians who were assigned to him, he worked gold mines and amassed a considerable sum of money. "God, who alone knows at what cost of Indians' lives it was obtained," says Las Casas, "will take account of it."

When matters were in this state, Alvarado returned to Cuba with the account of Grijalva's discovery of Yucatan. The news caused great excitement throughout the island. It told that there was a vast continent peopled by races far more civilized than any that had hitherto been met with. It held out a prospect of obtaining wealth far more speedily than even by the reckless employment of slaves in Cuba. There was, too, all the inducement which adventure offers to the explorers of an unknown country : and to these motives yet higher considerations were added. It was reported that some Spaniards, the remnant of a former disastrous expedition, were still living in Yucatan. Velasquez accordingly determined to fit out another fleet, and he selected Cortez to command it, as has been already stated.

The appointment of Cortez is said to have been due to the good offices of Amador de Lares, the royal treasurer in the island, and of Andres de Duero, the secretary of Velasquez; but there were many persons about the court who were incensed at having been passed over, and they did not fail to urge every kind of objection against sending Cortez on so important a mission. They reminded the jealous governor of his former quarrel with the new commander, and they employed Cervantes, the jester of Velasquez, to give utterance to their enmity. One day, when Velasquez and Cortez went to the sea-side to see how the preparation of the fleet was progressing, Cervantes cried out, " Diego ! look what you are about ; we shall have to go and hunt after Cortez." Andres de Duero answered angrily, " Be quiet, and do not play the rascal any more ; we know well that these malicious things, which pretend to be jests, do not come from you." But the jester went on saying, " Here's to the health of my friend, Diego, and his lucky captain, Cortez ! and I vow that I shall go with Cortez myself to these rich lands, that I may not see you, friend

Diego, crying at the bad bargain you have just made."*

It is certain that these insinuations had some effect on the mind of Velasquez, and Cortez found it necessary to hasten forward the outfit of his small fleet. He embarked his whole available fortune, and incurred large debts for this purpose. The prospect which now opened before him aroused all the energy of his character, and his own zeal seemed to be communicated to those who were to share in the expedition. It is not very easy to decide between the conflicting statements that have reached us of the circumstances of his departure. According to one account, he weighed anchor by night, without going to bid Velasquez farewell. It is more probable that the suspicion of Velasquez was as yet concealed, and that Cortez parted from him with all the semblance of cordiality. Yet so sudden was the leaving, that Cortez seized upon the cattle which were to supply Santiago with meat, and paid the butcher with a gold chain which he wore around his own neck. The parting from wives and children was hurried and tearful, and then, on the 18th of November, 1518, the fleet set sail. The banner of Cortez waved in the breeze, displaying a coloured cross on a black ground, and around the border were the words in Latin "Let us follow the cross and we shall conquer."

The armament was composed of six vessels, containing five hundred and fifty Spaniards, about three hundred Indians, and a few negroes, twelve or fifteen horses, and ten guns. Their leader was now in the vigour of manhood, and it may be well to give some sketch of his character at the outset of his career.

* Helps, vol. II. p. 250.

He was in many respects the model of a Spanish hero. Bold and courageous almost to rashness, his fine person well set off by his handsome dress and manly bearing, full of zeal and high expectation, and well acquainted with all those arts that win over and captivate the hearts of followers, no man could have been more likely to bring his undertaking to a successful issue. But in its truest and highest sense there was but little nobility in his aim and purpose. To amass wealth and fame is not a noble object: and thirst for gold was probably the prevailing passion in his own breast, as well as in those of his companions. There was the same profligacy of morals, and the same unscrupulous use of any means to gain his end, which had marked his early life. He was not wantonly cruel, but innocent blood was to be poured out like water, and thousands of lives were to be sacrificed, that he might establish his empire over the Mexicans. And all this was to be done in the name and under the sign of the Prince of peace, whose pure truth was not to be taught the people, but a dark superstition was to be set up in place of the sanguinary worship then established in Mexico.

As the fleet coasted along Cuba, Cortez carried off provisions from the king's stores at Macaca, and plundered a vessel that came in his way. On his arrival at Trinidad, he found an order from Velasquez to supersede him in his command. But it was now too late. Cortez had gained the affections of his little army, and refused to give up his office. Indeed, he was too far committed, and the order of Velasquez was most unreasonable. Cortez wrote him a letter with fair words, complaining of his unjust suspicions, and promising devotion to his interests; but he added that, on the next morning, February 10th, 1519, he should sail for Cozumel. Success alone could now justify his daring disobedience.

F.

A terrible storm fell upon the fleet, and the ship of Cortez, which stayed to convoy a disabled vessel, was the last to reach Cozumel. The natives, who had so gladly welcomed Grijalva, now fled to the interior of the island: for before Cortez arrived one of the captains had plundered their temples and terrified the simple inhabitants. Confidence was, however, soon restored; but all inquiries for the Spaniards, said to be in the island, were fruitless. One duty, however, was not to be neglected ere they sailed away. The islanders were harangued by Father Olmedo on the sin of idolatry and the excellence of the Spanish faith: and when they showed no disposition to change their creed, their idols were overthrown by the soldiers amidst the lamentations of the natives. But when the senseless images did not avenge themselves, as their worshippers had foretold, by destroying these impious foes with lightning, they consented, outwardly at least, to adopt the faith of the new comers.

Having secured a good store of provisions, Cortez, early in March, resumed his voyage; but one of the ships sprung a leak, and they were compelled to return to Cozumel. Soon after, a canoe, ferried by several Indians, arrived from the opposite shores of Yucatan, and one of the men asked, in broken Castilian, whether he was among Christians. This man was Geronimo de Aguilar, who had been one of a body sent from Darien to Spain some eight years before, but had been wrecked on the shores of Yucatan. He had been kindly treated by the cacique or chieftain into whose hands he had fallen, but was overwhelmed with joy at meeting with his fellow-countrymen. It would be difficult to exaggerate the advantages which Cortez derived from his discovery. His long residence among the people had made him familiar with their language, and he acted as interpreter during the expedition. The Spaniards so felt his value that they attributed to a miracle the accident which resulted in Aguilar's arrival amongst them. We may at least discern in it the working of God's mysterious providence, who had determined to open Mexico to the Spaniards at this time, and was thus carrying out his purpose according to the counsel of his own will.

Leaving Cozumel, and passing by the coast of Yucatan, the little armament entered the mouth of the Rio de Tabasco or Grijalva. The shore was lined with dense woods and deep groves of mangrove trees, and among these the Indians might be discovered prepared to oppose their landing. A short struggle ensued, but the superior strength of the Spaniards prevailed, and they established themselves upon the land. This first engagement was followed by a more severe conflict. The Tabascans were assembled in great numbers. "When we let off the guns," says an eye-witness, "the Indians uttered loud cries and whistling sounds, and threw dust and straw into the air that we should not see the damage we were doing them." But all their tactics were of no avail. The Spanish cavalry had been sent round to attack them in the rear, and when they rode into the battle the Tabascans, who had never before seen mounted warriors, were panic-stricken and fled. The slaughter in this battle is variously estimated at from one thousand to thirty thousand men. "And this," says Las Casas, "was the first preaching of the gospel by Cortez in New Spain!"

The defeat of the Tabascans was followed by the submission of the whole people; their principal caciques came to Cortez with various offerings of peace, and, among the rest, twenty female slaves. One of these, afterwards named Donna Marina, was of essential service to her new master. She was the daughter of a cacique of Painala, in the Mexican province of Coutzacualco. Her father having died while she was quite young, her mother had married again, and she desired to give to her son by this second husband the inheritance which belonged to Donna Marina. She accordingly had the child sent away by night, and pretended to her own people that she was dead. Marina passed into the hands of the Tabascans, and from them to the Spaniards. Cortez first had her instructed in the Roman Catholic religion, and after her baptism made her his mistress, with that perversion of the relation of faith and practice which may be traced throughout the whole story of the conquest. Marina's knowledge of the Mexican language proved invaluable to Cortez, whilst her own fidelity to him was worthy of a more sacred relation, and her constant sympathy and kindness to her fellow-countrymen in their misfortunes won for her their lasting gratitude and love.

The same scene of outward conversion that had taken place at Cozumel was repeated at Tabasca. The feast of Palm Sunday was kept with a solemn procession to the temple. The image of the idol was taken down and that of the Virgin Mary, with the infant Saviour, installed in its place. Mass was celebrated, and the soldiers joined in singing the chant: then, with the palm branches in their hands, they marched on board their ships, and sailed for the golden shores of Mexico. On the Thursday following, they cast anchor at the Island of San Juan de Ulua, that faces the port of Vera Cruz.

Scarcely had the ships come to their moorings, when

two canoes started from the mainland, and made direct for the admiral's vessel. A friendly intercourse was established, Donna Marina acting as interpreter, and such trifles as the Spaniards had brought with them for barter were exchanged for the gold trinkets and ornaments of the natives. Cortez having ascertained that their country produced gold in abundance, landed his forces and artillery the following day—it was Good Friday, April 21, 1519. The simple people aided him in these labours, and brought mats and cotton carpets to protect the new comers against the scorching rays of the sun.

Two days aferwards, Teuhtlile, the governor of the district, arrived at the tent of Cortez, to inquire in the name of Montezuma, the Mexican emperor, why the Spaniards had visited these shores. Cortez received him with all the pomp he could assume; and informed him that he had been sent by the emperor Charles, to hold communication with the Aztec sovereign, and demanded to be admitted to his presence. This request was received with evident astonishment and displeasure. "You have been but two days in the country," said Teuhtlile, "and you expect to see the emperor!" As Cortez, however, insisted on this point, the governor promised to communicate with his master. The presents were then brought in which had been sent by the Mexican court; they comprised fine cottons, mantles made of curiously wrought feather-work, and a wicker-basket full of golden ornaments. The cupidity of the Spaniards was awakened at the sight of these treasures. When Teuhtlile requested that a shining helmet, worn by one of the soldiers, might be sent to the emperor, because it was like that on the idol of Quetzalcoatl, in Mexico, Cortez assented on condition that it was returned filled with gold dust. When he gave as a reason for this request, that he wanted to compare the gold of Mexico with that of his own country, and further added, that the Spaniards' suffered from a heart complaint for which gold was a cure, we may imagine that the native ambassador saw through his excuses, and recognised the greed by which they were prompted.

During these negotiations, the Spaniards observed that a Mexican was making a picture of the new comers to be sent to Montezuma. Cortez was alive to the impression which would be produced by this representation on the emperor's mind. He accordingly ordered a review of his forces upon the beach. The Mexicans were unacquainted with the use of horses, and were filled with astonishment at the charge of cavalry; but when the artillery was discharged, the flash, the thunder, and the crash of the balls through the branches, well nigh overwhelmed them with consternation. The effect would be by no means weakened in its transmission to the court, and Cortez was persuaded of this as the embassy withdrew to wait for further instructions from their master.

The reply of Montezuma was unfavourable to the demand of Cortez. He refused to admit the Spaniards to his presence, but this denial was softened by the rich presents which his ambassadors bore. These comprised armour embossed and plated with gold, collars and other ornaments of the same metal, and adorned with pearls and precious stones, robes wrought in beautiful feather work, wagon-loads of fine linens, models cast in gold and silver of birds and beasts, of exquisite workmanship. The helmet was not forgotten, but was returned duly filled with gold dust; and to crown all, there were two circles of gold and silver "as large as the wheel of a chariot," and richly carved. The terms in which the Aztec monarch declined a visit from the Spaniards were couched in expressions which referred to the difficulty of the journey, and concluded with a request that they would return to their own land.

But the proofs thus afforded of the wealth of Mexico were the strongest inducement to the Spaniards to remain and make themselves masters of the country; their surprise and satisfaction were unbounded at the sight of treasures so far beyond their expectations, and all the feelings which urge adventurers to enterprise were aroused in their bosoms. To such liberality Cortez made but a sorry return, and he haughtily declared that he would not accept the emperor's refusal of an interview. So peremptory was his language that the ambassadors sent once more to learn the will of Montezuma. The Aztec prince gave the same reply as before, and although the message was accompanied by rich presents, the Mexicans retired immediately after their delivery, and none appeared the next morning to supply them with provisions. The place on which they had encamped was a region of burning sands, bordered by pestilent marshes. They suffered much inconvenience on such a spot, and had already lost thirty of their number. Whilst awaiting the return of the Mexican ambassadors, Cortez dismissed Francisco de Montejo to seek for a better position, and as he reported that he had been able to discover but one situation which was fairly sheltered, the Spaniards at once repaired thither.

But with this change of circumstances there sprung up a division in the Spanish camp. The rich presents, which testified to the wealth, were also evidences of the power of the Mexican emperor, and the more timid began to reflect upon the madness of attempting to oppose him with their present scanty forces. Their murmurs were swelled by the adherents of Velasquez, who were unwilling that Cortez should reap the glory and the profit to be derived from such a conquest. These discontents were aggravated by the evils they were suffering from the excessive heat, from the clouds of venomous insects, and the other discomforts of that burning climate. "It was high time," they said, "to return home and to report what they had learned to Velasquez: efforts could then be made to collect such a force as might cope successfully with Montezuma." The partisans of Cortez were not idle in this emergency. They urged that everything so far had gone on prosperously; that doubtless, in their new locality, the Mexicans would again begin to trade with them; that to sail now would be to lose all the advantages of their past toils, and to relinquish the prize at the moment it was placed within their grasp. They ought to establish a colony, with their leader at its head, and to take warning by the disgrace into which Grijalva had fallen from not having adopted such a course. At length, the contest became so violent that the party of Velasquez openly called on Cortez to lead them home, declaring that, although the others might stay, they were determined to return to Cuba, and demanding that the order for departure should be given.

Among the soldiers engaged in the expedition was Bernal Diaz, who was in the confidence of the leading supporters of Cortez. This man has ↳ an account from which we get an insight into the intrigues of the camp. We learn from it that a plan had been matured for forming a colony in the name of the emperor Charles V., and shaking off by this proceeding the authority of Velasquez. The consternation of its promoters may be readily imagined when Cortez assented to the demand of their opponents, and issued an order that all should be in readiness to embark for their return. They stirred up the common soldiers, who came with loud cries of discontent, and forced their way to the general's presence. An assembly was held, in which Cortez craftily dwelt upon the richness of the prize, whilst he professed his readiness to relinquish it; and then, with feigned reluctance, allowed himself to be persuaded to adopt the course which he most ardently desired. In order to give to these proceedings a semblance of legality, he desired that a requisition in writing should be presented to him, enjoining him to change the object of the expedition from that of trade to forming a settlement. Armed with such authority, he declared himself willing to obey their wishes.

A curious scene followed; but one in full accordance with the entire tenor of Cortez's behaviour during this campaign. In completing his revolt against the authority of Velasquez, Cortez observed a careful outward respect to legal forms. The arrangements for the new city were matured, and the name of the Rich Town of the True Cross (Villa Rica del Vera Cruz) was given to it. Its principal officers, alcaldes, regidors, and other functionaries, were then nominated by Cortez, the most important parts being filled by his firmest friends. Before them Cortez now appeared and resigned his office of captain-general, which he had received from Velasquez; and was then re-appointed by the council to the same dignity in the emperor's name. By this ingenious device the whole purpose of the expedition was changed, and Cortez was invested with powers that could only be taken from him by the Spanish sovereign. A stranger instance you will hardly find of men paying an outward homage to law whilst they were outraging its plainest commands. Yet it is not uncommon to attempt thus to satisfy the conscience, even whilst the will guides us to open disobedience.

There were some who remonstrated loudly against these proceedings, but Cortez was not slow to exert his new powers. He put the most active of them in irons, and despatched the remainder to seek for provisions. Meanwhile, every engine was employed to gain over the refractory; and when gold and promises had been liberally bestowed; when immediate want was removed by the return of the foragers with abundant supplies; and when, in addition, idleness, that most fruitful source of discontent in a camp was dispelled by the order to march for Cempoalla, and new fields and new hopes opened before them, the whole body acceded to the new arrangements. Whilst there can be no question as to the morality of Cortez's conduct on this occasion, there can be as little doubt of the boldness which could meditate on the conquest of Mexico with forces not only so small but so disunited, or of the wondrous tact with which he soothed their animosity and at last won them over to himself.

Before matters had been thus arranged, some Indians had arrived at the Spanish camp, and were brought before Cortez. They were natives of Cempoalla, the capital of the Totonacs, and were sent by the prince of that tribe to invite Cortez to pay him a visit. Their account of the treatment they had experienced from Montezuma, by whom they had been recently subdued, gave Cortez an insight into the jealousies by which the Mexican empire was weakened, and he at once divined the probable advantage of allying himself with the discontented states. He now, therefore, gladly directed the march to Cempoalla.

The spirits of the little army rose as they drew near to the city of their new friends. The sandy plains on which they had encamped, and on whose dreary wastes they had suffered so much, were exchanged for a green and fertile country. These rugged warriors were, perhaps, little moved by the glimpses of the blue Atlantic or the snow-clad peak of Orizaba, but they could not be indifferent to the superb and profuse vegetation of that tropical shore—to its groves of tall waving palms—to the thick underwood of aloes, interwoven with roses and honeysuckle—or to the festoons of graceful parasites that swung from branch to branch. Strange birds, of bright plumage; swarms of butterflies, with their delicacy of painted wing; and graceful creatures of the deer tribe, glancing through the woods, combined to form a scene of beauty which was enhanced by the memory of their recent privations. No wonder that they were extravagant in their praises of a scene which has enraptured every beholder, and termed it a "terrestial paradise;" or that, with a far depeer appreciation of its beauty, their thoughts flew back across the ocean to the scenes that were most dear to their hearts, as they fondly compared it to the choicest spots in their own fatherland.

A hearty welcome awaited them at Cempoalla. The love of flowers, which had survived their freedom, was already a characteristic of the natives, and they held out bunches of roses to the soldiers, and crowned their general and his charger with garlands. As they drew near to the town the whole population advanced to meet them, the men adorned with short mantles, the women clad in flowing robes that reached the ankles. The cacique received them at the entrance of his dwelling, whilst commodious quarters and abundant provisions testified to their good will.

What an unexampled opportunity was thus afforded if the Spanish had come to this distant region with the true message of the gospel of peace! If, taking advantage of their friendship, Cortez had declared to the Cempoallans that the God, "who sent them rain from heaven and fruitful seasons," had given a yet far more striking token of his love in sending his own Son to die for sinners; and if the lives and conduct of the Spaniards had been accordant with their doctrine, and they had shown their sense of God's love to themselves by the love which they displayed to others, what an unexampled opportunity—what a field for loving labour lay before them! Cortez, indeed, told the cacique, at an early interview, that he came to bring the knowledge of the true God, and to abolish their bloody and cruel rites; but the behaviour of the Spaniards was little calculated to recommend their teaching. With some words of truth upon their lips, and that truth sadly marred by Romish error and superstition, there was little of the influence of truth in their hearts.

From the cacique of Cempoalla, Cortez learned the condition of the Mexican empire, the hatred of the subject nations to their masters, and the cruelty and luxury of Montezuma; he learned also the great dread with which the Aztec sovereign was regarded. His armies were like the whirlwind, and slavery or sacrifice were the inevitable results of disobedience to his commands. This dread was called forth into action by the arrival of the Aztec nobles to collect the tribute from the people of Cempoalla. These officers deeply resented the hospitality shown to the Spaniards, and demanded twenty young men and maidens for sacrifice in expiation of their fault.

Cortez affected the strongest indignation on hearing of this demand. He bade the cacique instantly to seize upon and bind the Aztec nobles. When this was done, he repaired to them privately, and procured the release of two of their number, enjoining them to inform their sovereign of his generous return for the unkind treatment he had experienced. He subsequently required that the other Aztec chieftains should be placed in his hands, and then allowed them to join their companions. Such was the return of Cortez for the generosity of the Cempoallans. He thus continued to embroil them with the Aztec emperor, and to secure for himself the good will of Montezuma.

The Spaniards now proceeded to Chiahuitzlan, and a site was selected, between the two places, for his new city of Vera Cruz. The walls were marked out, public buildings designed, and, with the aid of their Indian allies, a town soon rose. Every man shared in the work—the general equally with the meanest soldier. The place was to serve as a retreat in the hour of reverse, whilst its harbour would give shelter to the vessels of any fresh comers.

The scene which had been enacted at Cozumel was now to be repeated at Cempoalla. In vain Cortez had urged upon the Totonacs the sin of their idolatry: they had replied, that their gods were good enough for them. When argument thus failed, he had recourse to violence. But the Totonacs were not disposed tamely to submit to such daring sacrilege : they eagerly assembled for the defence of their deities, and a battle seemed inevitable. Cortez, however, seized their chieftain, and declared that the first blow struck should be the signal for his death. The idols were overthrown, and the image of the Virgin and her Son installed in their places. Human sacrifices were forbidden, and the garments of the priests changed from black to white. Beyond this but little was altered, and the same priests were left in charge of the altars of the mass who had been wont to offer sacrifice to their heathen gods.

After this event, the Cempoallans were solemnly received as vassals of the king of Spain. It is amusing to observe the gravity with which this handful of men disposed of kingdoms, and claimed supremacy in the name of their sovereign over a vast and powerful empire. It is certain that Cortez had fully determined by this time to conquer Mexico, for in an account which he sent to Charles V. of his discovery, he declared he would take Montezuma dead or alive, unless he agreed to become a vassal of the Spanish crown. He now carried out a daring stroke of policy to further his plans. Conspiracy had again been detected in the camp, and he determined at once to crush it for ever, and to bind all his forces together by the bonds of necessity. The party of Velasquez wanted to sail away for further reinforcements, and to monopolize for their own side the advantages of their discovery: if departure were rendered impossible, they must all stand by one another, when surrounded by common foes in a foreign land. Cortez, therefore, determined to destroy his fleet. The stoutest hearts among the soldiers quailed when the order to sink the ships was given. They were now left, a handful amongst millions, escape was impossible, destruction imminent. Loud reproaches were raised against the leader who had thus brought them to perish in a strange country. Cortez stood unmoved, he calmly dilated upon the ever-welcome topic—the treasures of Mexico, which should soon be theirs. One vessel still remained, let those that quailed take that and sail away. They could wait at Cuba till their comrades, whom they had deserted, returned with the spoils of the Aztec empire. With a general impulse their confidence revived: "To Mexico! to Mexico!" was the universal cry.

Escalante, a trusty friend of Cortez, was left in command at Vera Cruz, and the army set out, on the 16th of August, 1519, upon its march to Mexico. Upwards of a thousand Indian warriors accompanied them, and as many porters were provided by the Totonacs to carry the baggage and drag the guns. Their course was directed towards the little state of Tlascala, whose enmity to the Aztecs has been already noticed. Cortez was alive to the advantages of securing their alliance, and sent an embassy asking permission to pass through their country, as they journeyed to humble the pride of Montezuma. He received an unfavourable reply. The council of the chiefs had deliberated long, but at length the deeply-rooted suspicion of all strangers and intruders upon their territory prevailed. By some strange oversight the Tlascalans left their rampart undefended; but, about four leagues further on, they assembled in dense masses, and offered a stern resistance to the Spaniards. A series of most desperate battles ensued, and, although the Europeans were victorious in every engagement, their position was becoming most critical; several of their number had been slain, all the horses were wounded, and the spirit of the foe seemed as defiant as ever. But discouragement was beginning to creep over the Tlascalan warriors; the pale faces of the foe, the horses, which were animals now first seen by them, and the thunder and flash of the artillery mingling destruction with terror, filled their minds with superstitious dread: and when a night attack, which had been devised as an extraordinary effort, was unsuccessful; when a number of spies sent to the Spanish camp under the pretext of a truce had been detected and dismissed with the loss of their hands; and when, after each victory, the politic Cortez offered terms of peace and friendship, the brave fellows at length consented to come to terms. They received the Spaniards with a loyalty and cordiality befitting the courage they had displayed; and Cortez, in whose camp complaints were again rife, and who had not a single unwounded soldier, was only too glad to find so serious an obstacle effectually removed.

At Tlascala another embassy arrived from Montezuma, accompanied, as before, by rich presents. The emperor besought Cortez not to ally himself with the Tlascalans, but to proceed at once to Mexico by the city of Cholula, whither orders had been sent for his entertainment. Cholula was the ancient seat of the Aztec religion, and its people were noted for their perfidy and superstition. The Tlascalans, now thoroughly united to the Spaniards by their common enmity to Montezuma, and by intermarriages which had been solemnized between them, warned Cortez that some treachery was intended. Agreeing with this estimate, the Spanish general yet determined to march to Cholula.

The whole army accordingly set out, accompanied by a body of the Tlascalans, 6,000 in number. Their path lay across one of those vast plains which are so striking a feature in Mexican scenery, and on all sides they saw evidences of the fertility of the soil, as well as of the industry and intelligence of its inhabitants. Large plantations of aloe and Aztec pepper, fields of tall waving Indian corn, broad sweeps covered with the rich flowering cactus and olive, rose on either hand. The country, now so bare of trees, was then shaded by deep woods; whilst natural and artificial streams of water supplied the moisture which its cultivation required.

On the banks of a stream hard by the city, Cortez halted his army for the night, and there received the Cholulan chiefs who came to meet and bid him welcome. At their own request he left the Tlascalans encamped on this spot, * until he should march forward to Mexico. Accompanied by only a few native servants the Spaniards entered Cholula. The entire population turned out to gaze upon the pale faced strangers. In no city, save the capital, had luxury reached such a pitch as at Cholula; the width of the streets, the size and comfort of the houses, the long white bournouses in which many were clad, the garlands of flowers and waving censors of incense, made up a scene that could not fail to inflame the excited feelings of the new comers. With what awe must they

* The Tlascalans, being enemies to the Mexican nation, were not allowed to enter.

have gazed upon the numerous temples in which the bloody rites of Aztec worship were performed; more especially as they drew near to the teocalli of Quetzalcoatl, whose summit had been visible for miles as they approached the city. This extraordinary edifice, to which reference has already been made,* was piled up to a height of 170 feet, in the form of a pyramid, composed of four terraces rising one above another. Some idea of its size may be gathered from the statement of Humboldt, that its base covered forty-four acres, and the platform on its summit was an acre in extent. On this was erected the temple of the deity, from whose altars there arose the smoke and flame in which his human victims were consumed. So terrible was the influence of their superstitions that six thousand human beings are said to have been annually sacrificed on the altars of Cholula.

For some days the Spaniards met with all kindness at the hands of the people of Cholula. They were quartered in one of the vast temples, an ample supply of provisions was furnished, and nothing seemed wanting to testify their friendship. On a sudden all was changed, and Cortez discovered that, at the direction of Montezuma, a plot had been formed for their destruction. They were to be assailed as they marched out of the city, and every preparation had been made to ensure the success of the attack. Streets had been barricaded, and pits dug, filled with stakes, to hamper the movements of the cavalry. But Cortez maintained his firmness under dangers before which the stoutest heart might have quailed. Having obtained full information of the plot, and of Montezuma's complicity in it, he sent for the ambassadors of the Aztec em-

* See page 14.

peror and reproached their master for his duplicity.
With his wonted cunning he affected, after an interval,
to believe their assurances that Montezuma had no
share in the design, and then telling them that he
would inflict signal punishment on the Cholulans, he
dismissed them under a strong guard. To the Cholulan
chiefs he only intimated that he would leave the city
on the following morning, and they readily acquiesced
in a proposal which seemed to further their own
designs.

After a night of no small anxiety, the Cholulan
caciques appeared at daybreak with a band of porters
far more numerous than Cortez had requested them
to provide. The Spaniards were all ready, drawn up
in martial array. The caciques were seized and sternly
accused of the conspiracy, which they were too much
confounded to deny. Then, at a given signal, the
Spaniards rushed forth and fired upon the unarmed
masses. Panic struck, and taken by surprise, the
miserable creatures were slaughtered like sheep; and
soon, in their rear, rose the shrill cry of their old
enemies the Tlascalans, who had marched into the
city at the summons of Cortez. A frightful scene of
massacre ensued, and its horrors were increased as
fire was set to some of the temples and houses, and
the flames spread rapidly along the wooden buildings.
The great temple was stormed foot by foot, and not
one Cholulan upon it survived the conflict. In abject
terror, the caciques at length persuaded Cortez to put
a stop to the plunder and carnage.

It is customary for those who have described such
scenes to offer some reflections upon them. Too often
these remarks are nothing more than a counterba-
lancing of opposing motives of worldly policy, or a state-

ment of some pleas by which the guilt of such actions may be extenuated. Yet to those who are accustomed to weigh all human actions in the balances of truth, there is only one decision possible upon the character of such a massacre. It is to no purpose to allege that like scenes have been elsewhere enacted, and that the annals of European warfare present us with spectacles of equal horror; for this only proves what terrible calamities are ever treading on the heels of war, and how weighty a burden of responsibility must rest on those by whom war is proclaimed. In the case before us, there is much less room for any hesitation. The conspiracy to destroy the Spaniards had been contrived at the bidding of a powerful master, and Cortez pretended to excuse the author whilst he took vengeance on the instruments whom Montezuma had employed. Even if his special circumstances had made some punishment appear inevitable, it had been enough to inflict it upon those of the chiefs who might be proved to have been the most active agents in the plot. There is nothing to excuse, hardly anything to palliate, the course actually adopted. Thousands of men were massacred, and a fair city laid in ruins, because their master justly distrusted the intentions of the Spaniards. This transaction is a foul blot on the fame of the conquerors of Mexico, and must for ever sully the glory which his admirers claim for their hero.

The interval of repose which followed the massacre was deemed a fitting season to set forth the tenets of the Spanish creed, although it could hardly be supposed that their practice was likely to commend their faith to the Cholulans. The great teocalli was purified and a huge crucifix erected on its summit, whilst an image of the Virgin (de los Remedios), was given by Cortez himself to adorn the temple. It was truly the blind leading the blind. Other embassies had arrived from Montezuma, loaded, as before, with rich presents, and furnished with specious reasons why the Spaniards should abstain from pressing on to Mexico. Cortez accepted the gifts, and politely evaded compliance with the expressed wishes of the giver. After a rest of some days, the little band resumed its march to the capital. The Cempoallans were afraid to venture into the country of their powerful foes, and were permitted to return home. With them Cortez despatched Escalante to act as his lieutenant at Vera Cruz.

The distance from Cholula to Mexico is about sixty leagues, and the road crosses the lofty ridge which divides the table-land of Mexico from that of the Puebla. As they mounted the sides of the sierra their march became excessively toilsome; cold blasts of wind swept down from the snow-clad sides of Popocatepetl. It had been dangerous to bivouac in such a region had not a large walled inclosure, intended for the use of travellers, afforded them the protection which, as children of the South, they required against the cold. But when, on a sudden turn in the path, the whole valley of Mexico lay stretched at their feet, all the toils of the ascent were forgotten in the beauty of the scene. Wondrous as is still the face of nature in that broad plateau, it then possessed features of beauty which have long since disappeared. Vast groves of luxuriant trees clothed with their rich foliage many parts that now are bleak and bare; cities, teeming with a numerous population, were dotted over the landscape; and the fields, which furnished a harvest for their support, carpeted the soil with their varied crops. The great lake on which Mexico then stood spread its waters over a wide surface, and many a rood of salt, barren marsh, now marks the space which it formerly occupied.* All the wealth of the Aztec empire was lavished upon this region, whose climate and fertility repaid with abundant gratitude the care bestowed on its cultivation. And as the eyes of the Spaniards ranged over the prospect, and they were able in the clear, dry atmosphere, to embrace a wide range of vision, until the view melted in the purple of the distant hills, overcome with its beauty they exclaimed, with cries of rapture, "It is the promised land!"

The news of their approach inspired vague but well-grounded apprehensions in the mind of Montezuma. All his entreaties had been unavailing, and as the Spaniards pressed on to his capital he had a mournful presentiment that the empire was about to fade from his grasp. Yet he aroused himself to meet the new comers with all the outward signs of cordiality, and concealed his fears beneath a smile of welcome. What must have been the thoughts that crowded into the minds of the Spaniards as they gazed upon the evidences of power and wealth by which they were surrounded! They had learned indeed that many of the emperor's subjects were ill-affected towards him, but how could so small a band as they cope with the resources of so powerful a sovereign? Did no misgivings suggest themselves as the Spaniards marched along the causeway through the lake, and as they crossed over the drawbridge to enter Mexico? They were placing themselves by their own act in the power of Montezuma, and retreat would be almost impossible. It was not the time, however, to parley with such fears.

* From the gradual drying up of the lake the city of Mexico is no longer an island, but stands upon its banks.

The major part would yield to the enjoyment of the present, without much thought about the future.

The scenes which followed are without a parallel in the history of nations. The Spaniards were courteously welcomed, loaded with presents, located in convenient quarters, and their every want supplied. There seemed to be no limit to the kindness and generosity of Montezuma, yet, in the midst of such treatment from him, Cortez suddenly determined to seize the emperor's person and to compel him to reside in the Spanish camp. The excuse alleged for so harsh a course was an attack made by Quauhpopoca, one of the Aztec nobles, upon Vera Cruz; and although Montezuma offered to send for the offender that he might be punished, it was in vain that he pleaded to retain his liberty. The unhappy prince was so overcome by his fears that he forbade his subjects to attempt his release: and Cortez even had the cruelty to place him in irons when Quauhpopoca declared that he had acted under Montezuma's orders. This last insult pierced the heart of the Aztec sovereign. He declined to return to his palace when Cortez—we know not with how much sincerity—offered him his liberty. Not long after, he avowed himself a vassal of the king of Spain, and, with his nobles, took the oath of allegiance to Charles V.

The frightful punishment of Quauhpopoca, who was burned alive, and the placing fetters upon his master, extort some words of condemnation from one of the most ardent admirers of Cortez. "It was," he says, "a politic proceeding to which few men would have been equal who had a touch of humanity in their nature." * Bernal Diaz, an actor in these scenes, after

* Prescott, vol. II. p. 152.

an interval of fifty years, thus recorded his reflections upon them. "Now that I am an old man, I often entertain myself with calling to mind the heroic deeds of early days, till they are as fresh as the events of yesterday. I think of the seizure of the Indian monarch, his confinement in irons, and the execution of his officers, till all these things seem actually passing before me. And as I ponder on our exploits, I feel that it was not of ourselves that we performed them, but that it was the providence of God that guided us. Here is much food for meditation!"

It was plainly impossible that matters should long continue in so anomalous a position. A crisis was brought about in an unexpected manner by the arrival of a fresh body of Spaniards. They had been sent by Velasquez, the governor of Cuba; and Narvaez, their leader, had express orders to arrest Cortez, and claim the profits of his discoveries for Velasquez. To support his attempt he had brought some 900 Europeans, with 80 horses, and about a 1,000 Indians. The condition of Cortez was indeed perilous. The Mexicans were inflamed against him. Montezuma had been alienated by his unworthy treatment, and had reason to question the truth of his representations when he learned that the new comers were opposed to him. The force of Narvaez far exceeded his own in numbers, and it was doubtful whether even the Tlascalans would stand firm when they saw the odds to which he was opposed. But the spirit of Cortez ever rose before danger. Leaving Alvarado in charge of Mexico and its captive monarch, he selected the trustiest of his comrades, attacked and conquered Narvaez, in a night assault, and with his usual address so improved the victory, that he speedily returned to the capital with the whole body of Spaniards that had lately arrived united to serve under his banner.

His presence was sorely needed at Mexico. Before his departure to meet Narvaez, his religious zeal had galled the proud Aztecs to the quick, for he had seized their principal temple for the celebration of Christian worship. All the prejudices of the people had been outraged by this proceeding, but they maintained a sullen attitude of submission. Now, however, news reached him that the Mexicans were in arms against him. They had burned the vessels he had built upon the lake, had besieged the Spanish quarters, and killed many of its defenders. In short, Cortez was implored to return if he would preserve the survivors.

This was a heavy blow to Cortez after his recent success. He hurried back to find the city almost deserted, and every sign of disaffection amongst the few that still lingered within its walls. The violence of Alvarado was the cause of this hostility. On the occasion of the festival of their war god, he had rushed in upon the unarmed worshippers and had committed a fearful massacre among them. This insane cruelty stung to the quick the pride of the Mexicans; they rose *en masse* with one long cry for vengeance on so perfidious an act. On they came by thousands, pressing forward heedless of the numbers that fell before the fire of their foes, and when the fury of the first assault was spent, they hemmed in the Spanish quarters on all sides, withdrew all supplies of provisions, and waited until they should be starved into submission.

Such was the posture of affairs when Cortez reached Mexico. Bitterly repenting his selection of Alvarado to govern in his absence, he had the littleness to vent his spleen upon the captive monarch who sent to him to request an interview. In all haste he despatched a messenger to summon aid from Vera Cruz, but it was too late. The man soon returned, sorely wounded, and announcing that the whole people were in arms. On they came in a surging tide, wave rising above wave, their banners flying, and their ranks marshalled under the most noted of their chieftains. As they approached in dense masses, the fire of the Spanish artillery made terrible havoc in their ranks, but they pressed forward undaunted, and tried to storm or batter down the wall behind which the Europeans were protected. Their flaming arrows soon set fire to the wooden buildings, whilst a cloud of missiles, hurled from powerful arms, inflicted much damage upon the foe.

Night brought some respite from the fatigue of the conflict, but next day it was resumed with unabated vigour. All the slaughter inflicted by the Spaniards failed to daunt the spirit of the enemy. It was in vain that they opened a murderous fire upon the thronging crowd, the places of the slain were instantly filled up by new comers. In vain did Cortez, and the most famous of his comrades, sally forth to charge them sword in hand: worn out with the labours of cutting down the enemy, they were fain to retreat after performing useless prodigies of valour. With bitter taunts the Aztecs pressed upon them as they withdrew behind their ramparts. "The fires of the sacrifice are waiting for you. No matter though a thousand of us should fall to one of your number, not one of you shall escape alive." Such words fell ominously on the superstitious ears of men wearied with fighting and sorely depressed in heart.

The battle was renewed next day; and now Cortez strove to bring the enemy to terms. He induced

Montezuma to address the people, and persuade them to desist, but the magic spell of his despotism was dissolved. The Aztecs reviled him as a traitor, and a shower of missiles fell around him. He was borne away by the Spaniards badly wounded, and their stern hearts must have been touched by the miseries of the unhappy monarch. This last indignity thoroughly crushed his wounded spirit. He refused all the kindness with which the Spaniards strove to comfort him; tore off the bandages with which they stanched his wounds; and nursed his proud sorrow in unbroken silence, until he felt his end approaching: then, summoning Cortez to his bedside, he solemnly intrusted his children to his care, "as the most precious jewels he could leave him, and expired in the arms of some of his own nobles, who still remained faithful in their attendance on his person." It was the 30th of June, 1520.

So died the mightiest monarch of the new world. The Spaniards found amongst the millions of the western hemisphere none like in power and wealth unto Montezuma. For more than seventeen years he had ruled over his wide dominions, successful in war, and wise in counsel, until, by his own people, he was regarded as more than a mortal man. The resources of the country, far and wide, were drained to minister to his wants. All that the earth produced of food or riches was assigned to him, but he fell in the fulness of his pride and luxury; he died dishonoured by his subjects, a captive in the hands of strangers. No wonder that he remained a heathen, and rejected all the entreaties of Father Olmedo; he had suffered too much cruelty and deceit from the Spaniards to have any confidence in the faith which they professed.

Yet there was that within him which, under the Holy Spirit's influence, would have gladly welcomed the message of a dying Saviour's love. We learn that in his last moments he declared that he bore the Spaniards no ill-will for the evils they had brought upon him. Surely such a mind, Divinely taught, would have prized highly the forgiveness which the gospel proclaims. His mournful end enforces and may serve to point the Scripture truth, " that none of us liveth unto himself." The selfishness of Montezuma's rule alienated the affections of his subjects, and so aided the march of the Spaniards to the capital. So true is it, even in worldly matters, that love is politic as well as right, and that if one member of a state suffer, all the members, however exalted, suffer with it.

The position of Cortez was now desperate. His overtures for peace were rejected, the fury of the enemy was unabated, and he learned that the bridges in the line of his retreat were broken down. It was determined to steal out on the night of the 1st of July, and by the aid of a portable bridge, which had been secretly constructed, to effect if possible their retreat to Tlascala. Arrangements were made for the conveyance of a certain portion of the treasure, and the rest was abandoned to the soldiers, many of whom fell victims in the night to the cupidity which led them to overload themselves with gold. With anxious hearts, we may well believe, they waited for the evening.

The night seemed to favour their retreat; it was dark, and drizzling. The foe had retired to their quarters, and the Spaniards gained the causeway (which connected the island on which Mexico stood with the mainland) almost unobserved. This causeway was crossed by three openings in the line of the Spaniards' march, and the bridges over these had been broken down by the Aztecs. Just as the causeway was reached they were discovered. No sooner was an alarm sounded than the priests took up the cry, and from the summits of their temples roused the whole city to arms. Cortez pushed on with all speed, but it was no easy thing to march the whole army over the bridge. Ere the last of their number had crossed the first opening, an ominous sound arose, and the waters on either side flashed beneath the strokes of a thousand oars, as the boats of the Mexicans bore them to the attack. The first opening, however, was passed in safety; Magarino, at the head of his engineers, advanced to raise the portable bridge and bear it forward to the second opening, but it stuck fast. The heavy weight that had been borne over it had fixed it firmly in the earth, and all efforts to move it were ineffectual. As this terrible news spread, a cry of despair arose from the Spanish force. Assailed in front, cut off in the rear, and attacked on both sides by numbers which increased every moment, their destruction seemed inevitable. Their wily foes rained thick clouds of darts on them, and rushing suddenly up the sides of the causeway grappled with them, hand to hand, and both fell together into the lake; the Mexican was quickly picked up by his friends, whilst the European was as quickly despatched. On they struggled, however, and presently the second opening was almost choked up with baggage, treasure, and dead bodies, mingled in dire confusion. Over this at length they scrambled, the enemy still hanging on their rear as they pressed forward until they reached the third and last opening in the causeway.

Here a fearful scene of confusion ensued. The

mounted cavaliers swam across, the infantry clung to the tails of their horses, or tried to find a place in which they might ford the stream. Many were drowned in the attempt, especially such as were over laden with gold. At length, the van and the centre got over, when word was brought that the rear-guard was overpowered, and, unless strengthened, would be entirely destroyed. With unhesitating gallantry the cavaliers dashed once more into the river to relieve their comrades; after a terrible struggle a straggling remnant effected a passage. Alvarado, unhorsed and hemmed in on all sides, hesitated for an instant at the opening, then placing his spear on the mass of ruin that choked the place he cleared it at a bound. The spot has ever since borne the name of Alvarado's Leap.

The Mexicans abstained from further pursuit, and Cortez was able to draw off his forces. They were sadly thinned. Little more than a third of the Spaniards, and a fourth of their allies, survived. The horses were reduced to twenty-three. All the artillery, all the treasure, all the baggage was lost. Hardly a musket remained. As he reviewed his shattered army, Cortez was unable to restrain his tears, so terrible was the disaster of the "Sad Night," as it has ever since been termed in Spanish annals.

The most determined spirit might have found abundant reasons for abandoning the attempt to conquer the country under the circumstances in which Cortez was now placed. His forces were thoroughly disorganized, and those of them who had come with Narvaez, began to utter loud complaints of the hardships they were enduring. It was doubtful how the Tlascalans would receive them, and when, shortly afterwards, a Mexican embassy arrived at Tlascala, a party in the city openly desired to make common cause with Mexico for the expulsion of the strangers. Their leader, too, had yet to learn how his conduct would be regarded at the court of Spain, and he must have reflected with bitterness on the loss of treasure which might have smoothed over many difficulties. But he was undaunted. He set himself to restore the confidence of his army. He trained it in a series of expeditions against the allies of Mexico. He gained complete control over the chieftains of Tlascala, and won the admiration of these fierce warriors by leading them to victories in which they took vengeance on their hated foes, and enriched themselves with plunder. He won over to his side two successive detachments sent by Velasquez, and permitted some discontented spirits to sail back to Cuba, thus doubly strengthening his army. He prepared for building a fleet of brigantines with which the siege of Mexico might be resumed. In such labours the six remaining months of 1520 were consumed. When the ships were sufficiently advanced, he chose Tezcuco as the head-quarters of the operations which he purposed to conduct against the capital. On the last day of the year, he marched into that city at the head of 600 Spaniards, well equipped, including forty mounted knights and nine cannons. Besides these, he had a force of Indian auxiliaries estimated at 100,000 in number.

The wide plain in which Mexico stands was then the seat of a vast and thriving population. Upwards of forty large towns, besides villages innumerable, were counted on its surface. Many of these towns had been, in former days, the capital of a tribe, whose chieftains still resided in them, and they consequently retained considerable social importance, although all political power had been grasped by the Aztec emperor. The capital, as we have already seen, stood on an island in the Tezcucan lake. The water of the lake itself was brackish, but a conduit, constructed with a double line of pipes, conveyed a plentiful and pure supply to the city. Three causeways, or dikes, built of stone, furnished the means of access from the city to the mainland, and it was the passage of one of these that had cost the Spaniards so dear on the "Sad Night" of their retreat. There were other smaller lakes scattered over the Mexican valley, with flourishing towns upon their borders. Their sites were occasionally protected by embankments from the incursion of the neighbouring waters, as the lakes thus restrained were on a higher level than the towns which stood upon their banks. These facts must be borne in mind by the reader as he follows the account of the siege.

Nearly opposite to Mexico, across the waters of the lake, but at the distance of half a league from its shore, rose Tezcuco, the head-quarters of the Spanish army. It had long been the rival of the capital, whose pre-eminence it still regarded with distaste. Its chief, Ixtlilxochitl, espoused the side of Cortez with a constancy that never wavered, even when the success of the Spaniards seemed most doubtful. This important acquisition gave Cortez a base of operations which was absolutely essential for the fulfilment of his plans.

It was plainly hopeless to attempt the reduction of the capital whilst it could draw resources and supplies from all the neighbouring towns. Cortez, therefore, determined to proceed against these first, in rapid succession, with the hope that their fall would induce the Mexicans to come to terms, and so spare him the difficulties of a siege and the destruction of the city. With this purpose he first marched against Iztapalapan, a city lying to the south of Tezcuco, and bordering closely upon the Tezcucan lake, whose waters were kept back by a strong sea wall. Here were the palace and beautiful gardens of the last Mexican emperor. It had a population of some 50,000 souls. A strong force was drawn up to oppose the Spaniards, but the fury of their onset carried all before them, and they rushed into the place after the fugitives, without regarding some canoes full of men, who were quietly and busily at work upon the mole or sea wall. A terrible massacre followed in the city, which was given up to pillage, fire and sword. No quarter was granted by the ruthless Tlascalans, and the Aztecs fought with all the energy of despair. Suddenly there rose a dull murmuring sound of rushing water, and the dread news was spread that the Indians had broken down the mole. Hastily was the retreat sounded. They were glad to flounder through the water as lightly burdened as possible, and to reach the mainland. All the plunder was lost, all the powder spoiled. Wearied and disheartened they returned to Tezcuco, the enemy still hovering on their rear. The Aztecs might be conquered, but they were in spirit unsubdued.

The attack upon Iztapalapan was followed by one of the most striking events of the war. Word was brought to Cortez from Tlascala, that the brigantines which he had ordered to be built were now completed, and he accordingly despatched Sandoval with 200 Europeans to escort them to Tezcuco. The vessels had been constructed and tried upon the lake Zahuapan. They were now to be taken to pieces and carried with the "anchors, iron-work, sails and cordage," on the backs of porters all the way to Tezcuco. In this manner, thirteen vessels of war were transported *nearly twenty leagues across the mountains.* The line of bearers, extending upwards of six miles in length, was protected by Sandoval's little army, and some 20,000 Tlascalans. The enemy, although they hung upon their march, did not venture to attack them; and the boldness of the conception which designed so extraordinary a manœuvre was only equalled by the success with which it was performed.

It was still necessary to dig a canal through which the brigantines might pass from Tezcuco into the lake. Leaving this work to be performed by the allies, Cortez turned his army northwards, and attacked the town of Xaltocan, the modern San Christobal. Its fall was followed by that of other cities (with most unpronounceable names), until, bending round the northern boundary of the lake, Cortez once more entered Tacuba. This town stood near the commencement of one of the causeways that led across the lake to Mexico. Along this the Spaniards now advanced, and it once more became the scene of an obstinate conflict. After each day's contest, Cortez offered the enemy terms of peace, but they were invariably rejected. His victories, indeed, seemed to bring him little fruit. The towns that were sacked furnished but little treasure. The gold had been buried or removed. It was plain that undying hostility had been awakened, and that he must strain every nerve to conquer or die.

For the present, then, Cortez returned to Tezcuco, where new cares summoned him in a different direction. The people of Chalco, a large town to the south of the capital, had been gained over to embrace the Spanish cause. They were now sorely pressed by the Aztecs, and their defection might be followed by that of other allies. To Chalco accordingly Cortez repaired. Not content with driving the Mexicans from that region, he crossed into the rugged districts of the Sierra, took the towns of Cuernavaca and Xochimilco, from which latter place he marched to Tacuba, entering it from the south, as he had formerly done from the north. He had thus completed the circuit of the lake, and everywhere had victory attended his arms.

Yet an incident at Xochimilco had almost ended his career. The Spanish forces were advancing on one of those causeways, built through the waters of a lake, which were so commonly the approaches to an Aztec town. On their route they were, as usual, assailed on both flanks by the Indians, who waded into the water, or fought from their canoes. On this narrow path, near the entrance to the city, Cortez and a small body of followers were suddenly overwhelmed. He himself fell from his horse, and immediately received a severe blow on the head. He was being dragged off by the enemy, when a Tlascalan warrior sprung upon the assailants, and being supported by Cortez's servants, rescued him from the grasp of the foe. A few days after this event, Guatemozin, the Mexican emperor, arrived at Xochimilco, and falling hastily upon some Spaniards who were bent on plunder, he took four of them alive. After offering them in sacrifice to the Aztec god of war, "their legs and arms were cut off and sent round to the different cities, with the assurance, that this should be the fate of the enemies of Mexico." *

The capital was not yet completely invested by the

* Prescott, vol. III. p. 56.

Spaniards, and as they marched from Xochimilco to Tacuba, they beheld the lake teeming with canoes, laden with the produce they were bearing to the markets. Some were piled up high with merchandise, others bore vegetables or the fruits of the country, others were crowded with the levies that had been called to the defence of the empire. So animated a sight surprised the Europeans who had lately joined the army, and they were enraptured at the beauty and activity of the scene; but the brow of Cortez darkened as he gazed across the water to the city that lay upon its breast, and he confessed that he was mourning, not for his own past losses, but at the thought of the misery that impended over that fair capital, and of the labours that were in store for his own followers. Such thoughts rise in all men's bosoms, and it is almost impossible so to steel the heart, that no such musings shall be able, at any point, to pierce its harness. But surely the responsibility of the misery which Cortez then deplored must be at his own door. He had voluntarily sought out and assailed the Aztec empire. If the lust of conquest had now involved him in a wretched necessity whence there seemed to be no escape, it does but forcibly illustrate how impossible it is for men to forsee the evils that will result from a first step in the path of sin.

From Tacuba the Spaniards passed on to Tezcuco; arrived here, they found the brigantines equipped and launched, and the canal finished. At this auspicious moment Cortez detected a conspiracy aimed at his life amongst his own soldiery. There were many discontented spirits in the army, and, as there was no opportunity for desertion, a plot was formed to assassinate Cortez and the principal officers, and then to seize upon the ships and sail home. It was revealed to the general on the day before it was to have been perpetrated. Villafaña, the leader, was apprehended, and the papers in his possession proved that some personal friends of Cortez were implicated in the design. With a ready discernment, Cortez at once destroyed the paper, and had Villafaña immediately executed. It would not do at such a juncture to allow any breath of suspicion to weaken the confidence of his men.

They were again to be diverted from brooding over their wrongs by active service. Twelve of the brigantines were manned (one having proved unserviceable), and sailed into the lake. A fresh muster of the allies was ordered, as many had returned home to house their plunder. Early in May the whole force was under arms, and the siege of Mexico was formally commenced. Sandoval was sent with a division to the south; Alvarado and Olid by the north to Tacuba. They were to push on from thence to Chapoltepec and destroy the aqueduct by which the city was supplied. Cortez set sail with his flotilla to strike a decisive blow, if possible, upon the lake.

In the first engagement on the water, the Aztecs were completely vanquished, and Cortez then sailed to Zoloc, an important station on the causeway from Cojohuacan. Alvarado occupied that which led to Tacuba, and Sandoval the third causeway to the north. Thus the blockade of the capital was complete.

The fiery cavaliers were, however, too impatient to await the effects of famine, and constant assaults were made upon the city on all sides. As the Spaniards advanced along the causeways they were supported on either flank by the brigantines, whose fire swept across the path of the enemy. Still the Aztecs retreated in good order, and fiercely disputed the passage at every breach in the path. When the Spaniards reached the city, a fierce conflict arose at each one of the numerous canals by which many of the streets were intersected. Much delay, too, was caused by the Europeans being obliged to fill up each breach over which they passed in order to secure the line of their retreat. Several days were spent in such conflicts, but every night the Mexicans pulled away the materials with which the breaches had been filled up, so that the work had to be begun all over again. This mode of warfare greatly dispirited the Spaniards. They had also to endure considerable hardships in the camp, where but few of them had any shelter against the cold of the nights. Poor old Bernal Diaz waxes quite eloquent in his recital of their sufferings.

Under these circumstances many of the officers urged Cortez to make a general assault upon the city, in conjunction with Alvarado and Sandoval. The general yielded against his better judgment, and gave instructions for the combined attack. Strict directions were given that in every case the breaches should be filled up, so as to allow the army to retire in good order.

Alderete, the royal treasurer, commanded the van of the division under Cortez. The Spanish forces advanced simultaneously, and the Aztecs, as usual, fell back before them. Drawn on by his ardour in the pursuit, Alderete hastily followed up the flying enemy, and rushed across a canal twelve feet in width without stopping to fill up the chasm. Suddenly, at the blast of Guatemozin's horn, the Aztecs turned upon their pursuers, and the shock threw them into disorder. Then ensued a terrible scene of confusion, the enemy showering darts upon them from the flat roofs of the houses as they tried to escape, and the retreating Spaniards crowding on the narrow path, till they thrust one another into the stream that girt its sides. Cortez, warned of their danger, hurried forward to the spot, and, standing at the edge of the canal, strove to save his men from drowning. He was quickly recognised by the Aztecs. With loud shouts, six of their number rushed upon him and endeavoured to drag him away captive. A desperate struggle raged around his person, but at length the superior strength and weapons of the Spaniards gained the mastery. Sorely wounded, he was mounted on a horse and led away by a Spaniard, who remarked, that his life was too valuable to be thrown away there; it was not before many of his comrades had been slain in his defence, and others had been carried into more dreadful captivity.

The assault had been everywhere a failure. Besides the killed and wounded, sixty-two Spaniards were captured, as well as two cannons and seven horses. A scene followed which filled the Spaniards with dismay. They were encamped so near the city, that in the clear atmosphere of the table-land they could distinguish what was going forward in the lofty temples. Day by day after this disaster, they beheld a solemn procession winding round the lofty pyramidal temple of the god of war. In the midst of the long file marched some of the white-faced strangers, ready decked out for the sacrifice. They were urged along by blows until they mounted to the summit, where the victims one by one were seized, stripped, and laid upon the sacrificial stone. Then, in the sight of their countrymen, the priest struck the prisoner with the sharp stone razor, thrust his hand into the wound and plucked out the palpitating heart, which he placed upon a golden altar. The body was then hurled down from the pyramid, and seized on to be devoured by the crowd. These scenes were repeated daily, until all the captives had been slaughtered; and at each sacrifice the Aztecs shouted in defiance, that so should all the enemies of their country be consumed.

Not only were the Spaniards disheartened by such horrors, but the confidence of their Indian allies was sorely shaken. In the sacrifice of so many Europeans, their superstitious fears saw the vengeance of their idols against the strangers who had dared to violate their shrines. The taunts, too, of the Mexicans, fell with an ominous sound upon their ears. "Go on in the work of destruction," they cried, as the Indians levelled the outskirts of the capital, "go on pulling down, you will soon have to build again. If we conquer, we shall make you build for us; if the Spaniards gain the day, you will have to build for them." The Spanish avarice and thirst for gold afforded many a bitter sarcasm, as they vowed, that if defeated, their treasures should not enrich their foes. "We will hide it where you shall never find it."

Yet the evil day of doom was but postponed by the victory of the Aztecs. Cortez now determined to proceed more cautiously, and to abandon all thought of preserving the city. Each breach in the causeway was to be so solidly filled up that it could not be re-opened. Each quarter that was gained was to be levelled to the ground, and the materials cast into the lake or the canals. With this ruthlessness of purpose, the Spaniards worked on steadily, and day by day the unhappy Mexicans saw a further portion of their capital destroyed, and themselves hemmed in within a more contracted space. Soon, too, the horrors of famine were added to the other sufferings of the besieged. In their extremity they devoured the most loathsome articles as food. The supply of fresh water was cut off, and they were compelled to drink the brackish water of the lake. Crowded together as they were into a narrow space, with such polluted food and drink, pestilence soon followed in the track of famine, and, with terrible rapidity, seized on their exhausted frames. They sickened and died in such numbers that the survivors no longer sufficed to bury the dead. Their corpses polluted the atmosphere of the city, and aggravated the sufferings of its unhappy people.

The cup of horrors was now filled to overflowing, but their spirit was invincible, they would rather die than yield. In their terrible extremity, the last feelings of tenderness were quenched, and mothers devoured their own children to satisfy the wolfish pangs of hunger. Gaunt and haggard creatures staggered through the deserted streets. As the Spaniards, day by day, made fierce assaults upon the city, the famine-stricken wretches gazed on them with frenzied eyes, or rained on them showers of missiles that fell powerless from their enfeebled arms. They perished by thousands in sullen obstinacy beneath the swords of their opponents. "Despatch us, do your worst;" was their only answer to all entreaties to surrender, and the savage Tlascalans, taking them at their word, slaughtered men, women, and children with undiscriminating violence. We may readily believe that the dead bodies strewed the streets so thickly that the conquerors marched over them to commit further devastation, since we are assured that on a single day no less than forty thousand perished.

The siege had lasted more than three months, when, on the 15th of August, 1521, Cortez, for the last time, led his troops against Mexico. Soon a cry arose that the emperor had escaped; the canoes that darted from the city were surrounded, and in one of these Guatemozin was discovered and brought before the general. He bore himself proudly in the hour of his fall, "I have done my best, now do with me what you will. You had better take my life at once." Cortez assured him of his protection and of honourable treatment; but he broke his word, and permitted him to be tortured in the hope that he would say where the treasures had been concealed. For the moment, however, he was kindly dealt with, and at his request the miserable remnant of the Mexicans were allowed to march out of the city and leave its ruins to the foe.

Thus ended this memorable siege, after a struggle unsurpassed in the annals of the world, for the indomitable spirit with which it was sustained. The conquerors might well exult at this termination of their toils, but they had little reason to rejoice in its immediate fruits. True to their declared purpose, the Aztecs had made away with all the treasures of Montezuma, and but a scanty portion fell to each man's share after all the privations of the long campaign. The city itself was one disordered mass of ruins, and immediate steps were necessary for its purification, or the consequences might be fatal to the visitors. Cortez gave directions for these works, and determined ultimately to build his new capital on the site of the old one. As years rolled by it was adorned with many beautiful and spacious buildings; but the special memorials of the Aztec civilization—the palaces, garden, and menageries —the pride of Mexico, were lost for ever.

THE STORY OF THE CONQUEST. 107

We wonder with what feelings Cortez thought upon his handiwork as he gazed upon the ruined city. Barely a year since, and it had welcomed him with hospitable cordiality within its walls. His own letters had borne testimony to the activity and prosperity of its people, to the marks of intelligence and civilization which rose on every side. These fruits of long and laborious years had all been blighted by his ambition, and he had made this return for the presents of Montezuma, and for the acclamations which had greeted his first entrance within its walls. With no enviable emotion must he have turned away. Had he known them, the words which the British chieftain applied to the Romans might have seemed applicable to himself, "They make a desert, and then call it peace."

The conquest of Mexico was completed with the fall of the capital, and, although some time elapsed before the more distant tribes were actually subjugated, the Spaniards were virtually masters of the country from the moment that they marched into the deserted town.

In the sketch that we have given of the varied steps through which this end was attained, our aim has been to indicate the many difficulties, in spite of which Cortez consummated his triumph. It is only by taking them into consideration that we can adequately conceive the magnitude of the enterprise, or the true greatness of the man who would persevere in the face of such accumulated obstacles. The power and resources of Mexico might have sufficed to deter any man from attempting to subdue it, unless he had been assured that the whole efforts of the Spanish government would be put forth in his support. Instead of having any such ground of confidence, Cortez entered the country with a mere handful of followers, many of whom were disaffected towards him, and regarded his success with no friendly feelings. That he won over to his side many such opponents is as great a proof of his ability as is a victory over the enemy in open field. Still this source of anxiety was never entirely removed, he had to suffer some of his forces to depart, and the conspiracy against his life, during the final siege, showed a wide-spread feeling of dissatisfaction amongst those that remained. His Indian allies were a care no less harassing; they were easily aroused, and only restrained with difficulty. Yet he managed them with such address that they stood by him in the hour of his need, shed their blood freely in his defence, and toiled under his orders when the conquest was secured. Besides all this, until the final struggle was passed he knew not how his conduct was regarded at the court of Spain; and his cares must have been terribly augumented by the consciousness that nothing, save victory, could excuse his insubordination: that defeat would inevitably be followed by disgrace. In no tragedy had man ever been portrayed as fighting against circumstances that seemed more hopelessly invincible.

It is here then that we must recognise the true greatness of the conqueror of Mexico, in the iron will and purpose that proposed to themselves a single end, and steadily followed it in defiance of all obstacles; in the bold courage that never blenched before dangers, let them come from whence they might; in the tenacity with which he grasped a definite design, and followed it out to its full completion. The lust of conquest, the carnage, the cruelty, the cunning, that marked his course—all these have found advocates, but in truth they admit of no defence. They are so many foul stains upon one whom the world has honoured because of his success. Their true character is not altered by the difficulties of the position of Cortez. It is the glory of righteousness that it has abided by the right in spite of all temptations; it must be the shame of wrong that in like circumstances it has failed.

We repeat that the greatness of Cortez consists in his singleness of purpose, and yet how his glory pales here beside that of the humblest Christian martyr, who, placing before himself God's glory as the one thing needful, has pursued that object at any sacrifice, even that of life itself. Singleness of purpose once attained, it is the end which ennobles it and gives it its true character. To conquer a vast region is not in itself a noble object, however stamped with the applause of men. To glorify God in seeking his truth for ourselves, or to make it known to others, is a far nobler aim than to tread, however gallantly, through the blood of thousands to such honours as those which were conferred on Cortez.

CHAPTER IV.

MEXICO UNDER SPANISH VICEROYS.

The new city—Subsequent career of Cortez—Mendoza, viceroy—Revolt of the Indians—Their sufferings—Sandoval, viceroy—Slavery of the Indians confirmed—Insurrections—Pestilence—Velasco, viceroy—Favours the abolition of slavery—Complaints of the colonists—Conspiracy against the family of Cortez—Occasion of its outbreak—Execution of the Alvarados—Peralta, viceroy—Intrigues against him—Munoz sent out as visitador—Pestilence in Mexico—Internal quiet—Velasco II., viceroy—The fowl tax—Repartimientos—Embankment and drainage of the lake of Tezcuco—Gelves, viceroy—His avarice—Outbreak in the capital—Strange scenes—*Auto-da-fe* at Mexico—English privateers—Count Revilla-Gigedo—Prosperity under his viceroyalty—Heavy taxation—Injustice to the natives—Famine—Avarice of the viceroy—New silver mines discovered—Galvez, visitador—Expulsion of the Jesuits—Indian indolence—Florez, viceroy—Incursions of the Apaches—Revilla-Gigedo II., viceroy—Anecdotes of his administration—Branciforte, viceroy—Discontent of the people—The beginning of the end.

FOUR years had not elapsed since the destruction of Mexico when a new city rose upon the ruins of the Aztec capital. The plans for the new town were laid out on a scale of great magnificence. Churches and palaces were erected in its spacious streets and squares, which were carried out in straight lines, so that the eye ran through them to rest upon the dark back ground of the surrounding mountains. A vast population was quickly gathered, and soon 2,000 Spanish families were settled in it, and more than 30,000 natives occupied the Indian quarter. All the activity of a thriving population was aroused within its walls, and the terrible desolation of the past was half forgotten in present prosperity.

The character of Cortez, too, appears in a more favourable light after the conclusion of the siege. Despite the opposition of Velasquez and Fonseca he was confirmed in his authority by a royal ordinance, dated October 15, 1522, and before its arrival Cortez was actively employed in consolidating his conquest. He showed such practical sagacity in his designs for the improvement of the country as raises him to the rank of a statesman, far above the level of a mere ruthless destroyer. Within three years several important expeditions to explore the country had been fitted out, and a territory of some 1,200 miles on the coasts of the Atlantic and Pacific had been reduced under the yoke of Spain.

We have not space to relate the adventures which befel Cortez in Honduras, nor those of Alvarado in Guatemala. It is the old story of Spanish adventure in the new world. Hair-breadth escapes were incurred and prodigies of valour performed by the Europeans, whose gallantry was, however, too, often sullied with cruelty, and Alvarado especially earned the detestation of the natives by his ruthless conduct. Strangely intermingled with such conduct, and with the avarice that characterized the first colonists, is the anxiety everywhere expressed and felt by them for the conversion of the Indians, and which gave to these expeditions the spirit of the crusades. The Popish tenets were generally accepted with all the semblance of outward compliance, whilst the Indians remained ignorant of the creed they had adopted, or still combined with it the secret worship of their former deities.

Although Cortez had been confirmed in his government, his adversaries still continued to heap up charges against him, and at length Charles ordered him to return to Spain that he might clear himself from all accusations. He met with every mark of attention and favour when he reached Toledo, in 1529. He was made Marquis of the Valley of Oaxaca, and large estates were conferred upon him, but he was not permitted again to resume his government. Perhaps he had become too powerful as a subject. At any rate, on his return to Mexico, he was forbidden to approach within thirty leagues of the capital, and after spending immense sums in projects for further colonization and exploration, which were never repaid by the government, he returned and died in his native land at Castilleja de la Cuesta, near Seville, on the 2nd of December, 1547.

When Cortez had been summoned to Europe, the government was intrusted to Nuñez de Guzman, with whom two officers, termed oidores, were associated; but, as the importance of the colony began to be more fully appreciated by the Spanish court, it was determined to send out a nobleman of high position and ability, with ample powers as viceroy; and in this form the country continued to be ruled as long as it remained an appanage of the Spanish crown.

Don Antonio de Mendoza, the first viceroy, arrived at Mexico in 1535. There were abundant sources of employment awaiting him. He began by reducing the clergy to order, suspending those whose lives were a scandal to their calling, and urging them to greater zeal in the conversion of the natives. The condition of the latter was the subject of much anxiety to the viceroy and the home government, and a code of laws was drawn up by the Council of the Indies to provide for their welfare. Unhappily the interests of the colonists were so opposed to those of the Indians that the authorities often found it impossible to enforce their enactments. But every credit should be given to the government for their zeal and their good intentions.

The viceroyalty of Mendoza was distinguished by the establishment of a royal mint at Mexico for coining money, and by the issue of the first book that had been printed in the country. The prejudices of the natives, however, greatly lessened the advantages which might have been derived from the former of these improvements. A large issue of copper coinage, valued by Torquemada at 200,000 dollars, was made, but it was so unpopular that severe laws were passed to insist upon its reception. Suddenly the whole of it disappeared. The Mexicans had thrown it into the lake. A small silver coinage was attempted in 1541, but it met no better success. Large quantities of it were collected and melted into bars; another portion shared the fate of the copper money.

The year 1542 was marked by a revolt of the Indians of Jalisco. The cause was traced to the oppression of the system of *repartimientos*, under which a number of natives were assigned to a European colonist, and were compelled to work on his farm or to labour in the mines. The clement viceroy was touched with the sufferings of the natives, and he entreated them to lay down their arms, but their experience of past wrongs made them reckless of danger. " We are lords of these lands," they answered, "and we wish to die in their defence." In the various actions which ensued such decisive victories were gained by the Spaniards, that the natives were fain to submit. They obtained very easy terms from Mendoza, who forbore from exacting vengeance for this violation of his authority.

The attention of the emperor was called by these insurrections to the condition of his American subjects. A council was summoned to look into the matter and legislate upon it, with due regard to the necessity of the colonists and the rights of the Indians. They ordained that, "there were to be no slaves made in the future wars of these countries; the system of *repartimientos* was to be abandoned; and the Indians were not, as a class, to be solely devoted to ignoble pursuits." The widest publicity was given to these humane intentions in Spain;* and officers were appointed to visit the colonies and see that the injunctions were carefully carried out.

Francisco de Sandoval, who was despatched on this mission to Mexico, reached St. Juan de Ulua in 1544. His arrival was the signal for the most strenuous efforts on the part of the colonists to prevent the publication of the decrees. On this issue hung the fate of the native population, and Sandoval declared his firm intention to maintain the emperor's commands, and in this course he was promptly seconded by Mendoza. The rage of the planters was unbounded. Their wealth was dependent upon their retaining the Indians in slavery; and at length their opposition grew so formidable that Mendoza allowed them to send a body of delegates to Spain, who might lay their representations before the emperor. Meanwhile Sandoval persisted in enforcing obedience to the decrees, and he removed several officers from their posts who

* Mayer's Mexico, vol. I., p. 143.

were convicted of cruelty to the Indians intrusted to them.

The whole history of Mexico would have assumed another complexion had the emperor remained firm on behalf of his Indian subjects. No engine was left untried by the proprietors to effect their purpose. "Money, influence, falsehood, and intrigue, were freely used to sustain the system of masked slavery among the subjugated natives; and at last a royal *cedula* was procured commanding the revocation of the humane decrees, and ordering the division of the royal domain among the conquerors. The Indians, of course, followed the fate of the soil; and thus, by chicanery and influence, the gentle efforts of the better portion of Spanish society were rendered entirely nugatory. The news of this decree spread joy among the Mexican landed proprietors. The chains of slavery were rivetted upon the natives. The principle of compulsory labour was established for ever, and even to this day the Indian of Mexico remains the bondsman he was doomed to become in the 16th century." *

From this time may be dated the undying hostility between the Indians and their Spanish conquerors, which still rages, and whose fruits may be traced in every portion of Mexican history, down to the conflicts which are being waged whilst we pen these lines.

It was not to be expected that the natives would be conciliated by such a policy; and, although Mendoza's authority was ever exerted to ameliorate the condition of the Indians, they continued to be illtreated by the planters, whose estates were scattered at wide intervals through the country, and who were almost uncontrolled by the authorities at the capital. The discontent of the

* Mayer's Mexico, vol. I., p. 144.

conquered people manifested itself in numerous insurrections which broke out during Mendoza's viceroyalty, and the sufferings of the natives were further aggravated by a pestilence which desolated the country in the year 1546, and is said to have swept off five-sixths of the whole population. The disconnected efforts of the Indians were, however, powerless against the superior strength of their masters. The numbers of the Europeans were constantly increasing, as grants of land were given to poor and deserving Spaniards, and the limits of the territory which they colonized were being constantly extended. Happy were those among the natives whose country was subdued by the preaching of the religious orders and not by the sword. Such was the fortune of the province of Vera Paz, whose name was given it to betoken that it had been converted to Christianity by the eloquence of the Dominicans, and not by the fiery zeal of the Spanish soldiery.

It was during the viceroyalty of Mendoza that Peru was added to the Spanish dominions by Pizarro; and, as the new colony required a governor of ability and discretion for its re-organization after the inevitable disorder of the conquest, Mendoza was transferred thither in 1550. His successor, Velasco, was sent out with instructions to endeavour to better the condition of the natives, and the struggle between the viceroy and the planters was renewed: the latter urged that the colony would be ruined if the system of forced labour was abandoned; that the fields would be untilled, and the necessary supplies for the colony would fail; more than all, that the royal revenues would be sacrificed. But Velasco was unmoved by these representations. He declared his determination "to relieve the Indians from the personal labours, tributes, and severe service in the mines with which they had been burdened. Their liberty he asserted to be of more importance than all the mines in the world; and the revenues they yielded to the Spanish crown not to be of such a character that all divine and human laws should be sacrificed to obtain them." *

It was nobly and truthfully spoken, but it raised a host of enemies against Velasco, and the accession of Philip II., on the abdication of Charles V., afforded an opportunity for undermining his power. Hitherto the viceroy had possessed unlimited authority. The jealous disposition of Philip was worked upon successfully, and he was persuaded to send out a decree that in future the viceroy should do nothing without the previous sanction of the Audiencia. It was not alleged that Velasco had misused his powers, but the conflicting statements sent home puzzled the government, and they sent out Valderrama as visitador of New Spain, to inquire into and correct abuses. How cruelly Valderrama exercised his functions may be understood from the title he acquired of "Molester of the Indians," and a powerful restraint upon him was removed by Velasco's sudden death. He had been ordered to undertake an expedition to the Philippine islands, and was organizing his forces when his health suddenly failed him. He died July 31, 1564. His memory was embalmed in the affections of the natives, whose cause he had maintained, and the remembrance of his loving sympathy for the oppressed still sheds its pure and gentle light around his tomb.

At the death of Velasco the government was administered by the Audiencia, until his successor should

* Mayer's Mexico, vol. I., p. 149.

arrive in Mexico, and the interval was marked by a tragedy which excited the deepest interest on account of the character and station of the parties concerned.

Among the noblemen then resident at Mexico, none was more conspicuous for wealth and popularity than the Marquis del Valle, the son of Hernando Cortez. How he managed to incur the hatred or jealousy of the Audiencia is not told us, but it is certain that they regarded him with aversion, and were eager to contrive his ruin. Some colour seemed to be given to their suspicions by the liberality and magnificence of the marquis on the occasion of the baptism of his twin daughters. The ceremonial was marked with unusual splendour. From the palace of the marquis to the cathedral a covered way was prepared, under an awning of rich cloths, and a salute of artillery announced to the assembled multitude the precise moment when the infants entered and left the church. A grand tournament, and a sumptuous banquet, spread in the streets, and to which all were welcomed, were maliciously construed as further evidence of a treasonable design to win over the affections of the populace.

On the evening of the baptism a grand entertainment, in honour of the event, was given by Don Alonso de Avila Alvarado, who, with his brother Gonzalez, was the intimate friend of the Marquis del Valle; and at this party a masque was performed, representing the first meeting between Cortez and Montezuma. Alonso played the part of the Mexican emperor, and as he placed a crown of laurel on the heads of the marquis and his wife, he exclaimed, "How well these crowns befit your noble brows!" On so trifling a foundation the Audiencia built up their accusation of treason against the first subject of New Spain.

The subsequent proceedings of the Audiencia are almost incredible. They pretended to have received information that a conspiracy was formed against the government, which was to take effect on the anniversary of the fall of Mexico. Armed bands were to be collected, under pretence of joining in the procession, and, at a given signal, Don Martin Cortez, the son of Marina, and half brother of the marquis, was to rush out and slay the Audiencia, and proclaim del Valle monarch of New Spain. The marquis was accordingly summoned by the Audiencia, under the pretext that a despatch had been received from Spain, with orders that it should be read in his presence. On arriving at the council chamber, without a thought of what was impending, he found himself surrounded by soldiers, and was taken prisoner on a charge of treason. He yielded, seeing that resistance was hopeless, and at the same time the two Alvarados, and the kinsmen of Cortez, were arrested, and their papers seized, in hopes that they might afford some evidence against them. Alonso's portfolio was found to be full of love letters, but did not contain one trace of treason. But their guilt had been predetermined by the Audiencia. In spite of the entreaties of the public bodies, and almost all the leading nobles in the city, the gallant Alonso, and his brother, were condemned and beheaded on the 7th of August, 1566. We are assured that the marquis only escaped from sharing the same fate by the arrival of Gaston de Peralta, the new viceroy.

Peralta soon discovered the iniquity of the proceeding, and having dismissed those members of the Audiencia who had been concerned in it, he penned a despatch to Philip II. giving a full account of the transaction. This despatch the suspended functionaries managed to keep back by bribing the viceroy's messenger; at the same time they sent out to Spain the most unfounded charges against the viceroy, accusing him of being remiss in his investigation of the conspiracy, and even of having provided an army of 30,000 men to support the marquis in his revolt. They confirmed their statements by a batch of depositions, one of which was to the effect that the witness had actually seen the forces adverted to. The sole basis of this tissue of falsehoods being a picture, containing a multitude of figures, which the viceroy had caused to be painted on a wall of his official residence.

The court of Spain was sadly confused on the receipt of these letters. It could not believe in the treason of Peralta, and waited for his reply; but when this was again intercepted it construed his silence into an admission of his guilt, and accordingly sent out a commission under Muñoz to take possession of the government and inquire into the matter. Peralta was thunderstruck at the arrival of Muñoz, and his own deposition from power, but he quietly yielded up his power and waited until his innocence should be established. Muñoz, on the other hand, abused his office frightfully. The prisons of Mexico were filled to overflowing, and so terribly did he signalize himself by his cruelty and reactions that a universal cry was raised for his recall. The same fleet bore back to Spain both Muñoz and Peralta, and at length the whole truth came out. In vain Muñoz tried to palliate his conduct. "I sent you to govern, not to destroy," was the answer of the king to his explanations. That same night Muñoz was found dead in his chamber. The Marquis del Valle had left Mexico for Spain, and, after a delay of seven years, during which his property was wasted by the crown officials, he also was acquitted and his lands restored.

Such an episode illustrates the dark state of society in Mexico, and we may well believe that the next viceroy, Alasanza, found it necessary to quiet the fears and distrust which were then widely prevalent. Yet a subsequent act of the home government could hardly be calculated to reassure the Mexicans. Religious disputes were raging in the capital, and needed a gentle hand to soothe them; but at this period Philip II. determined to establish the inquisition in Mexico, and sent out a grand inquisitor to organize the office. About the same period, 1572, the first Jesuit college was established in the city.

In 1576, Mexico was visited by a terrible pestilence, which carried off a vast number of the people. Its symptoms were violent pains in the head, succeeded by burning fever of so exhaustive a character that none were known to survive the seventh day of seizure. Nearly two millions are said to have perished. In the two years following, Alasanza endeavoured to lessen the miseries of the natives who had probably been the chief sufferers from the plague. He remitted the annual tribute, and gave directions for their more lenient treatment. It was in working the mines that they suffered most severely. "Their toil was incessant. Their task-masters gave them no respite in the bowels of the earth, for they wrought as if they designed to scrape every vein and artery of the colony's soil. Silver and labour were calculated with exactness, and no limit to the Indian's industry was prescribed, save that which was imposed by his capacity for work and his powers of endurance. The viceroy introduced a milder system, as far as he was able, among the leading miners of the colony. He insisted upon permitting the Indians regular repose, and he forbade their entire confinement within the mines, but commanded that they should be allowed time to breathe the fresh air on the surface of the earth, and suffered to attend to their domestic labours, or to toil on public works, for a competent recompense."* The terms in which the viceroy's orders are expressed enable us to conceive what the miserable condition of these poor creatures must have been.

Several years passed away without any incident of moment. Alasanza was removed to Peru, and succeeded by other viceroys in somewhat quick succession. Internally the country was agitated by religious disputes and the misconduct of officials. Beyond its coasts the terrible Drake hovered, hiding in the bays of California, and pouncing suddenly on the rich galleons that bore away the tribute, or came freighted with the precious products of foreign lands. Vast sums, however, reached the court of Spain: 3,300,000 coined ducats in silver, and 1,100 marks in gold, in 1585, and a still larger treasure in 1587, helped to liquidate the expenses incurred by Philip II. in his European wars. But, in 1594, the king's necessities induced him to resort to the system of forced loans, which were demanded of his American as well as of his European subjects.

Velasco, the son of the second viceroy, held at this period the government of New Spain. He undertook, with great reluctance, the task of increasing by four *reals* the capitation tax upon the Indians; and being anxious at once to alleviate the burden and to encourage them in rearing poultry, he agreed to receive three

Mayer's Mexico, vol. I., p. 162.

reals and *one fowl*, then valued at a real, in lieu of full money payment. The indolent and improvident natives allowed the time to slip by without providing themselves with any poultry, and they at last had to buy the required bird instead of selling it. The price of fowls rose in consequence to three reals; the tax-gatherers took advantage of the opportunity to press for the tax, and to make a market of their poultry, and so the unfortunate Indians were mulct in three times the amount through this scheme, which was devised in their behalf. An attempt to settle some of the wandering tribes in fixed abodes was not much more successful. The first Otomi who was compelled to live in a house killed his own wife and children, and then hung himself. For the present the Otomies were permitted to indulge their vagabond propensities.

Acehedo, count of Monterey, the successor of Velasco, abolished the fowl tax, and made most strenuous efforts to get rid of the system of *repartimientos*. The great hindrance to the enfranchisement of the natives lay in their natural indisposition to labour. It was impossible to raise the royal revenue save by a system of forced labour. It was equally impracticable to guard against the abuses to which that system was liable. It was a dilemma between idleness and tyranny. Plans were tried by which it was hoped that natives might be obliged to perform a fair amount of labour, and yet should be ensured the payment of their wages. Every Sunday they were to assemble in the market-place and enter into contracts for daily service; the viceroy in person attended on these occasions, and strove in his immediate neighbourhood to see the system fairly carried out. But a body of middle men came in. They hired large gangs on moderate terms, and then sub-let them at a profit. The Indians found themselves worse treated than under the old system, and we are told that they themselves begged that it might be restored. They were quite incapable of the effort of seeking for labour, and Monterey learned, like his predecessors, that it is impossible to help those who will not help themselves.

In 1607, Velasco was appointed viceroy for the second time. His administration was signalized by the attempt to save Mexico from the inundations of the neighbouring lakes, and it was under his direction that the system of drainage was commenced which we have described in the opening chapter. The only other incident of his rule that calls for notice was a revolt of the negro slaves in 1609. They assembled in large numbers in the mountains near Cordova, and a regular force had to be sent against them. The viceroy probably pitied the insurgents, for their treatment by their masters was intolerable. Yet, after several skirmishes, they were fain to submit and craved pardon, "because they had not rebelled against the king." An amnesty was immediately accorded them, and permission to settle in the town of San Lorenzo. It was stipulated that they should not afford an asylum to other slaves who might run away from the plantations.

Garcia Guerra, the next viceroy, died from the effect of an accident ere his term was expired, and the Audiencia succeeded to the government until the new ruler should arrive. It had generally been the fate of this body to distinguish its government by some act of atrocity, and it did not fail on this occasion to maintain its reputation. Hardly had they entered on their office, when the news spread abroad that the negroes were again in arms. The people were panic-struck. A terrible noise was heard by night in the streets of the capital, and the terrified citizens thought that the savages were upon them, and that they should be murdered in their beds. Inquiry proved that the alarm was due to the arrival in the darkness of a large drove of hogs. Yet, to excuse the public fright and their own credulity, the Audiencia had twenty-nine male and four female negroes put to death. "Their withered and fetid bodies were left to hang upon the gallows, tainting the air, and shocking the eyes of every passer-by, until the neighbourhood could no longer bear the stench, and imperiously demanded their removal."

Four years afterwards, the insurrection broke out in earnest in the state of Durango. It was the native Indians who now rose, under the leadership of a chieftain who called himself the "Son of the Sun, and God of Heaven and Earth." A terrible and indiscriminate massacre ensued of every European who came within their reach : neither sex, nor age, availed for protection. The churches were broken into, and many were murdered as they sought the sanctuary of the altars. Even the priests were not spared. At length, after three months of war and negotiation, peace was restored. It was gained more through the influence of the Jesuits than the arms of the soldiers.

A curious insight into the internal condition of Mexico is afforded us by the narrative of Father Gage, an English friar, who visited the country in 1625. Gage was at this period a Dominican monk, but no sooner was his English birth known at the court of Spain than strict orders were given to prevent his visiting the colony of Mexico. The worthy friar, however, concealed himself in a cask on board the galleon in which he was to sail, and did not emerge from his hiding-place until the vessel was some distance on her voyage. He subsequently renounced the creed of Rome, and after a series of adventures reached England, and was made chaplain to Fairfax. His book, now very scarce, abounds in quaint details, minutely describing the scenes which he had witnessed.

Gage gives us a lively picture of the sufferings of the Indians. Many were swept from their homes to the mines, and there perished under the severity of the labour imposed upon them. Forced service commonly prevailed. Travellers were entitled to demand without payment food for themselves and their mules, as well as porters to carry on their baggage. The amount due for these things was to be entered in a public ledger, and payment was not made for it by the government until the end of the year. So heavy were the burdens which the natives were required to carry, that when the strap which supported it was removed from the forehead, the skin not unfrequently came off with it. To all such incidental ills were added the existence of slavery throughout the land.

Each large proprietor might demand a number of workmen to till the ground or perform other menial offices. Every Sunday the native chief was obliged to bring a body of his followers to the market-place, and they were then assigned to the different proprietors. Only a certain number could legally be allotted each week; but as the officer who arranged the matter was paid by a tax of so much a head on each Indian, he was hardly likely to be restrained by such a regulation. The poor creatures were torn from their homes, and even then were commonly robbed of the payment which the law allowed them, under the pretext that it was due for the provisions with which they were furnished. At harvest time they were glad even to pay their masters for permission to return home, after half the week was spent, that they might get in their crops.

The patient endurance of the country people was not, however, tamely imitated by the city population. The Marquis Gelves was viceroy when Gage arrived at Mexico. His character was stained by insatiable avarice, and he determined to buy up all the corn in the country and then re-sell it at a great profit. He employed an agent, named Mesia, to purchase corn at the price fixed by the government for years of famine. It was soon discovered that there were no stores of food save in the viceroy's granaries. A panic quickly followed, and prices rose enormously. In vain the people demanded grain at 14 reals, the famine price as fixed by law. Gelves answered, that it was not a year of scarcity, and refused to interfere,

De la Serna, the archbishop, was now appealed to by the people. He promptly excommunicated Mesia. The latter disregarded his anathema, and raised the price of corn still higher. De la Serna then put the whole country under an interdict. The churches were all closed. The mills all silent. The priests went from house to house bewailing the affliction of the people. Still Mesia held out, supported by the viceroy.

At length the outcry became universal, and Mesia had to take refuge in the viceregal palace. In vain Gelves ordered that the interdict should be disregarded. In vain he ordered De la Serna to revoke his censures. The archbishop replied by excommunicating the viceroy himself. Gelves sent an officer to seize him. The prelate retired to the church of Guadalupe and awaited the arrival of the viceroy's minion at the altar; his mitre on his head, his crosier in one hand, and the sacrament in the other. He was dragged from the sanctuary, and sent as a prisoner to Spain.

At length, however, the passions of the people were roused to an ungovernable pitch. All Mexico rose in insurrection. The viceroy had to fly, and found refuge in a Franciscan cloister. The granaries were then opened, and peace once more restored; Gelves was recalled, but made "master of the horse" to the Spanish monarch. The noble-hearted De la Serna was degraded to the petty bishopric of Tamora, in Castile. Thirty years passed, during which little save palatial intrigues followed this disgraceful episode.

There were strange scenes occasionally at the vice-regal palace when a new governor was appointed to rule over the colony. When Muñoz was suddenly displaced from office he had to borrow from some citizens the money with which to hire a carriage to Vera Cruz. So, too, when in 1590 the viceroy Zuniga was supplanted by the bishop of Tlascala, the prelate seized all the property of his predecessor, and even withheld his wife's linen. On other occasions, the royal rescript appointing a new viceroy was kept secret until a fitting moment arrived for its disclosure, and the man who deemed himself the master of the country was awoke out of his sleep to learn that his powers had been transferred to another: this was the case with the Duke of Escalona, whose reign terminated in 1642. At the same time all his property was sequestrated and his jewels were sent to the treasury. Those viceroys who had been falsely accused generally succeeded in obtaining an aquittal, but the fact of their being subject to such treatment at all is a striking feature of the manners of the time.

There was little of interest in the history of the colony until the year 1659, when a grand *auto-da-fé* took place at Mexico, at which fifty human beings were burned alive. The Inquisition had been established by Philip II. in the mother country, and in this event we have some of the fruits of its labours. The horrid spectacle was witnessed by a dense mass of people, and the viceroy, in person, presided over the proceeding. Meanwhile the colony was extending its territories and growing in wealth and splendour. Various expeditions were fitted out to California and New Mexico. In many of the wildest border regions the civilisation of the natives was undertaken by the Jesuits, who carried out their task with a zeal and self-denial that were worthy of a purer creed. They settled amidst the savage tribes, ruled over them with an absolute authority, and derived no inconsiderable revenue from the tribute which their subjects paid to them.

During a considerable period, the weakness of the colonial government contrasted strangely with its internal growth and prosperity. Jamaica was captured by the English in 1656, and serious apprehensions were entertained for the safety of the Spanish ports. Nor were the internal frontiers of the country more secure. In 1680, a general rising of the Indians in New Mexico took place. They besieged Santa Fé, its capital, so closely that no one dared to show himself beyond the walls, and the beleaguered inhabitants only escaped by stealing in the night through the lines of the enemy. The city was levelled to the ground, and all hold over the natives was for the present lost. The sea was swept by the British privateers long after peace had

K

been proclaimed between the courts of London and Madrid. Still the internal resources of the country were developed. Crowds of emigrants landed on its shores, and the working of the mines resulted in a harvest of wealth hitherto unparalleled.

None of its rulers contributed more to this result than the Count Revilla-Gigedo, the first viceroy of his name, who held office from 1746 to 1755. The mining districts now were extraordinarily prolific, and no year of his government yielded less than 11,000,000 of dollars; the whole sum that passed through the national mint during his term being 114,231,000 dollars of the precious metals. The population of the capital amounted to 50,000 families, composed of Spaniards, European and Creole; 40,000 Mestitzos, Mulattoes and Negroes; and 8,000 Indians who inhabited the suburbs. This population consumed annually at least 2,000,000 arobas of flour, about 160,000 fanegas of corn, 300,000 sheep, 15,500 beeves, and about 25,000 swine. In this estimate the consumption of many religious establishments is not included, as they were privately supplied from their estates, nor can we count the numerous and valuable presents which were sent by residents of the country to their friends in the capital. The taxes of the city of Mexico, accounted for by the council, amounted to 333,333 dollars, whilst those of the whole viceroyalty reached 718,375 dollars. The income from *pulque* alone—the favourite drink of the masses—was 172,000 dollars, and their imposts swelled the gross income to the sum already indicated. It would be hard to say what corresponding benefit the country received in return for such exactions.

Of the taxes thus raised a very unfair proportion was exacted from the Indians, when their poverty and personal service are considered. The *alcaldes*, by whom the Indians were ruled in their respective districts, were made responsible for payment, and had to give security for it before entering upon their office. A census was taken of the natives in each district, and three *reals* each were collected from them three times a year, two natives being always assessed together, so that each might be liable for the whole sum. The whole year's tax, of eighteen reals for the two, was thus divided—eight were assigned for tribute, four for the royal service, four and a half as commutation for corn to the royal granary, half a real for the royal hospital, in which the natives were tended when ill, and the remaining real was divided between a fund for the cost of their law suits, and one for the erection of cathedrals. *

In 1749 and 1750, famine prevailed through all the country, save the metropolitan district of Mexico. The sufferings of the people were also aggravated by shocks of earthquake, which destroyed many of their villages, at a great cost of human life. So severe was the scarcity in the second year, that a *fanega* of corn was sold for twenty-five dollars in the region of Zacatecas, and the town population poured out into the forests that they might live upon the berries and roots which were to be found in them. The discovery of the silver vein of Bolanos, whose richness caused the merchants to bring to it large quantities of corn, afforded a considerable supply of work, and much alleviated the misery which would otherwise have been undergone.

The government of Count Revilla-Gigedo was able and successful, and the Court of Spain had every reason to be satisfied with the amount of tribute he exported thither; but his own character has not escaped the gravest imputations. It is asserted that he entered into every imaginable speculation; that he thought no commercial scheme beneath his notice which promised a large profit; that tables were spread in the vice-regal palace at which the courtiers might gamble, that their lord might profit by the loss of their doubloons. Yet such was his influence, that he was treated with respect notwithstanding such traits. So fearless was his bearing, that on the occasion of an outbreak he rode alone into the city, and awed the mob into subjection by his stern demeanour.

The discovery of the Bolanos mine, and the successful working of the veins at Zacatecas. excited the wildest expectations of wealth amongst the Mexicans at this period. Crowds of persons flocked to the mines with the hope of attaining rapidly to fortune, without the tedium of long and patient toil. A feverish spirit of restlessness seized many who were already deriving large profits, and on the announcement of fresh veins in New Leon, the miners of Zacatecas and Guanajuato flocked thither. Vast works were commenced, and a large outlay undergone, when the ores suddenly failed. In some quarters, penniless adventurers were raised to immense wealth. In others, those who had started with a competency found themselves reduced to beggary. Indeed, the whole history of the colony abounds in such violent oscillations of prosperity and adversity, of health and pestilence. In 1763, the small-pox broke out in the capital, and carried off 10,000 persons. On a former occasion it had raged so terribly that hardly an inhabitant could be found who was not marked by its ravages. Hardly had this pest subsided when a new form of disease appeared, which caused a continuous bleeding from the nose that commonly proved fatal. From the capital it spread to the country districts, where thousands perished without attendance, medicine, or care.

The administration of the Marquis of Criullas, from 1761 to 1766, excited much discontent at home and in the colony. Don José Galvez was accordingly sent out with powers as visitador, and under his able and searching rule the disorders were speedily remedied. Galvez was a man of extraordinary vigour, and of an industry that shrunk from no amount of labour. He soon dismissed some of the crown servants from their offices, and by his firmness successfully carried out his scheme for raising a revenue upon tobacco, an article of universal consumption with the Mexicans, the growth and manufacture of which had been hitherto unfettered. No small outcry arose at this proceeding. But Galvez would not be intimidated. He allowed the colonists to grow tobacco as they pleased, but all was to be sold at a fixed price to the revenue officers, and they disposed of it at a small advance, to be made into cigars.

Galvez was continued in his office after Criullas had been recalled, and his successor, De Croix, appointed; for the Spanish court had decided on a step which would need all his powers for its successful execution. A growing jealousy of the Jesuits had been springing up in Europe. In 1764, they had been expelled from France, and in 1766, they met with a like fate in Spain, and it was arranged that the brethren in Mexico should share the fortune of their order. Their influence in New Spain was immense. They had devoted themselves to acquiring power over the Indians, whom they ruled with a united civil and ecclesiastical authority. Their learning, their polished manners, their untiring patience, had won for them complete mastery over the natives; and they had so exercised their superiority that their subjects were kept in a complete state of pupilage and childhood. They made no effort to excite the Indians to self-exertion, and the natural apathy of the people induced a too ready acquiescence in a subordinate position. Zealous and self-denying as was the conduct of the Jesuits, their rule could only enervate and enslave.

So great, however, was the attachment of their flocks, that the court felt no small apprehension in carrying out its purpose. The distance between the various stations was accurately estimated, and messengers were dispatched in such a manner that the order to leave the country might reach them all on the same day, and so prevent any combined effort at resistance. On the appointed morning, troops occupied the streets that led to the chief colleges of the order; their halls were closed, their establishments dissolved, and they themselves were marched under an escort from Mexico to Vera Cruz. It was the 28th of June. They were followed through their journey to the coast by the tears of the people, but Galvez sternly repressed any expression of opinion as to their treatment. "It was not for the people," he said, authoritatively, "to say anything for or against the royal order; it was a matter only for the conscience of the king!"

In our rapid sketch of Mexican affairs we have not been able to advert to the influence of European politics upon its condition. This influence had become more marked since the accession of the Bourbon line to the throne of Spain, in 1701, from which period her fortunes were long closely linked with those of France. Consequently, the news of peace between

France and England was always received with pleasure at Mexico, as war left her coasts exposed to the ravages of English privateers. It was with considerable dissatisfaction, therefore, that the people learned that the home country had, in 1779, openly taken the side of the revolted American States against the government of George III. The Spaniard little dreamed he was helping to raise a spirit which should eventually deprive him of all his transatlantic colonies.

Some glimpses may occasionally be obtained of the inner state of Mexico at this epoch. With the immense increase of wealth derived from the mines, and which had doubled the revenue under Revilla-Gigedo, luxury and magnificence were seen in the capital. New buildings rose, a school of arts was formed, and the Mint, one of the fairest edifices in the capital, was raised. With these advantages came some desire to learn a little of the early history of the country, and archbishop Lorenzano, in 1760, published a meagre collection of Mexican antiquities. The learning of the country had been sadly lowered by the expulsion of the Jesuits, and so great was the suspicion of the rulers of the press, that special leave was necessary before types could be imported for printing. Violent jealousy prevailed between the religious orders, and their quarrels often called for the interference of the viceroy; but they grew in wealth and power, and immense gifts were constantly bequeathed to them. The mingled superstition and ignorance of the people were strikingly displayed in 1779, when the small-pox again broke out within the capital. The sick were carried to the churches and laid before the images of the saints, in expectation of miraculous cures. The healthy hurried to the same objects of veneration, trusting through their good offices to be preserved; and this indiscriminate intermixture aggravated incalculably the numbers seized by the disease.

The improvident and apathetic character of the natives is seen in the terrible effects which followed upon a single year of scarcity. The fruitfulness of many crops in Mexico surpasses anything of which we have experience in Europe. A little extra toil and labour might have secured such a reserve as should amply have provided for all probable contingencies. But no sooner did a single crop of maize fail than multitudes fell victims. Such was the case in 1785, when Bernardo de Galvez was viceroy. This ruler strained every nerve to succour the starving population. Large sums were subscribed to encourage agriculture, and many of the natives were employed on public works, the most prominent of which was the palace of Chapoltepec. The viceroy's humanity did not secure him from suspicions with regard to his object in raising this pile. It was remarked that he courted popularity, and especially aimed at securing the affections of the army. All such thoughts were cut short by his sudden death in November, 1786.

"At the period of the viceroy's decease his wife was pregnant, and it is stated in the chronicles of the day —as a singular illustration of Spanish habits—that the daughter of which she was delivered in the following month of December, received the names of Maria de Guadalupe Bernarda Isabel Felipà de Jesus Juano Napomucena Felicitas, to which was added, at the period of the lady's confirmation, the additional one of Fernanda. The Ayuntamiento of Mexico, in order to show its appreciation of the viceroy's memory, offered to become *godfather* of the infant; and the ceremony of baptism was performed with all the splendour of the (Roman) Catholic church, in presence of the court and of a portion of the army."*

Don Manuel Flores was viceroy of New Spain from 1787 to 1789, and turned his attention principally to the reduction of the Indians upon the northern frontier. The fertile lands around Chihuahua, and in New Leon and Texas, had attracted thither a large number of colonists, but neither their lives nor property were secure from the attacks of the native tribes. In vain were garrisons placed in the towns. The Apaches only shifted for awhile to some distant quarters, and then returning suddenly, when confidence had been restored, swept across the country, leaving everywhere death and desolation in their track. In vain were armies marched into the field; the Indians dispersed into the forests, whither none could follow them. As fruitless were the treaties arranged with them. They were only observed until an opportunity for plunder occurred, which always proved irresistible to the native mind. Flores accordingly proposed a war of extermination. He wrote to the Court of Spain that he would give "no quarter, time, or mercy." This ruthless purpose was carried into execution, and for a brief respite the frontiers enjoyed a degree of peace.

Flores was succeeded by the Count Revilla-Gigedo, the second of that name who held the office of viceroy. He was a son of the former governor, and avoiding his father's faults, he gained for himself the brightest name amongst the rulers of Mexico. Nothing escaped his active superintendence, and no obstacles daunted his stern and prompt will. He repressed assassination, the signal vice of Mexico, improved the roads and

* Mayer, vol. I. p. 256.

police, encouraged literature and science; in short, showed all the elements of an enlightened statesman. His keen glance discerned the value of the Californias, and he urgently pressed upon the Spanish court the need of fortifying so valuable a possession. Amongst other plans by which he might become acquainted with the real wants of the people, he placed a letter-box in a hall of the palace, into which all persons might throw their complaints; and of this box he always kept the key himself.

Two or three anecdotes may serve to illustrate the character and rule of Revilla-Gigedo II. He was in the habit of making nightly visits to the streets of the city to assure himself that his regulations were strictly carried out. Woe betide the unlucky officer whose failure in any item of duty was detected. He was summoned instantly to the spot, no matter what the hour of the night. "I await him here," was the customary expression of the viceroy, and it ensured a prompt attendance.

One evening, whilst walking through the city about sunset, he came upon a miserable street which terminated in a *cul-de-sac*. The houses which formed it were of the most wretched description. "Why," asked the viceroy, "is there no thoroughfare in this direction? and why are such hovels allowed to exist?" No one could tell. It had always been so, and it was nobody's business to interfere or remedy the evil. "Send the Corregidor instantly to me. I await him here." Soon that functionary arrived in breathless haste. He was ordered to open a broad and straight avenue right through the quarter to the city barrier; and it was to be ready the next morning, that the viceroy might drive through it on his way to mass. If not done, the corregidor should lose his office. With this pleasant assurance the great man marched away.

All night long the corregidor and his myrmidons worked at their task. A body of leperos were enlisted in the service, and for a small bribe the inhabitants assisted to destroy their own dwellings. By the light of a hundred torches pick-axe and crowbar were gleaming, and under their heavy strokes house after house was levelled and removed. Exactly at sunrise the viceroy's carriage reached the place, but the work was already done. Jolting over the fragments that strewed the path, and along the unpaved road, it yet was able to pass through the new street into the suburbs. The name of the Calle de Revilla-Gigedo still attests the truth of the story.

The power of the viceroy was absolute, and Revilla-Gigedo II. occasionally exercised it in the punishment of misdemeanors which are not usually amenable to law. Among the Creole nobles then resident in Mexico was a certain marquis endowed with immense wealth and two beautiful daughters. He had no other children, and it was hard to say whether he was caused most anxiety by his money or his heiresses. The elder, who bore her father's title, had fair golden hair and blue eyes, a very unusual style of beauty in Mexico. The younger was dark, with eyes like a gazelle, and hair black as the raven's plumage. Both were alike in one respect. They refused all offers of marriage. The marquis desired to see them well settled in life, and was quite worn out in persuading them to know their own minds.

One night the marquis was aroused from his sleep and summoned to the viceregal palace. What could he be wanted for at that unusual hour? He hurried to the viceroy's presence. "Marquis," said his excellency, "my superintendent of police complains to me that you did not take proper care to secure the doors of your mansion last evening." "Indeed, I assure your excellency that my steward locked both the great gate and the outer door last night." "But you have a postern opening into the street, and you were only saved by the watchfulness of my police from being robbed of your most valuable treasures—which I now restore to you." At these words a door suddenly opened, and there were the two daughters of the marquis, dressed in travelling costume, and locked in one another's arms. "And here are the thieves," he added; and in an opposite apartment were seen two of the most dissipated young men about the court.

The truth now flashed upon the mind of the father. "You see, marquis," said the viceroy, "that but for my police, you would have had the honour of being father-in-law to two of the greatest scamps in my viceroyalty. Look what a dilemma your carelessness has brought me into, my dear sir! I am obliged to wound the feelings of two of the most lovely ladies in my court to save them from the machinations of scoundrels unworthy of their charms, and I fear they will never forgive me! Farewell, marquis, take my advice and brick up your postern. Calderon was a wise man, and he tells us that a house with two doors is hard to keep. As for these young scapegraces, they sail in the next galleon for Manilla, where they can exercise their fascinating powers on the maidens of the Philippines." Transportation was rather a stern punishment for attempting to marry a fair and wealthy maiden.

This illustrious ruler was followed by Branciforte, who stands in unenviable contrast with his predecessor. Branciforte commenced a career of the most unprincipled extortion. Offices of high importance were openly sold; and as Spain was then at war with France, the viceroy thought it a good opportunity to confiscate the property of any Frenchmen that could be found in Mexico. The country was then so closed against foreigners that but few were discovered, yet what he could do in this way he did with unsparing avarice. The court was at once a scene of profligacy and of corruption. When at last the public dissatisfaction reached a height which imperatively called for recognition, Branciforte left the country loaded with the curses of the people, and carrying with him 5,000,000 dollars which he had plundered from them. Yet he was a favourite at court, and the king sent him (appropriately enough we think) the Order of the Golden Fleece. With all his profligacy he affected great reverence for the Virgin of Guadalupe, and paid her many visits, but no money. He desired to satisfy his conscience with the cheapest form of indulgence.

Three viceroys presided over New Spain during the ten years that intervened between the rule of Branciforte and the end of the viceregency. The internal prosperity of the country and its resources were still great, but various murmurings were ominous of the revolt now so near at hand. Azunza, who came after Branciforte, was personally popular, but the government of Spain, under the handling of Godoy, was ill-disposed to him, and he was removed to make way for Berenguer de Marquina, who had purchased the appointment. Two years elapsed, and, in 1803, Iturrigaray was sent to take the post. His term of office was signalized by the arrival of Humboldt in the colony, who received every assistance in his great work upon the state of Mexico, a work in which its resources and capabilities first became known to the outer world.

At this period a loyal feeling was prevalent in Mexico, and when, in 1806, the intelligence of the destruction of the combined fleets was received, the Mexicans gave 30,000 dollars for the widows of the fallen. But the patience of the country was sorely tried by demands for taxes to maintain the European war, and when Ferdinand VII. was displaced by Napoleon, all further hold over the country was virtually at an end. Through what struggles its independence was finally acknowledged will form the subject of our next chapter.

CHAPTER V.

MEXICO FROM THE REVOLUTION TO THE PRESENT TIME.

Loyalty of Mexico to Ferdinand VII.—Discontent of the Creoles—Pride of the Spaniards—Hidalgo's conspiracy—Its early success—Spiritual weapons employed against it—Hesitation of Hidalgo—Cruelty and success of Calleja—Hidalgo's capture and execution—Unconciliatory policy of Calleja—Junta of Chilpanzingo—Insurrection under Morelos—Renewed excesses—Siege of Cuautla—Noble behaviour of Bravo—Retreat of Morelos—Calleja viceroy—Death of Morelos and suppression of the rebellion—Romantic adventures of Victoria—Apodaca viceroy—Insurrection under Mina—Apodaca determines to suppress the constitution—Employs Iturbide—Defection of Iturbide—Plan of Iguala—O'Donoju viceroy—Acknowledges the independence of Mexico—Iturbide emperor—The new constitution—Revolt of Santa Anna—Iturbide in exile—His return, capture, and execution—His character—State of political parties—Federalists and centralists—Victoria president—The rival lodges—Pedraga president—Pronunciamento of Mexico—Guerrero president—Second revolt of Santa Anna—Bustamente president—Last efforts of Spain—Alaman prime minister—Internal prosperity—Third revolt of Santa Anna—His early history—military exploits—Clever stratagems—Outwits the Spanish general—Santa Anna president—War in Texas—Santa Anna a prisoner—Second presidency of Bustamente—French siege of Vera Cruz—Second presidency of Santa Anna—American war—Herrera president—Third presidency of Santa Anna—Comonfort president.

WHEN Spain was overrun by the armies of France, the authority of the Spanish government in Mexico was at an end. This was not, however, the immediate result of the intelligence that Ferdinand had been removed to make way for Joseph Bonaparte. At first, indeed, the Mexicans were inspired with a zealous loyalty to their transatlantic sovereign. All classes vied with one another in offering contributions for his aid, and in a few months seven millions were freely subscribed to support their king, their country, and their creed. But this loyal fit was of short duration. The prestige of the Spanish power was broken by the victories of the French. The distance between Spain and Mexico was too great to maintain enthusiasm in the cause of a prince whose ancestors had but small claim upon the sympathies of the Mexicans, and who seemed to be indissolubly wedded to misfortune. The bitter memory of years of oppression, insolence, and misrule, was refreshed by the prospect of deliverance; and gradually, without any suitable preparation in the habits of the people, and without fixed principles of action to guide its leaders, the nation suddenly found itself freed from the leading strings on which it had relied, without having acquired the strength needed for self support. Accordingly, from the period of the war of independence to the present time, Mexico has been the sport of various factions, each of which has grasped at power, but has been unable to retain it; each of which has constantly plunged the nation into war for its own selfish purposes, and ruled it, when victorious, for its own aggrandizement. No sadder spectacle can be found than that presented by this country, enriched with the precious metals and a luxuriant fertility, yet torn asunder by intestine strife, its credit destroyed, its industry paralyzed, its very vitals wasted, until its condition became so desperate as to call for some high-handed interference to put a stop to scenes which are a disgrace to the civilized world.

The first symptom of discontent was shown by the Creoles. This class was proud of the European blood which flowed in their veins. Many of them could trace their descent from the conquerors, and in intelligence and wealth they were quite equal to the Spaniards. The latter, however, excluded them with the utmost jealousy from all share in the government, monopolized all the offices in church and state, and treated all claims of the Creoles to participate in these dignities with supreme contempt. They would not even recognise them as fellow-subjects with themselves of Ferdinand, but asserted that the Spaniards were masters in Mexico over all the other classes. The municipality of Mexico was insolently informed that it had no authority except over the leperos; and Bataller, one of the imperial commissioners, used frequently to say that "whilst a Manchego mule or a Castilian cobbler remained in the peninsula, he had a right to govern the Americas."

Such expressions are generally felt to be more intolerable than the material evils of despotic government. They pass easily from mouth to mouth, and create an irritation which misdeeds often fail to awaken. The time, too, was ill chosen for such an assertion of authority, and the sudden outbreak of a wide-spread insurrection proved on how rotten a foundation Spanish power in Mexico was based.

A single spark set the whole country in a blaze. A conspiracy had been formed in 1810 against the Spaniards, and one of the band being at the point of death, sent for his confessor, and revealed the

L

names of those who had joined it; among them was Miguel Hidalgo, curate of Dolores, in the province of Guanaxuato. Hoping to crush the plot in the bud, the viceroy, Venegas, sent orders to arrest Hidalgo; but the priest received timely warning of his danger, and having won over Allende, captain of the forces in the neighbouring town of San Miguel, he boldly declared against the Spaniards. On every side the Indians thronged to the standard of Hidalgo. Down they came from their mountain chalets, swelling the force as it marched from San Miguel to Zalaga. A war of races seemed imminent, and the deadly hatred, engendered by centuries of oppression, burst forth in burning desire for revenge. As the mass swept along, every European was sacrificed, and the same fate befell the Creoles who hesitated to join them. Some of the latter had shared in the original conspiracy, but drew back in dismay from making common cause with so ferocious a mob. But their first advance was irresistible until some 20,000 undisciplined and half-armed savages reached Guanaxuato, shouting death to the Gapuchinos.*

Hidalgo called upon the town to surrender, and offered them favourable terms: but in vain. His horde threw themselves upon the place, carried it by storm, and commenced an indiscriminate massacre of its inhabitants. To no purpose were all his efforts to stay the slaughter or the plunder. For three days the work of destruction went on, until through very weariness the rebels held their hand.

It was plain that every effort must be made to crush the rebels. The insurrection was no longer under the guidance of the Creoles, but had passed into the hands

* A term of contempt applied to the Europeans.

of the Indians, and Mexico was threatened with all the horrors of a servile war. The viceroy despatched an army against them, under Truxillo, and strove to enlist the artillery of the church on the same side. From all the pulpits the priests were bidden to denounce the revolution as directed against the church and the Catholic religion. The archbishop excommunicated the whole rebel army. Truxillo attacked them at Las Crucĕs, and boasted that he had fought with the obstinacy of Leonidas, and had fired on those who came from Hidalgo with a flag of truce. But the arms of church and state combined were unavailing. Truxillo lost the whole of his artillery, and was compelled to retire to the capital.

The rebel host pressed on towards Mexico, and consternation prevailed throughout the city. It was utterly undefended, and a panic spread amongst its inhabitants, in which the viceroy is said to have shared. Once more he called in the aid of superstition. The image of the Virgin de los Remedios was carried in state to the cathedral, and thither went the viceroy with all ceremony. Dressed in full uniform, he approached the image, and imploring it to take the government in its own hands, laid his staff of office at its feet. He quickly resumed it, however, and proceeded to give instructions for the defence of the capital.

To so credulous a people as the Mexicans, it might well seem that the preservation of the capital was due to the Virgin de los Remedios. Certain it is that Hidalgo marched to within five leagues of the city, and then paused in unaccountable distrust of his powers. Perhaps he shrunk from renewing the horrors of Guanaxuato in the beautiful town of Mexico. Perhaps, as some accounts assure us, he was misled by feigned deserters, who informed him that the place was prepared to stand a siege. At any rate, he hesitated, and in his situation hesitation was fatal. After halting for some days in sight of Mexico, he withdrew his forces.

An army was sent in pursuit of him, under Don Felix Maria Calleja, consisting of about ten thousand disciplined troops, well furnished with artillery. The hostile forces met at Aculco, and a desperate conflict ensued. The Indians, as at Las Cruces, fought with the most reckless bravery. Dashing up to the mouths of the guns, they thrust their straw hats into the muzzles, and fell upon the ranks of their opponents with clubs and spears. It was a renewal of the old strife, and they fought almost as in the days of Cortez; but now, as then, discipline and military skill prevailed over numbers and unregulated courage. Hidalgo lost ten thousand men, of whom five thousand were put to the sword. The rebels fell back upon Guanaxuato, closely followed by Calleja.

The tide of fortune had now turned, and Hidalgo was again compelled to retreat. All the horrors which Guanaxuato had so recently experienced were renewed by the victorious Spaniards. The details of Calleja's cruelty are too horrible for us to sully our pages by recording. This man was a pitiless monster. The inhabitants of Guanaxuato, men, women, and children, were driven into the great square of the town and deliberately butchered. The great fountain flowed with human blood. Fourteen thousand perished in this way, and Calleja boasted in his despatches that by cutting all their throats he had saved the expense of powder and shot.

Such excesses on either side naturally produced

reprisals, and the circle of crime went on widening in its course. Hidalgo retired upon Guadalaxara, where he massacred 700 or 800 Europeans. To the Indian's recollection of past injuries there was now added the vindictiveness of despair; whilst the victorious Spaniards could urge no like plea. Again Calleja won the day at the bridge of Calderon, and his triumph was distinguished by the same massacres as before. Determined to stamp out the last embers of opposition, he issued orders "to exterminate the inhabitants of every town or village that showed symptoms of adherence to the rebels."

Hidalgo's force was now completely broken. He could still muster large numbers, but they were unarmed, and wanted all the munitions of war. He determined to leave Rayon in command at Saltillo, and with part of the plunder of Guanaxuato to sail to the United States and purchase what he required. At this juncture he was betrayed by Elizondo, one of his associates, and, after being degraded from the priesthood, was shot at Chihuahua, on the 27th of July, 1811. The regency at Cadiz rewarded Calleja with the title of count, and appointed him to succeed Venegas as viceroy of Mexico.

The death of Hidalgo closes the first scene in the story of the Mexican revolution. The enmity between the Indians and the Spaniards was too deeply seated to be suppressed, save after years of peaceful government, and by the long use of remedial measures. The Creoles, too, although the instinct of self-preservation had induced them to make common cause with the Spaniards, were determined to shake off the yoke which galled them. The whole country was broken up into factions, and a guerilla war was maintained throughout the northern and inland provinces. The only way in which a peaceful solution could be reached would have been by yielding something to the necessities of the times; and had Calleja been prepared to admit the Creoles to an equality with the Europeans, Mexico might have been saved to the Spanish Bourbons.

The new viceroy, however, was very far from entertaining any such intentions, and Rayon and the other leaders of Hidalgo's party seeing the necessity for united action, "assembled a junta, or central government, composed of five members, chosen by a large body of the most respectable landed proprietors in the neighbourhood of Zitacuaro."* This body held liberal opinions, but declared its willingness to acknowledge Ferdinand as king provided that he would come to New Spain and reign there in person. A still more important council was assembled shortly afterwards, under the name of the Congress of Chilpanzingo. They issued a manifesto in which they stated their demands to the viceroy, intimating that should they be rejected they were determined to appeal to arms.

The manifesto of the Congress of Chilpanzingo was couched in moderate terms. After dwelling upon the misery to which the country had been subjected through fifteen months of civil war, and asserting that a sovereign who was in captivity could exercise no authority by his officers over Mexico, they declared that the rights of Mexico were as indefeasible as those of Spain, that the two countries were in all respects equal, and that the one needed a representative assembly as much as the other. They offered, in conclusion, " that if the Europeans would consent to give up the offices they held, and allow a general congress to be

* Mayer, vol. I. p. 297.

assembled, their persons and property should be religiously respected, their salaries paid, and the same privileges granted to them as to native Mexicans." Ferdinand was to be acknowledged as the legitimate sovereign, and every effort made to aid him in his European wars.

These terms were contemptuously rejected, and the manifesto burned in the capital by the common hangman. Meanwhile the national cause was gaining strength, and a new leader appeared in the person of Morelos, who had held a commission under Hidalgo, and like him was a country curate. Matamoros, another priest, the two Bravos, Galeana and Guadalupe Victoria, were also leaders on the same side. The stream of rebellion again flowed down from the north towards the capital.

Calleja, who was not yet installed as viceroy, was sent against them. At his approach the junta fled from Zitacuaro, and the Spanish general razed its walls to the ground, burned all the dwellings except the convents and churches, and put numbers of its inhabitants to the sword. After this feat, he made a triumphal entrance into Mexico, and on the 14th of January, 1812, set out once more to attack Morelos, at Cuautla de Amilpas.

All the old scenes of atrocity and bloodshed were renewed by the royalists. Officers fell under the displeasure of their chief, unless they shared his sanguinary disposition. On one occasion, forty of the insurgents were captured unarmed in a wood. The royalist captain spared their lives and persuaded them to enlist in his service. Calleja was indignant when he heard of this humanity, and when, some days afterwards, eight of them deserted, he ordered the remaining thirty-two to be taken out and shot. To his honour the officer refused to obey this mandate, and the whole number, except four, effected their escape. Such an incident may serve to mark the spirit in which the struggle was carried on, and to account for the undiminished hatred with which Europeans are still held in the wilder regions of the country.

Morelos was shut up by Calleja in Cuautla, and stood a siege for two months and a half. He was greatly hampered in his command by the interference of the junta. His military talents were considerable, but he was not allowed to use them to the best advantage. He hoped, however, to prolong the siege until the rainy season should compel the enemy to retire. Calleja, on the other hand, hoped to starve him out before the heat set in, and cut off every way of access to supplies. Famine soon began to be felt. They had bread, but animal food fetched exorbitant prices.* A cat sold for six dollars, and a rat for one. The post at length became untenable. Not venturing to risk a general engagement, Morelos led out his forces by night, and succeeded in making his escape, although his whole army had to pass between the batteries of the enemy. Only seventeen men were lost in this manœuvre, but amongst them was Don Leonardo Bravo, one of the most gallant of the republican chieftains, who fell into the enemy's hands.

Bravo's son was commanding a force of the insurgents, and had just taken the town of Palmar by storm, when the news reached him that his father was a prisoner. He immediately offered the viceroy, Venegas, to give

* The wandering of a bullock between the lines of the enemy and the walls of the town was the cause of an engagement, in which nearly all the troops on both sides eventually took part.

up three hundred prisoners, captured at Palmar, in exchange for Don Leonardo. His offer was rejected, and his father sent to immediate execution. The brave young soldier at once ordered all his prisoners to be released, lest in the passion of his grief he should be tempted to exact a terrible revenge.

So stealthily had Morelos conducted his retreat that for some hours Calleja did not venture to enter the streets of Cuautla. He could not wreak his disappointment on the rebel army, but he could, and did, upon the innocent inhabitants. So pitiless was he in his cruelty, that years after, officers, who were present, spoke with horror of the scenes they witnessed; nor were the sufferings of the country confined to the immediate theatre of the war. Everywhere robbery and assassination prevailed; commerce was entirely destroyed; banditti infested all the public roads, and no person's life or property was secure. The mines were deserted. Most of the miners had joined the opposing forces, and the few that remained gained a scant subsistence by picking over the refuse of the ores. Agriculture was neglected, and corn of every species rose to famine prices. Disease followed on the heels of want, and all the vials of God's wrath seemed to be poured out upon the wretched Mexicans. Painful is it to think that the liberty born amidst such throes should have proved so doubtful a boon to its possessors.

The retreat of Morelos was but the avenue to fresh triumphs. He marched into Tehuacan, he captured Orizaba, he stormed Oaxaca. In these exploits he amassed large sums for the public chest, whilst his followers were gratified with full pay, and abundance of plunder. In the taking of Oaxaca, Guadalupe Victoria gained special notoriety. The town was surrounded by a moat, to be crossed only by a drawbridge, which was raised at their approach. There were no boats at hand, and entrance seemed impossible, when Victoria leaped into the moat, swam across, and landing in the face of the enemy, cut the ropes that held the bridge, which at once fell, and the insurgents marched over it into the town. These events occupied the years 1812 and 1813, in which latter the Congress of Chilpanzingo (of which we have spoken by anticipation) sent forth its manifesto.

From 1813 to 1816 Calleja governed Mexico as viceroy, and during this period the star of Morelos gradually declined. Morelos was anxious to effect the entire subjugation of the province of Valladolid, that he might have a secure base of operations, and a place of refuge in the season of adversity. He accordingly entered it with a considerable army, and Calleja despatched Llanos and Iturbide, who was at this time a royalist, to oppose him. We have not space to record all the evolutions of the struggle that ensued, nor are they of sufficient interest to call for their insertion. One by one the insurgent chieftains fell into the power of the enemy, and death was the inevitable penalty under such a man as Calleja, who was never known to spare. Matamoros, a greater soldier than Morelos, was the first victim. Every effort was made to save him, but in vain. The insurgents threatened a terrible revenge if his life were not conceded, and they executed it in the slaughter of all their prisoners.

These reverses had dispirited the liberal party, but a fresh accession of strength seemed to be springing up in La Puebla, and Morelos marched thither to foster its growth. His army was assailed in a mountain pass by General Concha, and sending forward Bravo to escort the congress to a place of safety he determined to keep the royalists at bay as long as possible, and then to sell his life as dearly as he could. "My life," he said, " is of little consequence provided the congress be saved : my race was run when I saw an independent government established."

The little band of Morelos held their position with much bravery, and the ground on which they stood was thickly strewed with the corpses of the foe. None was more terrible in this death struggle than Morelos himself; and it was not until he was left almost alone that the royalists succeeded in making him a prisoner. The soldiers treated him with a cruelty and indignity from which his gallant bearing should have saved him. He was stripped, loaded with chains, and carried, with many blows, to Tesmalaca. By General Concha he was more kindly entertained, but he knew that his doom was certain. On the 22nd of December, 1815, he was removed from the capital to the hospital of San Christobal, and after dining with Concha was marched out to execution. After thanking his captor warmly for his kindness, he walked with a firm step to the rear of the building, and with his own hands bound a handkerchief over his eyes. Kneeling down he prayed, saying, " If I have done well, Lord, thou knowest it. If ill, to thy infinite mercy I commend my soul." After these words he himself gave the signal to the soldiers who were drawn up to despatch him.

Among the victims who fell in the struggle for independence none have left a brighter reputation than Morelos. He had acquired at once the affections of the people and the confidence of his fellow-officers, and the cause languished so much after his death as to show how greatly it had been indebted to his energy and influence. General Teran dissolved the congress which Bravo had safely escorted to Tehuacan; Bravo himself was obliged to flee. His comrades were dispersed through the provinces. Victoria hovered about in the neighbourhood of Vera Cruz, and eluded all the efforts of the government to seize him.

The fidelity of the Indians to Victoria is one of the few pleasing incidents in this intestine war. Every inducement was held out to seduce him from the popular side. Rank and rewards were offered in return for his compliance. When all such attempts proved vain, a large force was sent to crush him. His band was dispersed, and a price set upon his head: but none were base enough to betray him. For thirty months he wandered amongst the recesses of the mountains, enduring incredible hardships. His food was the roots of trees, or the wild fruits of the forest, or even the bones of dead animals, which he found in caverns. His dress was worn away till nothing but a tattered cotton wrapper was left him. In this condition he was found by two Indians after the revolution of 1821, and he was welcomed as one risen from the dead; for the viceroy had been assured that he had perished, and that his body had been recognised. This account had been published by authority in the official Gazette.

The story of his discovery is no less remarkable. When abandoned by his forces, in 1818, he was asked by two trusty Indians where they should look for him if better days should ever come, and in reply he pointed out a certain mountain on which they, perhaps, might one day find his bones. The Indians treasured up this hint, and when Iturbide declared himself, in 1821, they set out in quest of him. For six whole weeks they sought him, maintaining themselves principally by the chase, but at length their bread was exhausted, and they were about to return, when one of them in crossing a ravine, which Victoria frequented, discovered the footprint of one who evidently had been accustomed to wear shoes (this always gives a difference of shape to the foot), and was, therefore, of European descent. Two days the Indian waited on the spot, and then, as provisions were failing him, he hung upon a tree all the little maize cakes he had in his wallet, and set out for his native village for more. He hoped that Victoria would see the tortillas, and would understand that some friend was in search of him.

"This plan succeeded. Victoria on crossing the ravine, two days afterwards, perceived the maize cakes, which the birds had fortunately not devoured. He had then been four whole days without eating, and upwards of two years without tasting bread; and he said himself, that he devoured the tortillas before the cravings of his appetite would allow him to reflect upon the singularity of finding them on this solitary spot, where he had never before seen any trace of a human being. He was at a loss to determine whether they had been left there by friend or foe: but, feeling sure that whoever left them intended to return, he concealed himself near the place. Within a short time the Indian returned: Victoria instantly recognised him, and abruptly started from his concealment in order to welcome his faithful follower. But the man, terrified at seeing a phantom covered with hair, emaciated, and clothed only with an old cotton wrapper, advancing upon him sword in hand, took to flight; and it was only on hearing himself repeatedly called by name that he recovered his composure sufficiently to recognise his old general." *

* Fay. Robinson's Mexico and her Military Chieftains.

We must resume the thread of our narrative. In 1816, Calleja was replaced as viceroy by Apodaca. The new governor was more prudent than his predecessor. He proclaimed a general amnesty to all who laid down their arms, and this induced numbers to come in. He left no means untried to crush those who refused to yield. The constitution sanctioned by the Spanish Cortes was now in operation, and it guaranteed the people some degree of liberty. From these various causes the revolution slumbered for a time. The general quiet, however, was disturbed for a season by the expedition of Mina.

Xavier Mina was a native of Spain, who had made himself a name in his native land. When the armies of Napoleon invaded the Peninsula, Mina organized a system of guerilla warfare, and although the French were masters of the open field he hung upon their rear, cut off their stragglers, plundered their convoys, and intercepted their despatches. With such success did he carry on his enterprise, that he was named Commandant General of Navarre, when his career was suddenly brought to a conclusion. He was taken prisoner, and did not obtain his release till 1814.

The arbitrary conduct of Ferdinand, when restored to the Spanish throne, quickly alienated from him the liberal party. Mina was implicated in a plot to restore the power of the Cortes, and obliged to escape. After passing some time in England, he crossed over to America, that he might aid the cause of the liberals in Mexico; and landed on the 15th of April, 1817, at Soto la Marina, with only about 350 men, chiefly North Americans, fifty of whom deserted him soon after his arrival.

Mina was not discouraged by the small number of

his band. In his early experience of guerilla warfare, he had learned how much may be effected by a few faithful followers, and he hoped to join the other popular leaders, and again to raise the mass of the Indian population. Leaving a third of his force at Soto la Marina, he boldly dashed into the heart of the country, and defeating several bodies of the enemy established himself at Sombrero.

The accounts which have been published by Mina's partisans reveal to us the causes of his ultimate failure. From the first moment his success was viewed with jealousy by Torres, who was then the most powerful of the patriot chieftains. His Spanish birth naturally occasioned suspicions amongst the ignorant and prejudiced people, and these were strengthened by his assault upon the hacienda of the Marquis of Jaral. This nobleman was extremely wealthy, and had uniformly espoused the royalist side, but as he was a Creole the plunder of his estate seems to have aroused the sympathy of the Mexicans. At any rate Mina failed to gain the confidence of the people, and without this he could not hope for eventual success.

News of the destruction of his force at Soto la Marina soon came to qualify Mina's satisfaction at his own exploits, yet their defeat was itself a triumph. Two thousand Spanish troops, under General Arredondo, were kept at bay by this band of one hundred men, and having been repeatedly repulsed, were glad to offer them honourable terms. Having got them into his power in this way, all the conditions of the capitulation were violated by Apodaca. Some of the unfortunate prisoners were confined in the most unhealthy cities of Mexico, while others were despatched across the sea in chains to rot in the dungeons of Ceuta and Cadiz.

Undismayed by the tidings of such disasters, Mina next made an assault upon Leon but was signally repulsed. He retreated to Sombrero, which was speedily invaded by the Spaniards under Linan. As he was unsupported by Torres, his numbers were unequal to the struggle, and Sombrero was soon found to be untenable. He cut his way through the enemies lines, but only fifty of his men survived the conflict. No quarter was shown by the ruthless Linan, who not only cut down all the insurgents in the field, but had the sick, who had been left in hospital, dragged from their beds and shot in the square of Sombrero. Mina threw himself into the fort of Los Remedios, and thence made an unsuccessful attempt on Guanaxuato. In flying from this place he was betrayed, taken prisoner, and shot by order of Apodaca, on the 11th of November, 1817. Although only in his twenty-eighth year, he had gained a reputation in both hemispheres.

The viceroy, Apodaca, fondly hoped that the rebellion was now at an end He was utterly unacquainted with the feelings of the people, and the deep-seated evils which made the Spanish yoke intolerable. In his fancied security he desired to emulate the despotic conduct of his European master, and he looked about for a fitting agent to carry out his scheme of doing away with the constitution. His own authority was hampered by its existence, and the exercise of the right of election seemed to keep alive the popular yearning after liberty. Meanwhile, he wrote to Madrid that Mexico was firmly secure to the throne of Spain, and that they need not send out another soldier to his aid.

Yet at this moment the embers were smouldering

beneath his feet. The insurrection was exhausted, not subdued. Many of those who had fought on the popular side entered the royal army after the proclamation of the amnesty, and spread liberal opinions amongst their new comrades. Despite the cruelties of which their friends had been the victims, the insurgents laid aside their enmity, and strove by every variety of seduction to win over their opponents. This state of affairs was well known to the generals, although Apodaca was unacquainted with it, and he gave it an unexpected opportunity for development when he selected Colonel Iturbide as his instrument to overturn the constitution.

A Créole by birth, Iturbide was well qualified to conciliate his countrymen, whilst from the brilliancy of his military achievements, he was more likely than any other to secure the devotion of the army. Moreover, he had commenced his career with an endeavour to throw off the Spanish rule; but in consequence of a serious disagreement, all communication between him and the insurgents was broken off, and he turned his hand against them. The severe blows which he inflicted on their cause in the battles of Valladolid and Puruaran seemed to render it impossible that the rebels and he could ever again act in concert. In addition to all this, Iturbide had won the esteem of the clergy, by professing "to expiate the excesses of his former life by a rigid course of penance and mortification."

To all appearance, therefore, a better choice could not have been made. Handsome in person, captivating in address, gallant in action, fertile in resources, Iturbide possessed exactly that combination of qualities which were requisite to carry out the viceroy's schemes. Hence, doubtless, it was that Apodaca intrusted him

M

with the command of a body of troops on the western coast, at the head of which he was authorized to "proclaim the re-establishment of the absolute authority of the king."

But the viceroy was completely outwitted. When Iturbide reached his command, he had very different plans in contemplation. He fully understood the position of affairs, and during the season of leisure, which three years quiet had afforded, he had convinced himself that the popular side must eventually prevail. Had this thought nothing to do with his ostentatious penance for his past misdeeds? we may well believe it had. He saw that if the Creoles would make common cause with the Indians, the yoke of Spain might be shaken off; and he employed all his talents in the contrivance of a plan which might unite the two parties against the Europeans.

The principal provisions of a declaration which he issued were drawn up to effect this object. It abolished all distinctions of caste, so that all subjects were to be united without distinction; declared the independence of the Mexican nation, and the establishment of the Roman Catholic religion. From these three articles it was termed the declaration of the "Three Guarantees." The government was to be a constitutional monarchy. The crown was to be offered to Ferdinand VII., and on his refusal, to either of the Infantas, and might, if necessary, be then conferred on a member of any reigning family. A junta, composed of leading men of all parties, was to act as a provisional government, under the presidency of the viceroy, until a congress could be summoned. In the meantime all persons who gave in their adhesion were to be confirmed in their posts. An army was to be enrolled for the defence of the "Three Guarantees," and the despotic power hitherto wielded by military commandants was to be destroyed. This proclamation was called the Plan of Iguala, from the little town whence it was issued. It appeared on the 24th of February, 1821.

Iturbide's army consisted of eight hundred men, who swore to support him in his enterprise. The Plan of Iguala, however, was not popular. The insurgent leaders did not at once join him. The Indians held back, and some of his own men deserted. With promptitude the revolution might have been crushed in the bud; but the viceroy's heart failed him; he was stunned by the defection of Iturbide, and neglected preparations for defence. The royalist party in disgust at his vacillation deposed him, and put Novella, an artillery officer, at the helm of government. These proceedings caused divisions to spring up, in consequence of which Iturbide was enabled to strengthen his position. He carried off a treasure of a million dollars on its way to the coast, he won over Guerrero, the chief of the old insurgents, and through him all the friends and veterans of Morelos. Victoria and others, who, as yet, knew not Iturbide's ultimate designs, combined with him to secure the independence of their country, and the revolution assumed a formidable aspect.

The army was in full march upon Mexico when news arrived that a new viceroy, O'Donoju, had just landed at San Juan de Ulua. Iturbide allowed him to advance to Cordova, and then proposed to him the Plan of Iguala as the only condition on which the throne of Mexico would be preserved to Spain, or the safety of the Spaniards in the country be secured. A treaty was drawn up, accepting these terms. Indeed, the viceroy had no other alternative, and the independence of Mexico dates from the 24th of August, 1821—the day on which it was signed. It is useless to inquire what authority O'Donoju had for such a step. The revolution was accomplished. The army entered Mexico in peace on the 27th of September, and a provisional regency of five, with Iturbide for president, immediately assumed the direction of affairs. A junta, composed of thirty-six persons, was appointed to contrive a scheme for electing a congress, and Iturbide was created generalissimo and lord high admiral, with a yearly stipend of one hundred and twenty-thousand dollars.

In drawing up the constitution there was a struggle for the mastery between the republicans and monarchists. The republicans gained the day. Iturbide desired to have two chambers, but it was resolved to have but one, and the Congress, thus constituted, met February 24, 1822. Each member swore to maintain the Plan of Iguala, but their real objects were soon manifest. There were three parties. The Bourbonists, who adhered to the sovereignty of Spain; the Republicans, who comprised all the old insurgent leaders; and the partisans of Iturbide, who desired his elevation to the throne. When the treaty of Cordova reached Spain, it was at once rejected by the Cortes, and with it fell the Bourbon party in Mexico. The struggle now lay between the other two. Violent recriminations and personalities disgraced the proceedings of the congress. All the discontents and animosities that have since ruined Mexico appeared in full activity; there was no self restraint, no moderation, no indication of capacity for self-government. At length, on the 18th of May, 1822, the army and the mob proclaimed Iturbide emperor, who after a brief show of resistance, accepted the crown.

Augustine I., such was the new emperor's title, swore to be faithful to the constitution, and the congress sanctioned his coronation. He reigned but ten months. No sooner had he seized upon the throne than Guerrero, Bravo, and Victoria, retired to the country, and began to organize their old followers against him. Nor were his acts likely to gain him fresh adherents. He was intoxicated by success. He demanded a veto on all the articles of the constitution; he squandered the public treasure, and, in violation of his own scheme, proposed military tribunals similar to those which the plan of Iguala had destroyed. When this proposition was rejected by the congress, he arrested fourteen of the deputies, and thus made the breach irreparable between himself and the representative assembly. Finally, on the 30th of October, he dissolved the congress, and appointed a junta of forty-five persons, selected by himself, in its room.

These proceedings naturally occasioned much discontent, and Iturbide in his turn became a victim to treachery very similar to that which he had himself employed against Apodaca. Among the most trusted of his friends was General Santa Anna, the governor of Vera Cruz, but on some suspicions of his fidelity Iturbide decided to remove him. Being apprized of this intention, Santa Anna assembled his forces, harangued them on the misconduct of the emperor, and urged them to join him in proclaiming a republic. No sooner said than done. Guadalupe Victoria, whose name was a tower of strength, descended from his mountain hiding-place to join him. General Echavari, who was sent against him by Iturbide, and who more than once defeated him, was won over to his side. And, on the 1st of February, the Act of Casa-Mata, arranged by the three generals and establishing a republic, was promulgated.

The power of Iturbide dwindled away as rapidly as it had grown. The whole country was soon in arms against him. Guerrero, Bravo, and the other generals declared for the Act of Casa-Mata. Why the emperor yielded without a blow is not very clear. His personal courage was undoubted, but all confidence was undermined by constant defections from his ranks. He placed his abdication in the hands of the congress, and it was at length accepted. He was furnished with a vessel in which to sail for Leghorn, and assigned a yearly pension of twenty-five thousand dollars.

It may be well to follow Iturbide to the close of his career, before proceeding with our narrative of Mexican affairs. Rather more than a year after his departure from the country, on the 14th of July, 1824, a British vessel touched at Santander, and the following day two gentlemen, calling themselves Poles, Count Charles Beneski and a friend, landed at Soto la Marina, and visited La Garza, the commandant of the district. They begged permission to travel into the interior, and it was conceded; but the suspicions of La Garza were excited, and as soon as the count's friend was stripped of his disguise he proved to be Iturbide. The unhappy man had been invited by some of his partisans to return, and ignorant of the law which condemned him to death if he should venture to set foot in Mexico, he had complied. The state legislature was then sitting, and they immediately gave orders for his execution. No respite for appeal to the congress was allowed him. He was led out on the evening of the 19th, and fell pierced by four bullets.

There is scarcely one of the actors in the war of independence concerning whom it is so difficult to speak as of Iturbide. With all his faults, he yet displayed such talents for government that in after years the people regretted his fall. Some consideration, too, was due to the successful leader who had effectually emancipated them from the yoke of Spain, and whose errors had some further palliative in the numerous dangers by which he was surrounded. So winning was his address, that a few days before his death he gained over all the escort that conducted him from Soto la Marina to the seat of the congress, and his hurried execution proves how much his foes dreaded the popularity of his name. A strange spectacle followed his judicial murder. His body was followed to the grave by the congress which had ordered him to be shot, and the man who had been executed as a traitor to his country was mourned by the government as a public benefactor.

When Iturbide left Mexico the chief power was lodged in the hands of Victoria, Bravo, and Negrete, and the old congress was hastily re-assembled until another could be chosen. The new congress sanctioned the Federal Constitution in October, 1824, which, with some short intervals of suspension, has since remained in force. From the very first, however, it was plain that the country lacked the necessary elements for so liberal a form of government. The state included only two large classes; the wealthy landed proprietors and miners on the one hand, and the miserably impoverished Indians on the other. Wealth and rags stood out alone in sad contrast, and there was no middle class to bind the two together. Yet some elements of order were not wanting. The church, the Creole aristocracy, and the army, were all conservative in feeling. Unhappily they were split up by internal divisions, and the weaker party appealed to the Indians for support.

These evils were exaggerated by other incidents. The upper class was almost as ignorant as its Indian fellow-subjects. The clergy were possessed of vast influence, which they strove to maintain by keeping the mass of the nation in a state of ignorance and superstition; and these elements they worked upon successfully in their own support when any attempt was made upon their vast possessions. The Bible was an unknown book in Mexico, and none could gather from its pages how men ought to govern themselves. There were wanting, consequently, all those indirect ameliorating influences which a knowledge of God's word invariably exercises amongst a people who reverence its teaching. All the fierce and unbridled tempers of the tropics were left without the check either of Divine authority or of a well-regulated public opinion. Amongst the many crimes for which popery is responsible, this is one of the most deadly, that, in depriving men of the key of knowledge, it leaves them slaves either to some despotism or to their own unfettered evil passions.

All these evils soon appeared in the history of Mexico. Nominally there were two contending parties, the Federalists, who favoured a constitution somewhat on the model of the United States, in which, besides a federal congress, each department should have its own representative body and should enjoy a large measure of self-government; and the Centralists, who desired that the whole country should be under the guidance of a general congress, the executive being wielded by military governors, under the direction of the president. In reality, however, the only principle which guided either side was their own selfish policy. The leaders advocated whichever scheme appeared at the moment most popular; and the clergy made common cause with either side alternately, in order to secure its own immense possessions from spoliation.

The general congress met early in 1825. Guadalupe Victoria was declared president, and Nicholas Bravo vice-president of the republic, which was established on a federal basis. It started with some strange notions of freedom. The Roman Catholic religion was declared to be for ever the creed of the country, and the exercise of all other religions was prohibited. Yet, at the same time, a loan was contracted in Great Britain. Great exertions were made to secure the aid of British capital in working the mines, and the Protestant countries of England and the United States were the first to acknowledge the independence of Mexico.

New elements of discord were soon at work. Victoria and Bravo were enemies, and openly endeavoured to thwart one another. Each of them was a brave leader in the field, but an incompetent statesman in the council chamber. Instead of soothing old animosities, and striving to unite all citizens together in a common bond of patriotism, the most prominent chieftains only fanned the fury of the respective factions. There were no past memories to which the country could look back to guide its future. There was no great statesman, not even any great political question, around which either side could muster its forces. Military distinction was the only ground of popularity, and this reduced all questions to the mere personal antagonism of the generals.

The rival factions sought to strengthen themselves by means of the masonic lodges. The secret organization of freemasonry was well suited to their schemes. The Scotch lodge was the head quarters of the Centralists, under Bravo, Pedraza, and Montagno. The York lodge, that of the Federalists, led by Victoria, Santa Anna, Zavala, and Bustamente. The latter was the more liberal party, and the most numerous; but it was opposed by the clergy, the wealthy landowners, and miners, and many of the highest officers in the army. The Scotch party were the first to violate the peace of the republic. At the close of 1827, Montagno effected the first *pronunciamiento*, as these risings are termed. The vice-president, Bravo, joined him. Guerrero was sent against them, and succeeded in arresting their progress, for they dispersed at his approach. In this state of confusion the presidency of Victoria came to its close.

At the election for a new president, Pedraza, the Scotch candidate, defeated Guerrero by a majority of two. The defeated side showed no more moderation than their opponents; but they were restrained from coming immediately to blows by the danger which menaced the republic. Spain had fitted out an expedition in Cuba to recover her lost colony, and all parties were united by the sense of a common danger. No sooner was this source of fear removed than all the old leaven began to work. In the autumn of 1828, Santa Anna, at Vera Cruz, raised the standard of rebellion, and in December he was supported by a *pronunciamiento* in the capital. The Spaniards were everywhere assailed by the mob, the houses of the Scotch partisans were plundered, the president, Pedraza, was obliged to fly; and, on the 1st of January,

1829, Guerrero and Bustamente were declared respectively the president and vice-president of the federal republic.

The administration of Guerrero was marked by a decree worthy of all honour. In commemoration of the anniversary of independence, slavery was abolished throughout the Mexican territories. All slaves were at once set free, and their owners were to be indemnified by the treasury for any loss they had incurred. But the payment was only to be made when the condition of the public funds would admit. This is the single act of Guerrero's government that calls for notice. He only held office two years. Bustamente, his former friend, declared against him on some pretext, and Santa Anna, who was sent to oppose the vice-president, changed sides and fraternized with him. Guerrero had committed the capital error of accepting the presidency, and Bustamente determined to snatch it from his hands. He had further the misfortune to be popular, and this steeled the hearts of his opponents against him. They had the meanness to pay a bribe for his betrayal, the audacity to put him on his trial for bearing arms against the government of which he was the rightful head, and the cruelty to execute him on this monstrous charge.

During the period of these internal conflicts, a Spanish force landed on the coast. It was the last expedition which Spain sent to recover her lost colony. Disease so weakened the troops that they fell an easy prey to Santa Anna, whose fame was much increased by this triumph; and shortly afterwards the garrison of San Juan de Ulua capitulated. It has been remarked by writers of the national history that General Miguel Barragan, to whom the castle was

surrendered, was married to the daughter of the last
direct descendant of Juan Andrade, the husband of
Montezuma's daughter; so that the husband of a lady
sprung from the unfortunate emperor of the Aztecs,
received the keys of the last stronghold held upon the
American continent by the countrymen of Cortez.

Bustamente's tenure of power was beneficial to
Mexico. It was only astonishing that he should have
consented to accept it under such questionable circumstances. For his previous career had been marked by
many good qualities. Originally a physician in a country
town, he had joined the Spanish army at the outbreak
of Hidalgo's insurrection; he was then about thirty
years of age. Almost the first act recorded of him
is in pleasing contrast to the horrors of the war: he had
the heads of Hidalgo and his comrades, which had
been fastened to stakes, taken down and restored to
their friends for decent burial. At length he became
too disgusted with the cruelties of the Spanish leaders
to co-operate with them any longer, and he went over
to the liberal side. In the varied fortunes of Iturbide
he had been always his faithful adherent. How he
was induced to ally himself with Santa Anna against
the government of Guerrero is more than we can
explain. His decision once taken, he carried it
out promptly. Remembering the scenes that had
disgraced the streets of the capital when Iturbide
assumed the government, he determined to prevent
their repetition, and marched on Mexico with a small
force. The city was then in the hands of Guerrero's
partisans. They had possession of the causeway by
which it is approached, and with a little vigour almost
every house would afford a separate basis of resistance.
The mode in which all these advantages were lost

affords a striking illustration of Mexican indolence. In the dead of the night Bustamente and his men arrived at the city gate, which was guarded by a sentinel of Guerrero's army. "Who goes there?" was his challenge. "Friends," was the reply. "Of what nation?" "Soldiers of Mexico." Without further inquiry they were suffered to pass, and in the morning the palace was in their hands, and the city quietly submitted. Such was the man to whom the government was now intrusted.

During the three years of Bustamente's rule Mexico enjoyed peace and prosperity, to which she had been long a stranger. The mainspring of the government was Don Lucas Alaman, who had been foreign minister under Iturbide. Under his administration various disorders were corrected. Smuggling, which had been practised to an unlimited extent, and with the connivance of the customs' officials, was repressed, to the great advantage of the revenue. The brigands, who then as now infested the highways, were either executed or terrified into good behaviour, and Alaman declared that he would not relax his efforts until he could leave his cloak in the open street at night with perfect confidence that it would be found untouched in the morning. These vigorous measures restored public confidence, and commerce again began to flow through its customary channels. Many of the mines were conceded to English companies, and Alaman showed every disposition of friendship towards our countrymen. A portion of the surplus revenue was assigned to the "Banco de Avio," which was established to promote arts and manufactures; from this fund advances were made at low rates to manufacturers, or machinery was purchased to be used without payment of any rent for it by those who were willing to establish new factories.

To such praiseworthy efforts to promote material prosperity Alaman added a terrible and unrelenting pertinacity in crushing his political opponents. His enemies indeed represent him as a monster, utterly regardless of the laws of God or man, by whom all the crimes of Cæsar Borgia would be committed without scruple. Certain it is that from his *bureau* in Mexico Don Alaman kept a watchful eye upon his foes. His arm was always ready to strike, even when the prey seemed quite beyond his grasp; and when once he had clutched his victim he was not the man to spare.

In the south, Guerrero was still in arms after Bustamente had seized upon the capital and the presidency. In vain Alaman strove to crush him. Surrounded by a band of faithful followers, and protected by the climate against a hostile force, Guerrero bade defiance to his efforts. There arrived, at this period, at the port of Acalpulco, a Genoese vessel, whose captain, Picalúga, insinuated himself into the confidence of Guerrero. One day the ex-president went almost unattended to breakfast with his friend. He was a little fond of wine, and partook freely of some that was placed before him. The meal finished, he went on deck to find that the vessel had weighed anchor, and himself a prisoner. He was tried at Oaxaca and shot, as has already been narrated. When Alaman was obliged to fly from Mexico, an order was found in his own handwriting to Picaluga for 50,000 dollars as the price of this treason. The Genoese blotted out the name of Picaluga from the roll of their citizens.

It was not likely that such changes as those introduced by Alaman could fail to earn him a good deal of enmity. Smuggling and highway robbery have always been the most popular of crimes amongst a half-civilized people. It is considered rather meritorious than otherwise to cheat the revenue officers; and no doubt amongst the thieves who infested the public roads of Mexico there were pre-eminent rascals who gained celebrity like that of Robin Hood and Richard Turpin. The taxes, too, were collected with a most unpleasant regularity, and the price of goods the owners of which had been obliged to pay duty was sure to be dearer than that of those which had been smuggled. These grievances might have been tolerated in another country, but the Mexicans had not been trained to submission. It soon was murmured that Bustamente was a tyrant and ought to be removed. A project of the government to make the wealth of the church contribute to the necessities of the state filled the cup of Alaman's iniquity to overflowing. Santa Anna took advantage of the cry thus given him; he came forward not only as the champion of the Catholic religion but also to assert the rights of Pedraza, and in December, 1832, Bustamente resigned his office, and Pedraza returned to serve out the remaining three months of his unexpired administration.

The history of Mexico for some years from this period is almost identical with the individual fortunes of Santa Anna, and no small portion of the perplexity and confusion in which it is involved is due to the strange combinations, contradictory policy, and varying line of action adopted by him. Accounts diametrically opposed to one another are given of him by the different parties in Mexico, and it is not easy to unravel the truth amidst the conflicting statements of contemporary writers. We must then confine ourselves to the principal facts of his career.

Santa Anna was the son of a Creole who possessed large estates on the road that leads from Vera Cruz to Jalapa, and resided at the hacienda of Mango de Claro. At a very early age he commanded a body of insurgent troops, with which he seized upon the town of Vera Cruz, and declared for Iturbide. His large possessions in this district naturally disposed the Indians to gather round him, and the rancheros, or Mexican farmers, formed a body of unrivalled irregular cavalry. Gifted with a fine commanding person, with attractive address, and a great command of language, Santa Anna was just the man to win popular admiration, and to carry himself with such tact as to manage all parties in the confused state of Mexican politics.

A grave act of insubordination soon brought him under the displeasure of Iturbide, and he was summoned to explain his conduct at Mexico. He went thither boldly self-reliant, but to his chagrin he was deprived of his command. For the moment he seemed to submit, but suddenly he appeared at Vera Cruz, where he denounced Iturbide as a tyrant, and raised his followers against him. He was not more obedient to the congress which subsequently assumed the direction of affairs; and the year 1828 saw him again in arms.

The incidents of the war which followed could hardly have occurred in any other country. In vain did the congress send out superior forces to reduce him to obedience. The hardy rancheros in Santa Anna's train had been bred and born in the *terra caliente,* the fever district of Vera Cruz. Seasoned as they were, fatigue and want seemed powerless to hurt them: whereas the vomito decimated the ranks of their opponents, or the heat struck them down upon the march. Still there were limits to a resistance to superior numbers even under such favourable circumstances. He was obliged to retreat and throw himself into the town of Camino de Oaxaca. Driven here from house to house, and from street to street, he at last took refuge with his men in the convent of San Domingo.

He well knew the people with whom he had to deal. The enemy would have massacred him and all his men without a scruple, but they would not injure the walls of a sacred building. Santa Anna, therefore, calmly lay down for his siesta, and when the firing was renewed, his men, secure behind stone walls, discharged their muskets with terrible destruction amongst the foe. All next day the strife continued on these unequal terms, the besieged party keeping close within their walls; but at night they dashed out from the gates and drove off a large herd of oxen into the courtyard of the convent.

Not far from the building which Santa Anna held was another convent crowned with lofty towers. No sooner had his men returned from their successful foray on the enemy's cattle than the gates of the convent were thrown wide open as for some religious procession. The enemy not questioning that Santa Anna was contented with the success he had already gained, awaited reverentially the coming of the monks, when, instead of a procession of priests, out rode at full galop a troop of rancheros and seized upon the second convent. The enemy by this manœuvre being placed between two fires was compelled to change his position.

It was not long before another stratagem convinced the loyal troops that they had to deal with no ordinary foe. "Is it possible," said the governor-general to his

N

aid-de-camp one morning, "that the long beards can have joined Santa Anna? Instead of soldiers I think I can see monks in the belfry." Soon after, the bells began to toll for service, as though the monks were going to pray for the deliverance of their house; and presently the cowls and hoods of the brethren were to be seen upon the roof. The general at once ordered his troops to advance and occupy the buildings, but when they drew near the monks suddenly let fall their robes, beneath which there shone out brilliant uniforms, and a deadly fire from both convents was poured upon the assailants with murderous effect before they could regain their quarters.

From his hazardous position Santa Anna was relieved by the revolution which deposed Pedraza. We have already seen the part he took in that movement. In the following year, 1829, he added to his former reputation by the masterly manner in which he checked the invasion of the Spaniards. General Barradas, at the head of four thousand men, had landed at Tampico to make one last effort for the subjugation of the country. Santa Anna, then minister of war, was at his post in Mexico, but he managed to elude the Spaniards, and to place himself at the head of a small force, with which he advanced upon Tampico. In the absence of Barradas, he attacked the place, which yielded after a struggle of four hours' duration. He had hardly entered it, when Barradas re-appeared with three thousand men. Retreat was impossible. A river lay between Santa Anna and the town, which he could only cross in the face of the enemy. Once more he had recourse to stratagem. He deluded Barradas into the belief that he had with him an overwhelming force, and accordingly the Spaniard agreed to come to terms. Santa Anna meanwhile crossed the river unopposed, as had been agreed on, and Barradas did not learn how he had been duped until it was too late. Every night the Mexicans attacked the Spaniards, who were thus kept at a distance until reinforcements arrived. Barradas was eventually glad to lay down his arms and sail back to the Havanna. Thus ended the last Spanish effort to reconquer the country.

By these exploits the name of Santa Anna became famous through the country, and when Pedraza's second term of office had expired, he was elected president. * He still professed to hold with the federal party, and was on the best terms with Gomez Farias, the vice-president, and a leader on the same side. The congress too, of 1834, was federal in character, but church matters again gave the signal for discord. A bill was brought into congress directed against the episcopal estates, and the clergy, in alarm, at once threw themselves into the arms of the Centralists. Bribery was largely resorted to in order to gain over opponents, and the president himself is said to have been thus induced to yield. At any rate, on the 13th of May, 1834, he dissolved the congress, in violation of the constitution, and immediately appealed to the people to maintain order and peace, which he represented as threatened by that body. Certain laws against the church were to be repealed, certain persons sent into banishment, and the whole constitution was to be remodelled. Until a new congress could be summoned for these purposes, Santa Anna was to have absolute authority. This revolution was called the *pronunciamiento* of Cuernavaca.

* On the 15th of May, 1833.

This new congress met in 1835, and the Plan of Toluca was the basis on which it reformed the constitution. The federal system was abolished, the state governments were annihilated, their legislatures dissolved, and all the states united under one government, whole and indivisible. Thus was formed the Constitution of Mexico, which has produced (says Mr. Robinson) all its later troubles, and is pronounced to be probably the worst that ever existed. Its features are these: A president elected for eight years; a house of deputies and a senate, the latter selected in the most complicated manner by electors thrice removed from the people; and a supreme court. It also embraces what is termed the supreme conservative power, with a veto on everything, composed of five members, and in the words of the organic law, "responsible to God and public opinion alone!" *

Violent opposition arose to this scheme immediately it was propounded, and a large part of the country took to arms. Yucatan broke off its connection with Mexico. Puebla, Jalisco, and Oaxaca all declared against it, and a serious insurrection broke out in Zacatecas and Texas. Santa Anna, however, did not bend before the storm. He despatched General Cos to reduce the Texans to submission. He went in person to Zacatecas, and gained the day, after a sanguinary struggle. The old elements of hatred once more broke loose on this occasion, and the track of the president was stained by the savage cruelty committed in the town of Zacatecas, and by the like misconduct of his troops throughout the province.

Having reduced this part of the country to obedience,

* Mexico and her military chieftains, p. 165.

Santa Anna set out with the flower of his troops to reconquer Texas. He was probably not unwilling to leave to others the unpopular task of getting the new constitution into working order, and he hoped to gather fresh military laurels. Texas stood on a somewhat different footing from the other Mexican states. The country had been originally colonized by a citizen of the United States, in 1819; conjointly with Cohahuila, it had formed one of the states of the federal republic, and in 1824 a general colonization law had especially invited foreigners to settle within its boundaries. A change of policy, however, had taken place, and the jealousy of Mexico had been excited by the number of settlers who came from the United States. Their neighbours were accused of a design to rob them of one of their most fertile regions, and, in 1830, an enactment passed the congress that no further immigration into the states should be allowed. To enforce its observance, a chain of forts was established in the country, and the people were thus brought under martial control.

The Texans were not disposed quietly to brook this interference with their liberty. They took up arms against the garrisons, and succeeded in expelling some of them from their posts. It was whilst the irritation thus produced was rankling in their breasts that they heard of the *pronunciamiento* of Cuernavaca and the overthrow of the constitution. They resolved to stand by their federal rights. The opening scenes of the war only served to inflame both parties, and so led to the final loss of Texas, and eventually to the conflict with the United States. The Mexican forces were at first victorious. The state legislature was dispersed by General Cos. Several small towns were taken, and in violation of the terms on which they had surrendered a number of Fanning's volunteers were butchered in cold blood by Santa Anna's orders. But these successes were soon checked by the battle of San Jacinto, in which the Mexicans were beaten, and Santa Anna himself was taken prisoner. "Sir," he said, addressing General Houston, on yielding up his sword, "yours is no common destiny; you have captured the Napoleon of the west."

The Americans were so enraged at the slaughter of their countrymen, that many of them urged Houston to send his prisoner to immediate execution. A council was held to deliberate upon his fate, and a somewhat improbable story has been circulated that his life was spared owing to the suggestion that Mexico would be more benefited than injured by his destruction. At any rate the side of mercy prevailed, and he was sent a prisoner to Washington. He was subsequently allowed to return to Mexico, on the understanding that he would use all his influence to secure the recognition of the independence of Texas.

Bustamente was elected president for the second time in January, 1837, under the new central constitution. He assumed the government at a season of much difficulty. The treasury was empty. The pay of the army was in arrear. The treaty concluded by Santa Anna with the United States was unpopular and the French government were pressing for some claims for injuries alleged to have been inflicted on their subjects. Bustamente was poor, and had not enriched himself by his former tenure of power; yet, to allay the impatience of the troops he advanced ten thousand dollars from his own funds. He promptly recognised the treaty with the government at Washington, and concluded another with Spain, by which the independence of Mexico was admitted. Such acts ought to have won him the affections, or at least the peaceable obedience, of the people. But the same inextinguishable spirit of disorder was still ripe throughout the country. In 1838, the Federalists once more rose in arms with Mexia at their head. Santa Anna, who had been living in privacy since his return from Washington, asked and obtained the command of the army sent against them. The opposing forces met near Puebla. The Federalists were conquered. Mexia was taken prisoner, and ordered to execution, with only an hour's respite, on the field of battle. "Santa Anna is quite right," was his reply when his sentence was made known to him, "I would not have given *him* half the time if I had gained the day."

Hardly had the danger from this source been overcome, when a more serious difficulty pressed upon the government. The French fleet, under Admiral Baudin, appeared at Vera Cruz in the winter of 1838, with demands for satisfaction, which they were prepared to enforce. The sum of 500,000,000 dollars was claimed as an indemnity for the past. The right of carrying on retail trade, and of exemption from certain imposts, were insisted on for the future. The unhappy Mexicans could not afford either to admit or to reject the claim. The fort of Vera Cruz was captured, and the city unsuccessfully assaulted. The failure of this last attempt, combined with the arrival of the British fleet to induce the French to lessen their demands, through the good offices of Mr. Pakenham, the English envoy, caused the belligerents to come to terms.

The successes of the French contributed greatly to the unpopularity of Bustamente. The Mexicans, as haughty as they are incapable, always attribute their misfortunes to the government, and take no share of the blame upon themselves. Commerce had been crippled by the blockade of Vera Cruz, by the war in Texas, and by the expenditure which was thus incurred. Still further taxation was now inevitable, in order to pay the French indemnity. The discontent thus caused reached its climax in 1840, when Generals Urrea and Farias declared against the president.

Some curious scenes followed, strikingly illustrative of Mexican politics. Farias' *pronunciamiento* was made on the 15th of July. His party rushed to the palace and seized upon Bustamente. He, however, contrived to escape the next morning, on which he published a proclamation complaining of the *incivility* to which he had been subjected in being made a prisoner. A series of declarations and counter-declarations appeared, each side zealously following up the other on paper. Meanwhile Mexico was devastated. There was a want of common necessaries in the capital, and many lives of peaceful citizens were sacrificed in the irregular firing of either party.

Urrea and Farias had relied on the aid of Santa Anna, but this wily politician declared for Bustamente. Nor had the president been lacking to himself in the most critical moment of the insurrection. After his escape he had recovered possession of the national palace, and was besieged in it by the insurgents. A breach had been effected in its walls, and his staff requested him to escape, but he refused. At this moment the rebels rushed into the room, crying "Death to Bustamente." He calmly stepped forward, threw off his cloak, and stood facing them undaunted. His boldness made them quail before him, and they retired without a hand being lifted against him.

During these internal troubles the Texans had been asserting their distinct nationality, and in 1844 they commenced negotiations to enter the American union. This proposal roused all the national pride of Mexico. In vain the president, Herrera, strove to bring about a friendly arrangement with the United States. At the end of 1845, he was obliged to resign in favour of General Paredes, and war against Texas was declared.

It was really war with the United States, whose forces were everywhere victorious. Matamoros was occupied by General Taylor on the 18th of May, 1846. Monterey, the key of the northern provinces, fell some four months later. Taylor then advanced, with only 5,000 men, to San Luis Potosi, where Santa Anna, now president once more, met him at the head of 20,000 Mexicans. This fine force was shattered in repeated efforts to force the strong position of the Americans in the gorge of Angostura. Meanwhile California had been seized upon by Fremont, and New Mexico by Kearney.

A still heavier blow was impending over the state. General Scott sailed at the head of a force aimed against the capital. At Jalapa, and at six other points in his march from Vera Cruz, the passage was disputed, and some fierce fighting took place. But nothing could arrest the progress of the United States army, which finally entered the capital on the 13th of September, 1847. This reverse compelled the Mexicans to yield to the terms insisted on by the United States. The independence of Texas was finally conceded, and with it California and New Mexico were added to the American union.

This disastrous termination of the war was for the time fatal to the popularity of Santa Anna, and he retired to Jamaica. It were quite hopeless for us to attempt to follow the constant changes that have since occurred. Every two or three years at most some new revolution has broken out, and this has frequently happened at much shorter intervals. Santa Anna fled in 1848. He was recalled in 1852, with a centralist constitution, and declared perpetual dictator in 1853. The very next year, a fresh *pronunciamiento* was made by General Alvarez. Santa Anna fled once more in 1855, and Alvarez was made provisional president. He resigned at the end of the same year, and General Comonfort succeeded him in 1856, who was welcomed by an outbreak within the first three months of his administration.

The names which have been prominent in the most recent disturbances are those of Juarez and Miramon. The former heads the liberal, and the latter the church party in the state.

Such has been the unsatisfactory issue of republican government in Mexico. Half a century has elapsed since the standard of independence was raised by Hidalgo, in the year 1810, and the condition of the country gradually deteriorated, until it reached a pitch which demanded the intervention of the European powers. In these fifty years no less than twenty-seven fundamental systems of law, or separate constitutions, have been enacted, and fifty-eight presidents have held the supreme power; but not one man amongst them has possessed the combined probity and vigour required to control and regenerate the Mexicans. Gradually all the bonds have been loosed, by which men of the same nation are united to one another, and universal anarchy has prevailed. The example of disobedience and disorder has commonly been set by those who, knowing the responsibilities of authority, ought to have been the most careful to yield to its requirements. The first necessary quality for command is to know how to obey, and there has been hardly a single occupant of the president's chair in Mexico who has been possessed of this essential qualification for his office; whilst the priesthood have fomented every outbreak which they hoped would help to prop up their failing influence, and to secure their property from bearing its due share of the burdens of the state.

This selfish policy has deservedly failed. An exclusive regard to their own interests, and an utter unconcern for the general welfare, have resulted in the ruin of those who have adopted so base a line of conduct. Every party has in turn seized upon the government by unlawful violence, and every party has found itself obliged to succumb to the same weapons which it has employed against its adversaries. The clergy, in their avarice, have overreached themselves. In the period of the greatest peril of their country, and when the nation was threatened with extinction; when the capital was held by the army of the United States, and their neighbours were demanding the annexation of their territory, the clergy refused to pay one farthing from their large revenues to defend their altars, their country, and their flocks. In the troubles that have since ensued their property has been involved in the general ruin. They have lost all the wealth which they grasped so greedily; a large portion of which they would most probably have retained had they been more generous in the hour of their country's need.

The whole history of the country may serve to illustrate a truth which it were well that some of our European rulers should ponder—a truth of universal application for all states and through all time. It is this. The welfare of every class in a community is inseparably bound up with the well-being of all the other classes; so that if one member suffer all the other members suffer with it. Spain endeavoured to rule Mexico by an exclusively selfish policy. As a consequence, she not only seriously crippled a territory which would have repaid a hundredfold any generous treatment, but inflicted injuries upon herself which gradually undermined her strength, and reduced her from the most powerful to the least influential of the European states. Since the declaration of independence each party in Mexico has similarly pursued an exclusively selfish policy. The result has been that this highly favoured land has become a byword to all the nations of the earth.

CHAPTER VI.

THE RELIGION AND RELIGIOUS CONDITION OF MEXICO.

Importance of the subject—Distressing features—Zeal of the conquerors — Influence of the priesthood — Ecclesiastical establishment in Mexico—Decline of church power and wealth—Churches and convents—Taking the veil—Irregular lives of the monks—The confessional—Tithes—Extortionate fees—Payments of miners to the clergy—Funerals of rich and poor, and the dissipation that accompanies them—Religious processions—Holy week in Mexico—Village festival —Superstition of the people—Our Lady of Guadalupe—The Virgin de Los Remedios—Sterner scenes of superstition— Public penances—The order of Santa Theresa—No prospect of tolerance—Privileges and responsibility of Protestants.

It would not have been unreasonable to expect that the first topic of inquiry with all professing Christians, when endeavouring to learn something about a foreign nation, would be their religious condition. If we take the history of the whole universe since man's creation, we find it separated into two great divisions by the coming of Jesus Christ. In his life we have the great central fact of the world's history, and the Bible teaches us that this fact has an interest of the deepest importance for all our fellow men. In Him the free salvation of God is offered to all that will believe; in his person and character the mind of God to sinners has been declared; and to the message of his truth, when faithfully uttered, is promised the accompanying influence of the Holy Spirit, so that it shall effectually work in the hearts of its hearers, and be productive of great results. And all this has been abundantly confirmed by the experience of the past. Although the progress of the gospel has been slow in certain cases, and missionary efforts have seemed for a time to fail, yet in every nation it has been found that the message of the Prince of peace is adapted to all the wants of the human heart, and brings the only true relief to a spirit burdened with the sense of sin. Everywhere there have been some who have believed on the Lord Jesus Christ. This of itself, one would have thought, should have aroused the attention of thoughtful men. Surely there must be something well worth knowing in that gospel which suits alike the civilized European and the savage dweller in the most barbarous lands. The true Christian understands the cause of such an influence, for as heart answers unto heart, he knows that the truth which is so inexpressibly dear to his own soul is equally fitted to cheer the heart of the wild Indian, who has learned to trust in Christ and be at peace. We wonder, therefore, that these results have not awakened more careful attention. The truth is the carnal mind is enmity against God and avoids instinctively such inquiries.

There is a further reason why the religious condition of a people should engage the notice of all men of observation, and it is this: that the inward reception of the gospel in the heart always has its effect upon the outward behaviour. Godliness hath the promise of the life that now is as well as of that which is to come. All experience proves it. Wherever the Bible is known and valued, there will be seen an industrious and thriving people. No conditions of climate or influence of race will explain away this result. In Switzerland adjoining cantons bear the marks of their creed as plainly upon the surface of their fields as in the interior of their churches. In our own land wherever the power of truth is brought to bear upon the long-neglected masses, an improvement in the habits of daily life invariably is the handmaid of an acceptance of the gospel. As a broad principle it may be affirmed that many a land with every natural advantage, but where God's word is withheld, is declining and falling into decay, whilst when the Bible is introduced the wilderness begins to flourish and to blossom as the rose.

The religious condition of Mexico will not, alas, present us with many pleasing features. A withering blight seems to have fallen upon the land, and in no respect has its influence been more deadly than in the power which a false creed has obtained over the minds of a people, who yet seem strangers to those practical virtues which that creed recommends. It may seem a harsh judgment to pass upon a whole people, but the Mexicans (with some slight exceptions that shall presently be noted), seem to have grasped all the superstitious usages of popery with the firmest tenacity, whilst they neglect those remnants of truth which are still retained in the Romish religion. You will find in Mexico no more obedient, nay abject, devotee than the lepero, who will kneel humbly to the host as it is carried by, and immediately afterwards plunge his dagger into the heart of a foe. Amongst the native Indians the shaven crown of the priest will meet with a respect which no sense of right or wrong could ensure for any moral or religious precept. It is true that since these countries shook off the yoke of Spain, there has arisen in each state a party who have desired to free themselves from thraldom to the priesthood: but even now the vast mass of the population is still a prey to the superstitious terrors and convictions by which their fathers were held in bondage.

In the early history of the Spanish occupation, we find a constant anxiety displayed by the home government for the conversion of the natives to the faith of Christianity. In theory at least, it was supposed that the pope had a right to confer dominions beyond the Atlantic upon European princes, on condition that they should bring over the idolaters to the Catholic church. Indeed, there seems to have been a genuine desire on the part of those in power to carry out this purpose, but their efforts and many of their edicts were hindered and disregarded by the sturdy cavaliers whose broad swords had won them dominion in the field. We find constant complaints from the good fathers who accompanied them, that the regulations of the Spanish court, on behalf of the conquered peoples, were constantly violated. Very frequent were the appeals made to the Spanish council by the priests on behalf of the natives of the New World, who were treated with much cruelty by the conquerors. It was, doubtless, owing to their kindness, and to the ready way in which they accommodated their teaching, so as to include many heathen superstitions, that the Indians first acquired that reverence for the priesthood which has continued to the present day.

From the period of the conquest ample provision was made for the ecclesiastical establishment in Mexico and New Spain. Friar Gage gives us some insight into the wealth of the church when he visited the country; and this was increased in subsequent years as the mines became more productive, and as wealthy individuals were induced to make large gifts to the religious orders. Humboldt estimated the clergy of Mexico at from 10,000 to 13,000. The secular clergy numbered about 5,000 parish priests; whilst the monks of all orders, with their lay brethren, might amount to 8,000 more, of whom 2,500 were to be found in the convents of the capital alone. The church was governed by an archbishop and eight bishops, and the tithes destined to the support of the clergy amounted to 1,835,382 dollars in the six principal bishoprics, no return being obtained from the other three. But, besides this average annual income, the church possessed a large accumulated capital, "derived partly from bequests and partly from surplus income, the whole of which was supposed, in 1805, to amount to 44,000,000 dollars." This sum was lent out on mortgage at a moderate rate of interest. Besides these sources of income the ecclesiastics held land whose full value did not exceed three millions of dollars.

The possession of such immense wealth by the clergy was one of the causes which contributed to the success of the revolution. It is easy to understand that the chief prizes in the church were eagerly sought after by Spaniards, whilst the vast mass of the priests, on whom fell the labour of ministering to the people, were of Creole and mixed origin. Hence arose a bitter distinction of *caste;* all the wealthier offices being filled by Spaniards, who were commonly sent from Europe, and returned thither after amassing a fortune, while those who bore the burden and heat of the day were left to toil on in ill-requited poverty. In many dioceses where the revenues of the bishop amounted to 100,000 or 120,000 dollars, there were parish priests who vegetated upon a pittance of 100 or 120 dollars in the year. No class threw themselves more earnestly into the revolutionary struggle than the great body of the Creole clergy.

We have no accurate statistics from which to describe the condition of the Romish church in Mexico at the present day. In 1826, the property of the church had been reduced by one half, partly under the administration of the Spanish government, and partly owing to the necessities and the confusion that arose during the revolution. The members of the clergy at the same period had diminished in a like degree to 5,595.

In endeavouring to estimate the influence which their creed still exercises over the minds of the people, we must not be misled by the facts which have just been narrated. With the enjoyment of political liberty it may be that many of the Mexicans have thrown off the abject obedience which they once paid to the priesthood, but this freedom has not been accompanied by any inquiry after a better system. The Bible is still, as of old, excluded from the country, and in the constant revolutions, with all their attendant miseries that have desolated the land, there has been but little opportunity for acquiring a knowledge of that gospel which is so sorely needed in such seasons of distress. As for the great mass of the population, they are accurately described by one of their own priests as "very good Catholics, but very bad Christians."

The churches of Mexico and of the principal towns throughout New Spain testify to the former wealth and power of the priesthood. In every part of the country large buildings were erected, and in the vicinity of mines now no longer worked, as well as dispersed in every region of Central America, the ruins of immense edifices stand as the mournful witnesses of past prosperity and present decay. Very striking is the effect of many of these dismantled churches which meet the eye of the traveller in the most deserted spots; the sole remaining monuments of busy towns whose very names have been almost forgotten. These churches are almost all of one type, being built in a debased style of classic architecture; and as they stand on some summit with their roofless walls and bare windows, they present a more picturesque appearance than they did at the period of their greatest completeness.

It is in vain that we search through New Spain for the elegant and noble proportions of our English churches and cathedrals. There are none of the slender, tapering spires and massive towers that adorn our home landscape; indeed such buildings would be out of place in a land so subject to earthquakes. The principal towns have each their cathedral, which is generally, as at Mexico, the headquarters of dirt, the floor commonly presenting a horrible spectacle, whilst beggars, filthy and diseased, and Indian market women, with screaming children, disturb the services and add to the discomfort of the place. At certain festivals, the floor of the churches is washed, and beggars are excluded. On these occasions well dressed persons venture to attend, otherwise it is but rarely that ladies intermingle with the crowd, although at times they do kneel on the foul floor, and then hurry home to change their dress as quickly as possible. So universal is this prevalence of dirt in the churches that most families of any position have an oratory, and employ a *padre* to perform the service for them in their own houses.

In strange contrast with this filth are the tawdry

ornaments by which many of the churches are overloaded, and the massive silver plate displayed upon the altar. Many of the more celebrated shrines in Mexico possessed at one time almost fabulous wealth in plate and precious stones, the cathedral of the capital, for instance, having such property worth several millions sterling. A part of these valuables has disappeared during the revolutionary period, but enough remains to make a strong impression upon the mind of a traveller, and to suggest at first sight ideas of magnificence which a fuller acquaintance with the churches speedily dispels.

Convents and monasteries are plentiful throughout every part of America that has been subject to Spanish dominion. Many of these are still richly endowed, and present an air of substantial comfort as well as considerable pretension to architectural beauty. In these will be found tolerable cleanliness, large and well furnished apartments, and gardens brilliant with every variety of flowers. We should indeed have been surprised if such establishments had not flourished amongst the Mexicans, whose natural indolence seems specially to adapt them to the ease of a monastic life.

Great are the preparations in wealthy families when a daughter of the house takes the veil. A large company of friends assemble, and the ceremony is preceded by a grand banquet, such as would come after a wedding with ourselves. The future nun is dressed in the most splendid array, and every appearance of satisfaction is maintained, although hearts may be aching at the prospect of the separation that is at hand, and at the severance of ties that can never be renewed. To our mind there are few things more horrible than this violent bursting of family bonds, ordained of God for our comfort in a sinful world, and this solemn devotion to a life apart from the world in which God has placed us. The religious ceremony of taking the veil is like that observed in the Roman Catholic countries of Europe. There is all the pomp of church music, the priests are dressed in their most gorgeous vestments, the altar blazes with lamps, and is adorned with gold and silver plate, and rich hangings of crimson and gold : amidst it all, between the long rows of nuns in their dark robes, kneels the novice, attired in her bridal dress of satin and lace and jewels. The curtain falls before the grating which shuts out the spectators from the choir in which the ceremony is being carried on, and when it is raised again the bridal dress is gone, and the maiden is seen lying prostrate, covered with a black cloth, and a solemn chant sounds like the last funeral dirge over one who is henceforth dead to the world. She is embraced on rising by all the nuns, is allowed to take one last look through the grating at the world beyond it, and then once more the curtain falls.

This is one of the few occasions on which sermons are preached in Mexico—the subject being naturally suggested by the event which the congregation is come to witness. In most extravagant terms the novice is praised for "having chosen the good part which shall not be taken from her," and all the Scriptural phrases which are applicable to those only who through the influence of the Holy Ghost have obtained a saving faith in Christ, are commonly applied to all who embrace a monastic life. It is painful to think how many a poor girl is firmly persuaded that by becoming a nun she is making sure of her salvation, and thus the voice of conscience is stifled, and any conviction of her own sinfulness is disregarded, whilst some are awakened, when it is too late, to the painful consciousness that they retain an unchanged heart beneath their new habit, and then despair of any hope from that gospel which they identify with the promises that have proved so delusive.

All travellers agree in testifying to the irregular lives of many of the monks. They are to be seen in the most disreputable places, at cock-fights and gambling tables, mixing in all the debauchery of the towns. Nor does such a manner of living destroy their authority. The Mexicans do not appear to estimate popery according to the behaviour of its clergy. The most worthless lepero, who has been stabbed in a drunken quarrel, or has been dangerously wounded at a bull fight, will confess with all solemnity to a priest who has been assisting at either of these pastimes, and will eagerly seek for absolution at his hands.

Were we able to penetrate the secrecy of the confessional, we should probably learn yet more startling facts concerning the religious condition of the Mexicans; but our readers will be able to form a fair judgment on this subject from what we have related elsewhere. It is no exaggeration to say that the false sentiments current amongst the people have caused the consciences of many to be so seared, that the violation of some superstitious rite is held to be a more serious crime than assassination: and a dying man will pass lightly over the murders he has committed, but will express remorse at the memory of some act of irreverence to the church or the relics of the saints. Nor will the priest to whom the confession is made, attempt to correct an estimate which he commonly shares with the penitent. It would be very unfair not to add that there are other priests whose lives adorn the church to which they belong, and who, although the upholders of a false creed, spend their days in visiting the sick and the poor, whilst their own habits are moral and self-denying.

The lower orders are now, in many instances, alienated from the priesthood, owing to the exactions to which they have been subjected. It is a fundamental tenet of the Romish church that the grace which is supposed to be received from sacraments can only be imparted through the hands of the priest; and advantage is taken of this tenet to gratify the cupidity of the clergy. Most exorbitant fees are demanded for marriage and baptism, whilst those payable at burials and masses are equally oppressive. "For instance, in states where the daily wages of the labourer do not exceed two reals, and where a cottage can be built for four dollars, its unfortunate inhabitants are forced to pay twenty-two dollars for their marriage fees, a sum which exceeds half their yearly earnings, in a country where feast and fast days exceed the number of days on which labour is permitted. The consequences are such as might naturally be expected. Immorality becomes rife, almost universal, under such a system."

The same system prevails with respect to baptisms and burials. In the mining districts every miner pays *weekly* half a real to the church, and an agent of the priest always attends when the wages are paid to receive his share of them. The only return which the miner enjoys for this weekly dole is the right of having a mass performed over his body after death, and even this he loses if his weekly payments are at any time discontinued. Some idea of the exorbitance of the demand may be gathered from the fact that in ten years six pounds ten shillings would be extorted for the honour of a funeral.

Ceremonies that are strange, and often exceedingly repulsive, follow upon the occasion of death in a household. It is customary for the dead body to lie in state, dressed in rich satin adorned with lace and ribbons, whilst all the jewellery belonging to the deceased is collected to add to the display. We even read of instances in which the diamonds of several families were *borrowed* to augment the splendour of the scene. Every acquaintance of the household is invited to visit the corpse ere it is borne to the grave. It was formerly the habit to bury the dead in his rich costume, but a plain dress is now substituted before the coffin is placed in the vault. To our mind there is something specially horrible in thus surrounding a dead body with all the vanity of this life, after the immortal soul has been summoned to the realities of the future world.

Very different scenes are to be witnessed in the dwellings of the lower orders. There the hospitality commonly exercised at this time degenerates into revelry and debauchery. In the same room with the corpse will be gathered a number of persons half or wholly intoxicated, quarrelling over a gambling table, as the piles of copper coin pass from hand to hand. In the midst of such orgies, protracted beyond the hour of midnight, the whole party will pause for a few minutes as the clock strikes twelve—the hour of the souls in purgatory. Amusements are suspended, and every one kneels to go through a fixed form of prayer. This over, all return again to their interrupted dissipation; and if there seem for a moment to be a somewhat subdued manner in the guests, it is quickly lost in the uproar and excitement which follow.

With that strange adherence to the letter of Christianity, whose spirit they so little understand, a Mexican parent will profess satisfaction at the loss of a child who has been called away from earth "before he was old enough to displease the God of heaven." Visitors are then expected to offer their congratulations, and the poor mother tries to hide beneath a forced smile the grief with which she inwardly mourns her bereavement. We would· not question that the spirit of a darling child is accepted through the death of our Saviour, and those who have learned to realize the love of God in Christ, may be glad that their children dying early have escaped the many sorrows of a sinful world. But it is most unnatural not to grieve for the loss of those whom every tie of affection makes most dear to us, and tears will and should flow freely, even while the heart acquiesces and rejoices in the Divine will.

When the body is borne to the church there follows all the pageantry with which the Romish system loves to feed the eye and inflame the feelings of its devotees. If the family be wealthy, the whole building will be hung with black, priests in robes of white and black velvet embroidered with silver minister before the altar, and the thrilling tones of some solemn mass add to the effect of the ceremony. On a lofty bier in the centre of the church the coffin is placed, long rows of tall candles lining either side, whilst incense burners or massive lamps of silver shed their perfume and their flame. A full band of music, a long procession of monks bearing lighted tapers, and figures veiled and clothed in deep mourning, all lend a solemnity to the scene; and all this while the soul has gone to its account. Oh to have at such an hour the only needful garment, the robe of Christ's righteousness to cover human guilt, and the only music that can fall joyfully upon the ear, even the glad welcome of "well done, good and faithful servant, enter thou into the joy of thy Lord."

The streets of Mexico, and indeed of all the towns of New Spain, are constantly visited by religious processions. On fête days there are to be seen long lines of priests, and banners emblazoned with the emblems of the saints: and almost every religious service serves as an opportunity for some such display. Whenever a dying Catholic desires to receive the sacrament, there appears a coach with an eye painted on the panels and drawn by six mules, and within it are seated the priests bearing the host. As the carriage moves forward a bell is sounded incessantly to give warning of its approach, and all instantly fall upon their knees: buyers and sellers in the streets, and ladies sitting out upon the balconies of private houses all kneel alike, and to refuse compliance would expose you to the fury of the mob. The Protestants commonly turn aside out of the way, and even then do not always escape the angry comments of priests and people.

During the whole week preceding Easter Sunday all Mexico is engrossed in religious ceremonial. From every quarter crowds of country people throng the city, booths are erected in the squares, garlands and tapestry hang from the balconies, shops are shut and business suspended; whilst all the churches are adorned with the greatest splendour. On Palm Sunday the cathedral is the great centre of attraction, and multitudes resort thither to see the ceremony of blessing the palm trees. When all is ready there appears a long line of Indians, each bearing a palm tree at least seven feet high. Some of them have travelled many a weary mile bearing their strange burden, which of course has lost all vitality by the way and is now carried with its leaves curiously plaited together: on they come sweeping through the crowd until they reach the place where the priests are assembled who are to bless the trees, and these are afterwards taken home as treasures highly prized to adorn their huts. It is curious to mark in every land what toil and pains men will undergo to obtain some fancied blessing, a striking mark that the sense of sin is no unreal thing even where men are strangers to the blood of Christ, by which alone sin's guilt can be removed.

The occupation of the Mexicans at this season is to hurry daily from church to church, kneeling a few minutes before some altar in each and then passing on to another, or else to assemble in some friend's house which commands a good view of the various processions. The scenes which the interior of the churches present are very strange to English notions. Large images of the Virgin Mary, dressed in magnificent robes of silk and embroidered with lace and jewels, are conspicuous in almost every edifice; in the chapels of the saints there are similar figures; whilst the high altar is variously adorned according to the taste of the parish priest and his assistants. In some a large wax figure of the Saviour is surrounded by other figures to represent some occurrence in the life of Christ; in another, perhaps, the infant Jesus is represented as lying in the manger at Bethlehem. Large flowering shrubs of exquisite beauty, roses in full bloom, orange trees laden with fruit and blossom, and immense vases of cut flowers adorn the altar.

Pictures borrowed from convents or private houses line the walls, on which are also hung cages of singing birds,—add to this the strains of music, the brilliancy of a tropical sun, shining through stained glass windows, or at night the blaze of a thousand tapers, and the mingled perfume of incense and flowers, and you may understand how powerfully the Romish church acts upon the feelings of an excitable people. The aim of all this pomp is to produce a vivid impression on the senses, and to effect this no pains is spared. Hence many of the scenes are such as would be revolting in our eyes. Ghastly pictures or models of our Lord's sufferings, with the blood trickling from his wounds, are not uncommon. To be painfully affected at such a scene, to believe all that the church teaches, and to leave everything else to the care of his confessor, is to be a model of Christianity under such a system.

Each day in the week has its special programme, but that of Thursday is looked forward to with the most eager expectation. No carriages are permitted, and the ladies walk through the streets in all the magnificence of velvet and jewellery—diamonds flash amidst a crowd which includes ragged Indians and Poblana peasants in their picturesque costume—little children absurdly overladen with finery contrast strangely with the miserable and dirty urchins that trot by the sides or are tied on the backs of their Indian mothers. It is not till evening that the grand procession begins. Large figures of the Saviour in the different incidents of the passion, images of the Trinity, and all the apostles, "from St. Peter with the keys to Judas with the money bag," and more than all the "Virgin of Sorrows," as she is termed, enthroned in state, and covered by a canopy of velvet, form the principal features of the train, whilst a long cavalcade of priests, monks, and laymen, bearing torches and tapers, light up the procession as it passes by. Such a scene is varied by the mourning attire in which every one is dressed on the following day. Saturday is mainly devoted to the purchase and explosion of "Judases," as firework images meant to imitate the betrayer are called; and Easter day is ushered in with the sound of booming cannon to celebrate the triumph over death of Him who then burst its gates and opened the kingdom of heaven to all believers.

The other great festivals of the Romish church afford a like opportunity for a kind of religious drama. At Christmas it is customary to give performances in private houses, in which all the scenes of Bethlehem are enacted. Persons dressed as the Virgin and Joseph appear on a stage representing a cold, dark night, and demand admittance to the inn. From within are heard voices which refuse to let them enter, until the Virgin declares that she is Queen of Heaven, when the doors are thrown open. We cannot transfer to our pages a full account of all the details so childishly enacted. Priests take part in the performance, ladies dressed as shepherds, and children with wings to imitate the angels are not wanting. It is concluded by a priest taking a wax figure of the infant Saviour and placing it in a cradle. Then the whole party in the same dresses, "angels, shepherds and all," pass into another room and dance till supper time. After all this we are hardly surprised to learn that they mark Christmas day in Mexico by having *no* service in the churches.

The priests find in the poor natives very docile disciples; but they are often strangely at fault in their performance of the elaborate ceremonial of popery

Mr. Ruxton strolled into the village church at La Xuage to see what was going on. "The priest, equipped in full canonicals, was engaged before the altar praying with an open book, and at particular passages gave a signal with his hand behind his back, when half a score of Indian boys outside immediately exploded a number of squibs and fire-wheels, and a bevy of adult Indians fired off their rusty 'escopetas,' the congregation shouting vociferously. At the time when one of the salvos should have taken place and a huge trabuco fired off, which was fastened for safety to the door of the church, the *padre* rushed out in the middle of his discourse and clapped a match to the bunghole, giving a most severe look at the neglectful bombardier, and banging off the blunderbuss, returned book in hand to the altar, where he resumed his discourse."

Throughout Mexico the population is exclusively Roman Catholic, and very ignorant and bigoted disciples they are. In the principal towns every house has its figure of the Virgin or some tutelary saint; whilst billets of paper, on which short prayers are written, may be seen upon the doors. The system of selling masses for the dead is extensively carried out in Mexico. An American traveller in the country, Mr. Waddy Thompson, relates that one day his washerwoman begged him to lend her two dollars. "What do you want them for?" he asked. "Because to-day there is a special mass to be said, which relieves the souls in purgatory from ten thousand years of torment, and I want to secure its benefits for my mother." "Do you really believe this?" he asked again. "Why, yes," she replied, "is it not true?" with a countenance of as much surprise as if he had denied that the sun was shining.

What can be the religious condition of those who, instead of looking for pardon of sin only through the blood of Jesus Christ, are persuaded that it may be obtained by the grant of an indulgence. Be it remembered that an indulgence is defined to be a remission of the punishment due for sins, and then imagine the blasphemy of the following notice which was pasted up in the church of our Lady of Guadalupe on the occasion of her festival:—

"The faithful are reminded that the most illustrious bishops of Puebla and Tarazora have granted an indulgence of eighty days for every quarter of an hour during which the images are exposed, and five hundred days for each Ave Maria which is recited before either of them. Lastly, the most excellent Fr. Jose Maria de Jesus Belaumzawn, for himself and for the most illustrious the present bishops of Puebla, Mechoacan, Jalisco, and Durango, has granted an indulgence of two hundred days for every word of the appointed prayers to our most exalted lady, for every step taken in her house, for every reverence performed, and for every word of the mass which may be uttered by the priest or the hearers; as many more days of indulgence are granted for every quarter of an hour in which these images are exposed on the balconies, windows, or doors, for public adoration."

Other instances may illustrate the power of superstition throughout these regions. In Mexico there are two rival claimants for popular favour, the "Virgin de los Remedios" and "Our Lady of Guadalupe." The latter is, perhaps, the most patronized at the present time, since she has been adopted as patroness by the republican party; and to her intercession almost every favourable event is commonly attributed. The cathedral of our Lady of Guadalupe stands on a hill at some distance from Mexico. Some four years after the conquest, so runs the story, the Virgin appeared to an Indian, named Diego, and directed him to go to the bishop, and say that she desired to have a shrine erected to her upon this spot. Diego's first attempt to see the bishop failed, and the Virgin then appeared a second time and gave him more peremptory orders; but the bishop refused to believe Diego's report unless he brought with him some token from the Virgin herself. Once more the holy mother appeared, and on learning the bishop's reply, she bade Diego go to the summit of the hill and gather her some roses. Off went the Indian much wondering that he should be sent to a barren rock for roses, but although there was no other sign of vegetation near, he found the rose blossoms, and brought them back with him. The Virgin took the flowers, and throwing them into his *tilma*, told him to show them to the bishop, and inform him that these were the credentials of his mission. Arrived at the palace, he opened his *tilma*, when, behold, there was discovered upon it the picture of our Lady, to which miraculous powers have ever since been ascribed.

The portrait so strangely procured is a coarse daub representing the Virgin in a blue cloak spangled with stars, and a garment beneath it of crimson and gold, and to this paltry piece of painting the people betake themselves in the hour of their trouble. If the state is torn by intestine strife, as when the Mexicans revolted against the yoke of Spain, if some unlooked for domestic calamity threatens to desolate the home of a Mexican family, or if far away from the mountain on which her temple stands the storm-tossed sailor is terrified at the immediate presence of death, in all such cases the mind is turned not to the love of the Father who sent his Son into the world to save sinners, nor yet to the sympathy of the Saviour who, having ascended in our nature to God's right hand, still pities men's infirmities and answers men's prayers, but the Mexican, ignorant of these resources, betakes himself for succour to the intercession of our Lady of Guadalupe.

Equally absurd and foolish is the legend of the Virgin de los Remedios. The image was brought over by Cortez, and placed by him in the great idol temple in Mexico; but on the "night of sorrows," it disappeared, and was subsequently discovered *in the heart of a large maguey tree* on the top of a barren treeless hill. The figure so strangely preserved, and recovered under circumstances that sound somewhat contradictory to Protestant ears, is a hideous wooden doll about a foot long, with rude holes for the eyes and mouth— "no Indian idol could be much uglier"—and holds in its arms a smaller doll of similar workmanship. When drought prevails for any length of time in Mexico, it is customary to bring this figure into the city, and carry it in solemn procession through the streets. In the days of Spanish rule, the viceroy used to march on foot before it, whilst the image itself was borne in a splendid coach driven by a nobleman of the highest rank, and in this fashion a visit was paid to each of the principal convents in the city. It is still stoutly asserted that plentiful rains invariably follow the performance of this ceremony.

During the period of the revolution, the Virgin de los Remedios was selected as patroness of the Spanish party, and was conducted into the capital with much ceremony, dressed in the uniform of a general officer.

P

Her assistance, however, proved unavailing. The Spaniards were beaten, their general was taken prisoner; her sash was torn from her, and her passport signed with an order that she should leave the republic. This last disgrace was spared her, and the Mexicans still pray for rain to the miserable image that could not protect itself against the fury of its foes. A lady, who was astonished at the ugliness of the image, asked the attendant priests how it was that no attempt had been made to improve its appearance, when she was gravely informed that several artists had begun the work, but each one had immediately sickened and died. So the frightful wooden thing remains in all its primitive ugliness, dressed out in satin and pearls, and encased in a large silver maguey.

The favourite saint in some districts seems to be Santa Lucia. When it is deemed desirable to stir up an extra amount of religious enthusiasm, the image of Santa Lucia is carried round to the different villages and country towns, and her arrival is the occasion of general rejoicing. She takes up her abode in the hut of some poor Indian, and thither resort all the peasants of the neighbourhood. Santa Lucia is the patroness of matrimony, and is firmly believed to grant any desired lover to the prayers of her devotees. Such a power would be secretly invoked in most places, but here there is no such bashfulness; and as young men and maidens assemble in great numbers at her festivals, which afford an opportunity for much gaiety and for a large intermixture of people with one another, there can be no doubt that the fête of Santa Lucia does often conduce very materially to establish her reputation.

It may be well now to turn to some of the sterner

scenes of superstition that are witnessed in New Spain. The manifold errors with which popery has encumbered the truths of the gospel, has not been able at all times to soothe men's consciences or to satisfy that inner longing after reconciliation with God which rises in a heart burdened with the conviction of sin. It is one of the deepest wrongs which Romanism has inflicted upon mankind, that instead of pointing the penitent sinner to the cross and bringing him into immediate and personal intercourse with the Son of Man, it thrusts the priesthood between the sinner and the Saviour, and would quiet the conscience by undertaking all its responsibilities, thus reducing the mind to a mere machine under the guidance of an ordained director. As might be expected in every country, there are stronger minds that cannot submit to such leading strings, who feel with overpowering force, of conviction that as their sin is essentially personal and individual, so its guilt must be removed by some personal act, and cannot be committed to the agency of any human deputy. Taught this truth by long experience, Romanism has adroitly availed herself of it to turn such conviction into a channel in which priestly influence may be maintained, whilst the heart is lulled by its own voluntary sufferings into the quiet of a false security. Man's natural disposition is always prone to seek for peace with God through its own action rather than through the blood of a crucified Redeemer, and this propensity has found abundant exercise in the bodily mortification so highly extolled by the Romish church.

In the autumn a season of public penance is proclaimed, and is accompanied by strange ceremonies. The two sexes go to church separately; the women at early morning, the men at night. In the morning service the women kneel for about ten minutes with their arms stretched out in the form of a cross. But when the men's turn comes a far more painful discipline is undergone. The congregation, which is rarely very numerous, first listen to a sermon from some preaching friar, the burden of which is generally an elaborate description of the pains of purgatory and the torments of hell. This over, a penitential chant follows, and suddenly every light in the church is extinguished, save where a carved picture of the crucifixion hangs illuminated with the blaze of many lamps reflected upon it. Then a voice cries out through the church, "My brothers, when Christ was fastened to the pillar by the Jews he was scourged." At these words the bright figure disappears in total darkness, and directly after the sound of lashes may be heard falling upon the bare backs of the assembled penitents. Horrible scenes occasionally ensue, as the excited devotees, each belabouring himself with an iron scourge, work themselves up to a frightful energy, excited as they are by religious enthusiasm and by the gloomy scene by which they are surrounded. Blood flows freely until the preacher, remounting his pulpit, calls upon them to desist, assuring them that God's anger is satisfied, and that no further suffering is required. But it not seldom happens that the priest is unable to control the excitement which he has awakened, and there have been cases in which death has followed upon these self-inflicted torments.

Repulsive as is this ceremony, we deem it inferior in horror to the discipline of the most severe conventual establishments. The order of Santa Theresa is perhaps the strictest in New Spain. Sad and silent is the life passed by the poor women, who, by enrolling themselves in this community, hope to gain a higher place in the favour of the Almighty. A bare board for a couch, and this crossed by bars on the days of special penance, a log of wood for a pillow, a girdle studded with iron nails to tear the flesh, and a cross with similar nails pressed against the bosom—such is the daily mortification of the nuns of Santa Theresa. On particular occasions a crown of thorns is worn by one of their number, who lies prostrate on her face and submits to other tortures. It is sickening to read of such terrible discipline, especially as we remember it is borne in His name who came to alleviate and cure bodily as well as mental suffering. Day after day goes wearily by, and the feeble strength of many a sister declines under the severity of the rule; but in the fevered state of mind engendered by so unnatural a regimen, she longs for further torments, and seems to rise above all earthly things in the suffering to which she subjects her weak, mortal frame. Oh for some voice to calm the fluttering spirit of such an one, and to tell the welcome truth of that surpassing love which embraces every repentant sinner,—to point to the Good Shepherd who, far from exacting such cruel self-infliction, gathers the lambs in his arms and carries them in his bosom.

The sketches we have given may serve to convey some idea of the religious condition of New Spain. In the republic of Mexico the various political changes have produced very little alteration of feeling in religious questions. In the revolution which severed the country from European domination, the great mass of Creole priests took so active a part on the liberal side, that their authority was not weakened by the success of the moment, and they have used it to instil into their people the same principles of intolerance which everywhere accompany the Romish system. There is consequently, at the present day, no more generous feeling towards Protestants in Mexico than in the most bigoted period of Spanish rule, nor are there any indications that may lead us to anticipate the dawn of a better state of things. Amongst the upper classes ignorance or superstition is only varied by indifference to all religious questions; amongst the lower, fanaticism widely prevails, and the cry of heresy will arouse them to the bitterest hostility towards those against whom it has been raised. We mourn over the sad prospects of a country possessed of every natural advantage, but in the dark horizon of whose religious condition there breaks forth no single ray of light. Yet above the policy of rulers and the ignorance of nations, the Lord God omnipotent reigneth, and in his own time and way He may be pleased to reveal his truth to this now benighted land.

To those who know and love the truth nothing can be more painful than to dwell upon the results of such dense darkness as now covers the whole territory of Mexico. It would be difficult to find any country which is acquainted with any portion of Christianity wherein so few hopeful signs can be discerned. The prospect for the future seems little better than the retrospect of the past, and only one sadder condition can be imagined: it is that of those who in more highly favoured lands neglect the salvation which is freely offered them. More tolerable for Sodom and Gomorrah in the day of judgment than for Chorazin and Bethsaida—such were the words of Him whose truth remains unchanged through the course of time. If to possess the light of truth be our blessed privilege, to take heed that we are walking in the light is no less our bounden duty. The fear of the Lord is the beginning of wisdom; the love of Christ is its sum and substance. But to possess, and not to have loved, the truth is the saddest condition of all for the heart of sinful man.

CHAPTER VII.

MINES, COMMERCE, AND CIVIL CONDITION.

Importance of the silver mines—Scenery of the mining districts—Romantic history—Production in former years—Mining under the viceroys—Hindrances—Strange discoveries—Fortunes of the Counts of Valenciana and Regla—Career of Laborde—Prospects of the silver mines—Commerce of Mexico—Restrictions under Spanish rule—Absurd legislation and its cost to the Mexicans—Smuggling—Imposts upon internal trade—Upon papal bulls—Changes consequent upon the revolution—Depressed condition of native manufactures—Civil condition—Courts of law—Prisons—Population—Absence of national feeling—Peonage—The peasantry—National character.

THE silver mines of Mexico are proverbial for their richness. Long before the Spanish occupation of the country great quantities of the precious metals had been extracted, and after the conquest the amount obtained was enormously increased. From 1690 to 1803 the value of the produce is estimated at upwards of £284,000,000 sterling. Yet the mines have never yet been worked with such scientific knowledge or mechanical appliances as to test their actual capacity.

The richest lode of silver in the world, that near Guanaxuato, lies within the stony bosom of the Veta Madre, on the ridge of the Cordillera. Fertile plains and well cultivated fields alternate with the rugged porphyritic rocks whence the silver is drawn. In the rainy seasons torrents sweep down the mountains side, bearing a thick detritus to enrich the valleys. In dry weather the clear liquid sky stretches like a deep blue ocean over waving crops of corn and trees of varied foliage. "The Peruvian tree, the gum tree, the golden flowered *huisache*, amidst whose blossoms scarlet-plumed parrots scream, shade and perfume the roads."* Such is the treasure-house in which lie hid the wealthiest resources of this wealthy land.

In other mining districts, such as that of Catorce, the veins of ore are found in rugged and barren mountains. Far and near there is no sign of verdure, save a few stunted shrubs; no road, save a badly marked track sprinkled with rocks, over which the horses are constantly stumbling; no variety to the unbroken barrenness, save where a straggling patch of sand is covered with thin brushwood. Once and again the scene is chequered by some ravine of startling beauty where a stream fertilizes the soil: then there spring up pepper trees and roses, and clustering vines. Here, too, cypresses raise their lofty heads with a thousand garlánds of parasites waving from their branches.

Many a romantic story might be told of the strange adventures which have befallen those who sought for veins of silver. No fairy tale ever surpassed in its wild extravagance the sudden transitions of fortune in those mountains. Some solitary traveller or a few labouring men would light upon a lode of the precious ore, and then, however remote the spot, large towns would spring up and huge churches rise upon the mountain side. Vast wealth in many instances was rapidly amassed, and then squandered as rapidly in the pursuit of further gain. At one time the generous

* "Vagabond Life in Mexico," p. 236.

soil would yield enormous profits, at another would greedily swallow up all without making a return. What a history of wild excitement, broken hearts and fortunes, and brains turned alike by prosperity or adversity too great to bear, the full narrative of the Mexican silver mines would comprise! That narrative will never now be written. The materials of which it should have been composed have been lost beyond recall.

In an early age it is not easy to gain accurate statistics, and it is not till a comparatively recent period that we are able to compute the enormous amount of silver that was annually obtained from the mines. The most trustworthy authorities assure us that, for fifteen years preceding 1810, the registered coinings averaged nearly 23,000,000 dollars annually, whilst the uncoined produce must have reached at least a million more. From 1810 to 1825, a period of revolution and commercial disturbance, the annual produce of the mines fell to 11,000,000 dollars, but some idea of the immense importance of this source of wealth may be gathered from the statement that this last return of 11,000,000, raised during the worst times, is more than double the highest average produce of any other Spanish colony at the period of its greatest prosperity.

The silver obtained in such vast quantities was the great staple of foreign trade in Mexico, and was exchanged by her with the mother country for European products and manufactures. From 1796 to 1810, about 22,000,000 dollars were exported annually to Spain, and the influence of the mines was hardly less important upon the internal trade. Large towns, as already noted, sprang up in the vicinity of the mines, and called much labour into activity to supply their wants. Agriculture received an impulse in distant regions, as the immediate neighbourhood was rarely capable of maintaining the miners. Luxury with all its minute requirements followed upon the heels of wealth, whilst thousands of mules were needed to work the mines, to drain the shafts, to pulverize the ores, and to carry the silver to the mint. Thus the prosperity of the whole community became largely involved in the successful production of the precious metals, and wide-spread was the ruin that ensued upon the insecurity engendered by the revolutions. This fact may explain the sudden collapse which has befallen a country the most opulent in the world in mineral treasures. A variety of circumstances, to be presently adverted to, have combined to check for the present any adequate realization of the advantages which may yet be derived from the same source.

It would be quite impossible for us to enter upon a history of the mines at a remote period. Soon after the conquest the only object of Spanish colonists was to amass a fortune as quickly as possible, and then return with it to Spain. The custom was at first to grant to individuals a mine and a number of Indians to work it. As the mineral wealth of Mexico became more fully understood a much wiser system was adopted. In theory all mines were the property of the sovereign, but any person might obtain permission to work a vein which he had discovered and "denounced," as it was termed, to the authorities. The only condition with which he was fettered was one to secure that the mine should be worked effectually. Exclusive possession of a certain number of yards was given to the discoverer, and it was only withdrawn upon its being proved that he had not attempted to extract the ore within the time appointed by the royal ordinance. Indeed all the government superintendence seems to have been carried on with good faith, impartiality, and moderation. There were heavy dues to pay, amounting to a tax of 16½ per cent., but there was full scope for individual exertion, and every encouragement was offered to make it successful, a part of the tax being devoted to Avios, or advances made to needy persons in order to assist them in carrying out their operations.

The peculiar location of the veins of silver in Mexico gave a special character to mining adventures in that country. Many of these lay close to the surface, and since they did not require that any large outlay should be incurred in preliminary works, the ores were dug out by men who were glad at once to sell them for ready money. They were accordingly purchased by a class of middle men at the mouth of the mine, who reduced them and extracted the silver. These Rescatadors again sold the bars of silver to the merchant at a rate far below the price at the mint. By the system of Avios above mentioned, and by this facility of immediately disposing of the ores, an impetus was given to mining operations which is quite unparalleled. The great hindrance to the success of the plan arose from the fact that there was only one mint at which the silver could be coined. The expense and risk of its conveyance thither had to be undertaken by the merchants, and considerably reduced the miner's profits.

Other drawbacks there were of less importance, but which still were felt at times. The gunpowder used in blasting the rocks, and the quicksilver employed in amalgamating the silver, were both government monopolies; and, although they were supplied at a fair price, yet in times of scarcity the wealthier miners commonly influenced the governor to give them a supply in preference to their poorer brethren. But these evils, tolerable in times of security, became insurmountable during the revolution. The expense of escorts for the silver from the mine to the mint, and the exactions of the officers who commanded them, quickly reduced the value of the ore to the miner so much, that it no longer repaid the cost of raising it, until first the poorer veins and then even some of the richest were entirely abandoned to the gambusinos, as the class is called, who gain a precarious livelihood by picking over the refuse ores. It was not until the introduction of foreign capital, in 1825, that works on an extensive scale were resumed.

A few examples may serve to illustrate the extraordinary results that were attained in the silver mines of Mexico. At the Veta de la Biscaina, in the district of Real del Monte, Bustamente and Tereros began a level to drain the works, which was not completed until 1762. The former died before the works had been finished, but Tereros, afterwards Count de Regla, obtained a nett profit of £1,041,750 in the first twelve years. Besides two ships of war which he presented to Charles III., one of them of 120 guns, he lent £208,350 to the Spanish court, which was never repaid. The expenses of the works at Regla amounted to £416,700, yet he left immense estates to his children, as well as a huge sum in ready money.

The fortune of Obregon, Count of Valenciana, was yet more astounding. Arriving in Mexico, in 1760, at an early age, he began to work the Valenciana vein, in Guanaxuato, a spot then believed to be destitute of precious ores. The young adventurer had no capital, but friends were induced to make some small advances, and with these he continued his operations. For six years he toiled on, during which his expenses considerably exceeded his profits, but nothing could induce him to abandon his enterprise. In 1767, he persuaded a petty merchant at Rayas, named Otero, to join him, and in the year following success began to crown his labours. As the shaft grew deeper the richer portions of the vein were reached, and for forty years, from 1771, the Valenciana never yielded less to the proprietors than from £80,000 to £124,000 per annum. And there have been years so productive that the nett profit has amounted to £250,000 sterling.

M. Obregon (says Humboldt*) preserved in the midst of immense wealth the same simplicity of manners, and the same frankness of character, for which he was distinguished previous to his success. When he began to work the vein of Guanaxuato, above the ravine of San Xavier, goats were feeding on the very hill which ten years afterwards was covered with a town of seven or eight thousand inhabitants.

The career of Laborde presents still more astonishing fluctuations. He was a French miner who came to Mexico in great poverty, and for some years pursued his occupation with but indifferent success. Suddenly, in the year 1743, he acquired immense wealth from the mines of La Cañada, in the district of Tasco. Superstition and avarice seem to have contended for possession of his heart, and at length divided it between them. He built a church at Tasco, which cost £87,507 sterling; yet he compelled his daughter

* Essai Politique.

to enter a convent that he might leave all his fortune to an only son. Fortune, however, deserted him, and stripped him of the treasures she had conferred. He was reduced to the lowest poverty in working the very same vein whence all his wealth had been derived, and from whence he had drawn annually from 130,000 to 200,000 lbs. troy of silver.

In his distress he was permitted by the archbishop to sell a golden circlet, enriched with diamonds, which he had presented to the church at Tasco. It fetched some £22,000, and with this sum he withdrew to Zacatecas, and began to clear out the famous mine of Quebradillas, which had long been left unworked. In this attempt he again lost almost all his property, and seemed once more to be threatened with beggary.

He set to work, however, with the scanty remnant of his fortune, and lighted upon the vein of La Esperanza. Wealth again poured in upon him, and at his death he had amassed £125,000. The son, for whom he had disinherited his daughter, eventually retired into a monastery, and Laborde's hopes of founding a great name and family were blighted. A more striking instance we shall hardly find of the vanity of this world's treasures.

Most baneful is the influence produced upon the mining population by these fluctuations. The great mass of the working miners refuse regular wages, however high, and insist upon a share in the profits of the enterprise. They pass accordingly from abundance to the extremity of poverty, and their lives give evidence of the recklessness produced by such alternations. When labour becomes a mere gambling speculation we may expect that the passion for hazard, thus whetted, will extend to their amusements. A month's hard toil sometimes scarcely produces enough to live upon, and then again a day's success recompenses all his past privations. The gold thus suddenly acquired is scattered with a lavish hand, and the miner goes back again to work only when his last penny has been lost at play. The same spirit spreads contagiously amongst the other inhabitants of a mining district. "'Will Don B. pay me?' asks one man of business in confidence of another. 'Yes, I think he will; he won 5,000 peros yesterday,' is the kind of reply."*

We can only just allude to the future prospects of the silver mines of Mexico,—a subject of no small interest to many of our fellow countrymen. No general decision can be arrived at on this point, which would not admit of very numerous exceptions. Mines that have proved most prolific in former years have yet failed to return a profit under the superior management of British agents. The enormous expense of conveying machinery to the mines, the absence of any adequate supply of fuel for steam engines, and the obstinacy with which the Mexican labourers are wedded to their old method of working, at times present insuperable obstacles. We regret to add that, in many instances, the Cornish men who were sent out have proved more unmanageable than the natives, and by their misconduct have enhanced the prevailing intolerance of foreigners. At the same time there can be no question that there are immense stores of silver yet unextracted. Rich veins abound which have scarcely been touched, and there seem to be almost inexhaustible resources which only await happier days for their development.

The system of trade enforced under the viceroys was

Froebel, 378.

of the most oppressive character. All commercial intercourse was interdicted with any other than the mother country. "All imports and exports were conveyed in Spanish ships, nor was any vessel permitted to sail for Vera Cruz or Porto Bello, her only two authorized American ports, except from Seville, until the year 1720, when the trade was removed to Cadiz as a more convenient outlet. By the peace of Utrecht, in 1713, Great Britain with the asiento, or contract for the supply of slaves, obtained a direct share in the American trade, by virtue of a permission to send a vessel of 500 tons annually to the fair at Porto Bello. This privilege ceased with the partial hostilities in 1737. But in 1739, on the restoration of peace, licences were granted to vessels, called register ships, which were chartered during the intervals between the usual periods for the departure of the galleons. This was followed, in 1774, by the removal of the interdict upon the intercourse of the colonies with each other; and this again, in 1778, under what is termed a decree of free trade, by which seven of the principal ports of the peninsula were allowed to carry on a direct intercourse with some of the colonies. Up to the period when these modifications were made the colonists were forbidden to trade either with foreigners or with each other's states under any pretext whatever. The penalty of disobedience and detection was death." *

The object of such restrictions was to retain the whole carrying trade in the hands of the Spaniards. A still further effort was made to secure an exclusive market to Spanish manufactures. The cultivation or manufacture of articles that could be procured or made in Spain was forbidden in Mexico. It was illegal to

* Mayer, vol. I. p. 131.

erect factories or to cultivate the vine or the olive. Even some kinds of provisions which could have been more easily obtained at home the Mexicans were compelled to send for across the ocean.

The amount of wasteful expenditure thus occasioned is almost incredible. Through the great influx of the precious metals into the peninsula the people grew idle, and the Spanish manufactories gradually declined. The Spaniards were then obliged to go to other countries for goods to supply their colonies, and this became a source of fresh exactions. It was reckoned that the cost of British goods was raised a hundred per cent. through their having to be brought first to Cadiz and shipped from that port. They had to pay duties on entering and fresh duties when they were embarked for the New World; whilst the merchants who enjoyed the exclusive trade to Mexico could exact any price they pleased to put on their commodities.

The effects of such a system may be easily understood. "The merchants took advantage of the wants of the colonists, and were at one time sparing of their supplies, that the price might be enhanced, and at another they sent goods of inferior quality at a price much above their value, because it was known they must be purchased. It was a standing practice to send out European commodities in such scanty measure as to quicken the competition of purchasers and command an exorbitant profit. In the most flourishing period of the trade from 'Seville the whole amount of shipping employed was less than 28,000 tons, and many of the vessels made no more than annual voyages. A motive on the part of the crown for limiting the supplies was, that the same amount of revenue could be more easily levied, and collected with more certainty and despatch on a small than on a large amount of goods."*

Such a system offered irresistible temptations to smuggling. We accordingly find that an illicit trade was so largely carried on, that at least three-fourths of all commerce was contraband. English, French, Portuguese, and Dutch, all strove to steal away some share of the profits which the Spaniards were so eager to monopolize. The risk was great in consequence of the distance to be traversed and the naval power of Spain at that period. The expense, too, was enormous, as heavy bribes had to be given to the Spanish customhouse officials. From these causes smuggled goods were not much cheaper than others in Mexico; but the colonists had the benefit of a larger supply. At length the evil became so flagrant that a royal company was formed with extraordinary privileges, to drive the smugglers from the market by underselling them. The project failed, and the company itself was at last detected in carrying on, with the Dutch at Curacoa, the very practices which it was pledged to suppress.

To the evils caused by this absurdly restrictive system others were added by the insecurity of the seas. English privateers lurked in the bays and unfrequented inlets of the New World, and dashed out upon any straggling and unsuspecting galleon. The name of Drake was terrible to the Spaniards, from the audacity and success with which he had plundered their vessels in the reign of Elizabeth. His successors were scarcely inferior in courage and daring. Whilst the mother country suffered from these losses to some extent, their chief weight fell upon the colony.

The home trade of Mexico was fettered by similar

* North American Review, vol. XIX. p. 177.

enactments. Royal duties, taxes and tithes, were exacted on every imaginable pretext. Nothing escaped the clutches of the revenue. Every kind of merchandise was subject to a fresh impost every time that it changed hands, and merchants and tradesmen were obliged to give in, on oath, a record of their transactions. A few eggs, a jar of oil, a handful of vegetables, were all included under the *alcabala*, as well as the sale of large estates and mines. Nothing could be more burdensome than these minute and petty exactions. Their tendency was to demoralize the people into a nation of cheats and perjurers.

In addition to the *alcabala*, there were transit duties through the country, under which it has been alleged that European articles were sometimes taxed thirty times before they reached the consumer. The king had his royal fifth of all the gold and silver, and monopolies of all tobacco, gunpowder, salt, and quicksilver. Offices, both civil and religious, were openly sold, and the prices paid for them were of course exacted from the people, in addition to the legal salaries. Every agreement had to be drawn upon stamped paper, some of which cost six dollars a sheet, and formed an engine for considerable extortion in the complicated system of Spanish legislation. Besides these sources of revenue, a poll tax of five dollars was imposed on every native. But the most extraordinary imposition in the whole catalogue of Spanish taxes was that laid upon papal *bulls*.

"These *bulls* were issued every two years, sent over to America from Spain, and sold by the priests under the direction of a commissary appointed to superintend this branch of the revenue. They were of four kinds: —1st. The bull for the living, or Bula de Cruzada, so called because it has some traditionary connection with the bulls of the crusades. It was deemed essential for every person to possess this bull, and its virtues were innumerable. Whoever purchased it might be absolved from all crimes, except heresy, by any priest; and of heresy he could hardly be suspected with this shield to protect him. On fast days he might eat any thing but meat, and on other days he was exempted from many of the rigorous injunctions of the church. Two of these bulls, *if they had been paid for*, communicated double the benefits of one. 2nd. The bull for *eating milk and eggs during Lent*. This was intended only for ecclesiastics, and persons not holding the first, which entitled the possessor to all the advantages of both. 3rd. *The bull of the dead*, Bula de Defuntos, which was indispensable to rescue departed souls from purgatory. It was bought by the relations of a deceased person, as soon as possible after death: and poor people were thrown into agonies of grief and lamentation if they were not able to purchase this passport for the spirit of a relative suffering the miseries of purgatory. 4th. *The bull of composition*, which released persons who had stolen goods from the obligation to restore them to the owner. One slight condition, it is true, was attached to this bull, which was, that the person when stealing had not been moved thereto by any forethought of the virtue of a bull to make the property his own, and his conscience white. Bating this small condition, the bull converted all stolen goods into the true and lawful property of the thief. It had the power, moreover, to correct the moral offences of false weights and measures, tricks and fraud in trade, and in short all those little obliquities of principle and conduct to which swindlers resort to rob honest people of their possessions. 'It assures to the purchaser,' says Depons, 'the absolute property in whatever he may have obtained by modes that ought to have conducted him to the gallows.' The price of these bulls depended on the amount of goods stolen : but it is just to add, that only fifty of them could be taken by the same person in a year."*

The commerce of Mexico has not expanded so much as might have been anticipated since the declaration of independence. The restrictions which we have been describing were removed, indeed some of them had been modified by their Spanish rulers. The trade of the country was opened to the civilized world, and the relations of Mexico with Great Britain in her mining operations naturally attracted some British manufactures to this market. Factories were also established in the country and several branches of trade were carried on successfully, especially the manufacture of cigars, hats, glass, and earthenware.

The country offered unusual advantages for such efforts. Manual labour was cheap, the workmen submissive and skilful at imitation, the country productive of abundant raw materials. Cotton could be raised within its territory. Wool might have been supplied almost indefinitely. The silkworm could have been reared with extraordinary facility. These resources in almost any other region would have called forth and rewarded the energies of a manufacturing population. But the Mexicans are utterly devoid of enterprise, and strangers cannot be induced to settle in a land where property and life are insecure. So great is the suspicion entertained of foreigners, that success would be sure to be attended by the aversion of the people, and would

* North American Review, vol. XIX. pp. 186-7.

probably be followed by pillage in the first popular tumult. And so Mexico only possesses a few coarse manufactures, and imports foreign fabrics in exchange for her precious metals.

The few factories that are in existence are most miserably mismanaged. The interior is more like a prison than the workshop of honest and industrious men. The workmen are treated with extreme severity and subjected to corporal punishment. The truck system, found to be so injurious in England, prevails universally: and tobacco, spirits and food, are furnished by the employer at exorbitant prices. No wonder that the operatives only comprise the most ignorant and worthless portion of the population. Their handiwork is wretched. Leather, paper, cutlery, are all of the worst description, and it is not long since there was only one watchmaker in all Mexico. There is the most obstinate prejudice against any improvement, and the commonest mechanical appliances are almost unknown. We should have thought that their native indolence would have induced the Mexicans to avail themselves of modern inventions designed to save labour, but they will have nothing to do with them. M. Chevalier tells us that even the wheelbarrow is not to be found in Mexico. When some merchants had imported two wheelbarrows to aid in conveying goods from the custom-house the men refused to use them.

The commerce of Mexico labours under some natural disadvantages in consequence of the rapid ascent from the sea coast to the interior, but an efficient government and an industrious people would quickly have overcome these obstacles. Indeed, the Spaniards maintained some admirable roads, but during the various revolutionary outbreaks these have been considerably damaged, and are not yet repaired. This is the case even on the highway between Vera Cruz and the capital. The state of things is much worse in the interior and northern provinces. It was almost impossible to convey to the mines the machinery sent out to work them under the English companies. In many instances paths had to be cut through forests, or shelving planes dug to the beds of the rivers, down which the wagons were let gently on one side, and then dragged up on the other by the united force of the whole party. In the dry atmosphere of the table-land the woodwork of the stoutest carriage wheels snaps upon the slightest strain, and the lazy drivers would at times purposely direct a wagon over some rough place in order to produce such an accident. As neither wheelwrights nor forges are to be met with for leagues in the interior, the whole caravan would then be detained, perhaps some days, until the fracture was repaired.

At present, then, Mexico presents the spectacle of a country on which the greatest natural gifts have been lavished in vain. Although almost three centuries and a half have rolled away since the final subjugation of the country, it is a question whether the land has progressed in any one item of material civilization.

The civil condition of the people is equally unsatisfactory. The Mexican law courts have retained all the procrastinating habits of the old Spanish tribunals. The laws of the country are at present in a most complicated and disorderly condition. Decisions of the most contradictory character have been pronounced, and the legal writers make the darkness yet more oppressive by their lengthy and unmeaning commentaries. The uncertainties, delays, and expenses of a Mexican law suit are proverbial, and have given rise to the maxim, that "a bad compromise is better than a good law suit."

Nor are the glorious uncertainties of the law the only hindrance to justice in Mexico. Bribery is often resorted to. Witnesses are either bought off or intimidated, and the judges themselves are accused of corruption. When such means fail perjury is commonly employed, and an accusation is rebutted by the foulest falsehood. So flagrant are these evils that in many instances notorious criminals are allowed to go unpunished. Rank and position often avail to protect those who have disgraced such advantages. In 1839, a colonel in the army, who was also one of the president's aid-de-camps, was convicted of being the chief of a band of robbers, who infested the high roads and the capital at the very time that their master was living in the palace. In this instance the attorney-general resisted the threats and bribes of the friends of the criminal, and justice took its course: but the prosecutor died shortly afterwards, and it was believed that he had perished through foul means.

The prisons of Mexico are on a level with its law courts. A strong military guard presents the appearance of unusual precautions from without, but within all is clamour and disorder. "Passing through several iron and wood-barred gates you enter a lofty corridor running round a quadrangular courtyard, in the centre of which is a fountain of troubled water. The whole of this area is filled with human beings—the great congress of Mexican crime. Some are stripped and bathing in the fountain; some are fighting in one corner; some are making baskets in another. In one place a crowd is gathered around a witty story-teller, relating the adventures of his rascally life. In another a group is engaged in weaving with a hand-loom. Robbers, murderers, thieves, felons of every description, and vagabonds of every grade and aspect, are crammed within this dismal courtyard, and, almost free from discipline or moral restraint, form a most splendid school of misdemeanor and villany."*

The population of the country, in 1850, was estimated at seven millions and a half. Nearly four millions and a half were Indians, about 1,100,000 whites, 6,600 negroes, and 2,100,000 Mestizos or mixed races. The three original races are the European whites, Mexican Indians, and negroes, and from their intermixture in different degrees, no less than twenty-two different castes are specified, besides the produce of other unions which have no specific name. The children of a white father are called Mulattos if the mother be a negress; Mestizos if she be an Indian; and Creoles if she be a Mestiza. These are the most important distinctions.

The maintenance of these distinct classes has been a leading cause in the misfortunes of the country. There is no amalgamation between the three great races. There is no such thing as national feeling in Mexico. This state of things is mainly due to the period of Spanish government, when the Europeans strove to monopolize the wealth of the country, and in the insecurity which has since prevailed in Mexico there has been no arrival of strangers who might gradually fill up the intervals by which the classes are now separated. At the present day, whites, Creoles, and Indians are as widely alienated from one another as when the independence of the country was pro-

---

* Mayer, vol. II. pp. 150-1.

claimed. Ominous murmurs have been heard from time to time, uttered by the Indians, that they would soon expel the Creoles (as the Creoles had driven out the Europeans), and assume their rightful mastery of the country.

We have already noticed that slavery is abolished by law in Mexico, yet it exists in fact through the system of *peonage*, as it is termed, by which a debtor becomes the slave of his creditor. The recklessness of the Indians is often purposely encouraged by their masters, that they may be thus reduced to actual slavery under an altered name. The actual working of the system will be fully understood through the following illustrations, selected from M. Froebel's narrative.

M. Froebel accompanied a friend, named Don Guillermo, from Chihuahua to Temosachic in search of a fraudulent debtor. Don G. had been accustomed to give the debtor's father credit for a few hundred dollars, and at his death the son brought a letter apparently written by his dying parent, asking him to accord the young man a like indulgence. Don Guillermo willingly granted the request, and goods amounting to a few hundred dollars were delivered. "Three years elapsed, no payment was made, and nothing was heard of the young man; and now his creditor appears suddenly in Temosachic. 'Where does Natividad Andrada live?' asked Don G. of the first person as we rode into the village. 'There is his mother's house,' was the answer. We rode on to the open door, at which a respectable old woman appeared. 'Is Natividad at home?' 'No, sir.' 'Is he in the neighbourhood?' 'He is in the village.' 'Let him be called. I must speak with him.' In two minutes he came. He was a young man of more than middle height, well formed, and with good regular features, on which an irregular life now began to show its traces. 'Natividad,' said Don G., 'as you have not come to me I have been obliged to come to you. Why have I never seen you again in Chihuahua?' 'I was unable to pay, your honour.' 'Can you pay now?' 'No, I am poor, I have nothing.' 'Do you know how much you owe me?' 'Not exactly.' 'Three hundred dollars.' 'It is so, since your honour says so.' 'Cannot you pay me at least a portion of it?' 'I have nothing.' 'Then you must come with me and work for me.' 'I am ready. I believe your honour's demand is just.' 'Then get ready, I cannot wait.' 'I *am* ready, I wear all that I possess.' This consisted of an old straw hat, a coarse cotton shirt, wide unbleached cotton trousers, sandals, and a gay-coloured ragged woollen blanket, with which the poorest man gracefully covers his rags.

"During this conversation, which deeply affected the fate of several persons, we had not got off our horses, and the old woman had not spoken a word. She now burst into tears, and turning to Don G., said, 'Your honour claims your right; but how miserable am I in my old age! He is my only child. But I have long seen that he would not be the comfort of my declining years: he has not followed his father's example. But will not the gentlemen dismount and enter my poor house?' she added, with the politeness which the lowest of the Spanish race never forget. 'Yes,' said Don G., as we entered the small clay hovel, 'your husband was a worthy man. How has his son fallen into so miserable a position?' 'Ah, sir, he has gambled away everything.' 'I should have given him no credit but for the letter of his father. How could he recommend a son whose bad character he must have known?' 'Ah, sir, my husband never wrote that letter; my boy forged it at the instigation of his bad companions.' 'Then it is right that you should be punished,' said Don G. to the young man, 'and you, señora, must comfort yourself.' 'As the lad now is, he can never give your honour any help.' 'I will take charge of him. I will teach him to work and to live like a respectable man; and the time may come when he will return to you an estimable character. You will go with me to Texas,' he then added. 'Wherever your honour pleases.' After a short stay, during which the old woman regaled us with tortillas and frijoles and Natividad took leave of a young woman and kissed a child, we left the place and set out on our return.

"It deserves special notice that this transaction, which did not occupy half an hour, was settled without the interference of any public authority.

"A similar proceeding with regard to another debtor of Don G.'s took place at the Villa de la Concepsion. The second man was just as willing to follow his creditor as a peon, although he looked upon his fate rather differently. 'What do you sigh for man?' he said to his companion in misfortune. 'Regret is of no use. Begin a new life. Does not Don G., a distinguished cavalier, open the door of the world to you? What have you known of the world as yet? Nothing. Now you will get acquainted with it. You will see the United States. You will be a man! You will pay your debtor, and when, after an absence of some years, you go back to your native place, your mother may be dead, but your children will have grown big, and who knows but their father may become alcalde of Temosachic?'

"When we remounted to leave Temosachic, it was extremely painful to me to see that Natividad was obliged to follow us on foot, and in a quick trot to keep up with our horses. But I could make no alteration, and would only watch with surprise how, like a faithful dog, he trotted on, now before and now behind us, and again at our side. Vargus, the other debtor, joined him at the Villa, and though at first his speed was insufficient, he soon taught his legs to move when he saw he must either keep up with our carriage or run the risk of being scalped by some wandering Apaches. This treatment of the two men was assuredly cruel, but it is not thought so in Mexico. An extraordinary rapidity and endurance in running is common to all Mexicans of the lower class."

This long extract gives us an insight into some of the most characteristic features of the Mexicans. The recklessness with which the debt was incurred and its proceeds spent in gambling, despite the debtor's knowledge that he was liable to be reduced to slavery, and the calm, stolid indifference with which he yielded to so terrible a penalty are common elements in the popular character. An Englishman would naturally be disposed to question whether such a servant would not cause more trouble to his master than he was worth; but M. Froebel states that he subsequently travelled over some thousands of miles with these two men, and that they were both distinguished by their perfect goodwill, their untiring activity, and irreproachable honesty. In these instances, however, there may have been some incentive to good conduct in the expectation of regaining their freedom. The commoner result of the system of peonage is that the creditor designedly involves his debtor to an amount that he can never repay, and then retains him as his bondsman for life. Slavery in fact, though not in name, prevails throughout the country districts. The peasantry are in serfdom to the great landowners, and there is little reason for the latter to dread that they will ever be called to account for their treatment of the natives.

The most painful contrasts of wealth and absolute indigence is another marked feature of Mexican society, and, save a few shopkeepers in the larger towns, there is no intermediate class to connect the high and low together.

The national character has been necessarily much modified by such a state of things. The Mexicans rank low in the scale of humanity. One who has travelled much amongst them * describes the people as "treacherous, cunning, indolent, without energy, and cowardly by nature. Inherent instinctive cowardice," he adds, "is rarely met with in any race of men, yet I affirm that in this instance it certainly exists, and is most conspicuous." They have a brutish indifference to death, and a capacity for the endurance of excessive fatigue, qualities which would render them stubborn soldiers in the hands of a good general, but even then they could not be expected to behave more than tolerably well. The national character will, however, be more clearly reflected in the minute details of social life which will form the subject of the next chapter.

* Mr. Ruxton.

CHAPTER VIII.

SOCIAL CONDITION OF MEXICO.

Mexican houses—Quarter of the leperos—Callers—Visits and visitations—Ceremonious politeness—Mode of salutation—"Quite at your disposal"—A doctor's farewell—Indian etiquette — Servants — Their indolence and untidiness — Strange dress of children—Education—Reading—No newspapers—Street cries in Mexico—Mexican market scene—Indian costumes — The fashionable world — Evening promenade—The lepcros, their indolence, rags, etc.,—Frequency of assassination—The head quarters of dirt—Amusements—Dancing and singing — Country towns — Home life in a hacienda—Bull marking—Bull tailing—El Gallo—Duels and bloodshed—Amusements a true test of character—Travelling—Mule caravan—Slight delays—A desert journey—Perils and delights of the way—Insecurity of the roads—News by the way—a Mexican stage coach—Mud—Mexican inns and their landlords—A half-witted traveller—Visitors at a vehta—Crosses on the road side—Jealousy of the government—Ignorance and intolerance—The only remedy.

How shall we attempt to describe every-day life in Mexico? Which shall we begin with among the many items that make up the common existence of the multitude? This is one of the hardest portions of our undertaking. Foreigners for the most part see little of the true home life of the people with whom they sojourn, and those who write for their fellow countrymen do not think it worth while to give details with which every one is familiar.

if you desire to mix in society. Cards are sent round containing the announcement that Mr. and Mrs. —— inform you of their arrival in this city, and put themselves at your disposal in the street of ——. Then come visits of etiquette paid in all the splendour of evening costume. We select the following description of morning callers, given by Madame Calderon:— " Señora B—. Dress of purple velvet, embroidered all over with flowers of white silk, short sleeves, and embroidered corsage: white satin shoes and *bas à jour;* a deep flounce of Mechlin appearing below the velvet dress, which was short. A mantilla of black blonde, fastened by three diamond aigrettes. Diamond earrings of extraordinary size. A diamond necklace of immense value, and beautifully set. A necklace of pear pearls, valued at twenty thousand dollars. A diamond sévigné. A gold chain going three times round the neck and touching the knees. On every finger two diamond rings, like little watches. —No Mexican lady has yet paid me her first morning visit without diamonds. They have few opportunities for displaying their jewels, so that were it not on the occasion of some such morning visit of etiquette the diamonds would lie in their cases wasting their serene rays in darkness."

Callers in Mexico are not got rid of so easily as in countries in which time is esteemed of value. The old Spanish politeness and hospitality, combined with modern Spanish indolence, make these morning visits at times no small burden. They rarely last less than an hour, and sometimes extend over the whole day. Gentlemen visitors look in at all hours, join in any meal which may occur in its course, walk out with you and return home, perhaps to spend the evening, notwithstanding the obvious inconvenience that such habits must at times entail. At the same time the genuine hospitality which can endure such a system must not be overlooked. All agree in testifying to the openhanded liberality with which friends are welcomed to a Mexican table.

Another remnant of Spanish manners is the ceremonious formality with which compliments are passed, and which is pronounced to be " beyond measure tiresome." When a lady calls she is warmly embraced by the mistress of the house, and led to a seat, the person of most consequence being carefully placed on the right side of the sofa: and in strict correctness the following dialogue ensues: "How are you? Are you well?" "At your service, and you?" "Without novelty, at your service." "I am rejoiced, and how are you, señora?" "At your disposal, and you?" "A thousand thanks, and the señor?" "At your service without novelty." This interesting exchange may be kept up with slight variations to any extent, and may be applied to other members of the family. Before taking a seat there will be another contest of politeness. "Pray be seated." "Nay, you pass first, señorita." "No, madam, pray go first." "Well, to oblige you, without further ceremony. I dislike etiquette and compliments." If it be in the morning you should add—"How have you passed the night?" with the usual reply—"In your service." The visit over, both parties again open fire. The lady accompanies her friend to the top of the stairs, another embrace follows, and—"Madam, you know that my house is at your disposal." "A thousand thanks, madam. Mine is at yours, and though useless, know me for your servant, and command me in everything you may desire."

"Adieu, I hope you may pass a good night." When the first landing-place is reached the visitor turns round and goes through a mitigated repetition of the adieus. We suppose that the hostess returns to her drawing-room with a feeling of relief, but custom soon reconciles us to the strangest modes.

It is the fashion that all ladies, married and single alike, should be addressed by their Christian names by both male and female acquaintances. Married ladies add their husband's name to their own maiden one, and are more commonly known by the latter. The invitation to a funeral mass is sent in a printed form, stating that certain relatives of the deceased, who are named, request you to assist at the suffrage of the funeral honours. Time and place are then given. Marriages are announced by a printed note which tells that Señor A. and Anna B. beg to inform you that they have contracted matrimony, and have the honour of offering themselves to your disposal. Englishmen in Mexico often complain of the insincerity of this expression, which is a mere habit, and Mexicans are equally indignant that they have been occasionally taken at their word by foreigners, who have carried off some article which had been placed "at their disposal."

Madame Calderon mentions an absurd mistake she made through ignorance of another Mexican custom. She had been inquiring for servants on her arrival, and had just succeeded in completing her arrangements, when the porter of a lady came with the señora's compliments, *and she had another servant at Madame Calderon's disposal.* The answer returned was that Madame C. was much obliged, but she had just hired a chambermaid. The porter opened his eyes in astonishment at this reply, and said nothing, but on inquiry after his mistress' health he gave answer that she *and the baby* were coming on very well. Then only was it understood that this was the established mode of informing friends of the birth of a child.

This elaborate etiquette appears especially burdensome in a sick room. Imagine your physician as he rises to take his leave. "Madam, (this by the bedside,) I am at your service." "Many thanks, sir." "Madam! (this at the foot of the bed,) know me for your most humble servant." "Good morning, sir." "Madam, (here he stops beside a table,) I kiss your feet." "Sir, I kiss your hand." "Madam, (this near the door,) my poor house and all in it, myself, though useless, included, all I have is yours." "Many thanks, sir." He turns round and opens the door, again turning round as he does so. "Adieu, madam, your servant." "Adieu, sir." He goes out, partly re-opens the door, and puts in his head—"Good morning, madam."

Such ceremony is not confined to the higher classes. Indians when they meet take off their hats to one another, and humbly kiss the hand of any female friend. A drinking bout, which will end in quarrelling and frequently in assassination, is commenced with the same regard to etiquette. Even the poorest persons you meet bow, and wish you "good day," holding their hats in their hands till you have passed. It is thought more polite to say señorita than señora, even to married women, and servants always call their mistress La Niña, the little girl, whatever her age.

The Mexican ladies are loud in their complaints about their servants, who seem to be especially censurable for dirt and idleness; but their mistresses generally neglect the precaution of requiring a character from the place where they were last in service, and it is not thought a reproach to have lived in a dozen families, staying no longer than a month or two in each. This negligence leads, at times, to very serious results, as the worst characters become servants that they may more easily carry out schemes of robbery on an extensive scale. At the root of the idleness of servants is the general indolence engendered by the warmth of the climate and the cheapness of provisions. An old woman, with six children, was hired to wash at twelve dollars a month, but at the end of the first month resigned her post, and soon after used to come with all her family to beg. When asked why she left her place, she answered, "Señorita, if you only knew the pleasure of doing nothing!" Their love of finery is the only stimulant to exertion, but when a girl has earned enough to buy an embroidered garment and a second-hand pair of satin shoes, she will throw up her place and go home to display her wardrobe.

Madame Calderon endeavoured to train up a young girl, twelve years old, as a good servant. The child was taken from her family, who lived by begging, and her instruction in reading and sewing commenced. Once a week she was visited by her mother, a tall, slatternly woman, with long matted hair, and a cigar in her mouth, accompanied by several friends and a tribe of children. The whole party would get some dinner from the housekeeper, and then, all lighting their cigars, would sit and howl in chorus over the unhappy fate of Josefita in having to go to service. After these visits it is needless to say that Josefita was fit for nothing, and used to sit on a mat in the most listless idleness. One day she went to see her mother at home, and, instead of returning, a very dirty note was despatched saying, "she needed to rest herself." Very many of their class deem begging much less degrading than service.

One very disagreeable custom of the women-servants is that of wearing their hair long, uncombed, and always in the way. But, in this respect, they often only follow the example set by their mistress. This habit makes the thought of a female cook exceedingly repulsive. Yet these women have their good qualities: they keep the house clean, though not their own persons, and are the perfection of civility, humble and good-natured to excess. In large families their superintendence devolves on a housekeeper, and the family comfort is almost entirely in her hands. In the roomy dwellings of Mexico a number of men-servants, coachmen, footmen, gardeners, and porters, with wives and children, all find shelter and swell the number of inmates.

The relation of parents and children is one of the pleasing features of Mexican life. In no country are more devoted obedience and respect shown by sons and daughters, even when they are married. In many instances the married children continue to live in the father's house, and unite in perfect harmony. There is very little general society, and such families become all in all to one another, refusing all invitations to travel abroad, and knowing no happiness save where parents and relatives are to be found. There is too much reason to believe that conjugal fidelity is far less strictly observed, and much time is misspent in intrigue and its attendant crimes.

We do not get many glimpses of the children belonging to the upper classes. Occasionally they may be seen accompanying their parents to some religious ceremony, and are frequently as much over-dressed as the lady whose costume was described above. "Long velvet gowns trimmed with blonde, diamond ear-rings, high French caps, befurbelowed with lace and flowers, or turbans with plumes of feathers. Now and then the head-dress of a little thing that could hardly waddle alone might have belonged to an English dowager duchess. Some had extraordinary bonnets, also with feathers and flowers, and as they toddled along top-heavy one would have thought they were little old women, till a glimpse was caught of their lovely little brown faces and black eyes." When plainly and becomingly dressed, with their long black hair uncovered and falling down in plaits, the children are remarkably pretty; and their regular features have a childish beauty which fails, from lack of expression, to be as striking when they grow older. Their complexions are pale and their eyes black or hazel—indeed, beautiful eyes are a drug at Mexico, but good complexions much rarer than diamonds.

Education is at the lowest level in Mexico. Little boys and girls are sometimes sent to a day school held in a large room. The mistress marches up and down in a very inelegant undress, her long hair trailing on the ground behind her back, brought round with a good switch every time she turns. The little ones gather from the lesson as much as they can, or as much as they please, and no more. Sometimes the father gives an occasional lesson to his children, but very little permanent good is effected on such a plan. Nominally the young ladies can all read and write, and manage a little music and sewing, but the greater number are very deficient even in these rudimentary accomplishments, and very few know how to spell.

They seem to have no inclination to learn; the climate disposes them to be idle, and since other girls know no more, they are content. They leave off all lessons at an early age. One lady, on being asked if her daughter went to school, replied, quite shocked, "Oh dear! No! she is past eleven years old." After this age there are very few that read a book through from one year's end to another.

Notwithstanding an ignorance of those modes of occupation which are now common in almost every English cottage, the Mexican lady can yet contrive to make her society agreeable. They are never awkward, often graceful, always self-possessed, and have the French art of conversation on trifles. Yet this elaborate idleness is the source of much evil amongst them. A lax system of morality is traceable to this as one of its causes, that the mind having no other subject of thought dwells much on its own evil inclinations. The freedom of association with their own circle of friends and their fidelity to one another help both to cause and to conceal many breaches of duty. And under a cover of outward decorum, even stricter than that which is observed elsewhere, an amount of licentiousness prevails on which it is most painful to dwell.

There are certain institutions both in Mexico and Central America which are dignified with the name of colleges, and are intended for the instruction of boys. But, with hardly an exception, they are most inadequately supplied with masters, and a really good education can only be had by sending boys abroad. Of course under these circumstances the general ignorance is at once melancholy and profound. Nor are there any of those other elements which, amongst ourselves, so greatly enliven the intelligence of all classes. Though a republic in form, there is no political freedom. So miserable is the condition of party strife that men grow weary of struggles which are rife with blood and plunder, but which are not conducted in behalf of any known political principle. "What is the news?" in Mexico means nothing more than, has any one been recently robbed or murdered? There are no newspapers in our sense of the word; a few pamphlets, filled with vehement personalities and gross abuse, are all that the press throws off. Of literary society there is none. Although there are good shops in Mexico (if they have not been ruined by recent and repeated revolutions), yet commerce is in too primitive a condition and communication is too insecure to afford material for a price-current or a "city article." There is neither a harvest of original thought nor a supply of reliable facts; so men live on in the same routine of daily existence without concern about the outer world.

Whilst mental life thus stagnates, the city is all alive with the activity of animal existence. An extraordinary number of cries begin at dawn and continue till night, uttered by hundreds of discordant voices. You are aroused from sleep by the shrill cry of "Carbon, señor?" pronounced "Carbosin," inviting you to get up and purchase coals. Then comes the grease man, "Mantequilla lard! Lard! at one real and a half!" This somewhat unctuous dainty for a hot climate is followed by the equally alluring cry of "Good salt beef!" announced by the butcher. The woman who buys "kitchen stuff" breaks into the chorus with "Hay cebo-o-o-o-o!" and stops to chatter with your cook, who is next assailed with "Tejocotes por Venas de chile!" by a female who would barter her small fruit for pods of hot pepper.

We must let Madame Calderon portray the rest of the tribe in her own words: "A kind of ambulating pedlar drowns the shrill treble of the Indian cry. He calls aloud upon the public to buy needles, pins, etc. He enters the house, and is quickly surrounded by the women, young and old, offering him the tenth part of what he asks, and which, after much haggling, he accepts. Behind him stands the Indian with his tempting baskets of fruit, of which he calls out all the names, until the cook or housekeeper can resist no longer, and, putting her head over the balustrade, calls him up with his bananas, and oranges, and granaditas, etc. A sharp note of interrogation is heard, indicating something that is hot and must be snapped up quickly before it cools. 'Gorditas de horna caliente!' 'Little fat cakes from the oven, hot!' This is in a female key, sharp and shrill. Follows the mat-seller, 'Who wants mats from Puebla? Mats of five yards!'

"At mid-day the beggars begin to be particularly importunate, and their cries, and prayers, and long recitations, form a running accompaniment to the other noises. Then above all rises the cry of 'Honey cakes!' 'Cheese and honey!' 'Requeson and good honey!' (Requeson being a sort of hard curd, sold in cheeses.) Then come the dulce men, the sellers of sweetmeats, of meringues, which are very good, and of all sorts of candy—'Caramelos de esperma! bocadillo de coco!' Then the lottery men, the messengers of fortune, with 'The last ticket, yet unsold, for half a real!' a tempting announcement to the lazy beggar, who finds it easier to gamble than to work, and who may have that sum hid about his rags.

"Towards evening rises the cry of 'Tortillas de cuajada,' 'Curd cakes,' or 'Do you take nuts?' succeeded by the night cry of ' Chesnuts, hot and roasted!' and by the affectionate venders of ducks, 'Ducks, O my soul, hot ducks!' As the night wears away the voices die off, to resume next morning in fresh vigour."

Perhaps the streets of no city in the world present so diversified a picture as those of Mexico. Every variety of costume, civil and religious, Indian and European, of the city and the country, is intermingled in the crowd. At early morning the lake of Chalco is covered with hundreds of light canoes, in which the Indians are bringing their goods to the markets of the city. The light craft is pushed along over the water by an Indian woman, very slightly dressed, with her long black hair (very different from that of the negro) trailing down her back, on which a little infant is often tied. Piles of fruit of every description, loads of meat, poultry and wild ducks in extraordinary profusion, Indian corn cut in the straw as forage for mules, and other commodities weigh down the frail bark to the water's edge. A quantity of flowers is, in most instances, thrown lightly over the cargo, and adds to the beauty of the scene as the boats glide by in the morning sun. If there be a man on board he rarely performs any more active service than singing some Indian ditty to the music of the banjo or guitar.

We follow them to the market, and a most animated scene is presented to the eye. Indian women in chemises of white and blue striped cotton, men clad some in nothing but a pair of drawers, others in their *sarapes* —a kind of blanket with merely a hole in the centre for the head, and dyed of bright and varied colours. Bronze coloured fellows, with only a cloth around their loins, carrying basins on their heads which match the hue of their own skins. There comes the water-carrier bending beneath the heavy load contained in the large earthen *chochocol* on his back, the whole weight of which hangs on the broad leathern strap across his forehead. There come others with the various dainties we have spoken of in describing the street cries. At intervals women with short petticoats, which, though commonly in rags, are sure to be fringed with a border of lace, and their unstockinged feet thrust into dirty-white satin shoes, invite you to purchase a glass of *atolli*—a drink made of maize and tinged with some bright colour. Up trots a spirited little Mexican horse, on which sits the rancherita, the farmer's wife of Mexico, riding before her husband, whose arm encircles her waist. They are followed by the postman from some country town, laden with parcels, parrots, monkeys, —with everything conceivable except letters.

If it be a *fête* day, the Indian population will appear in all their most gaudy finery, their long hair, rarely disturbed by the comb, now adorned with a wreath of flowers. Among them all the prettiest costume is that of the Pueblana peasant. "A white muslin chemise trimmed with lace around the skirt, neck, and sleeves, which are neatly plaited; a petticoat shorter than the chemise and divided into two colours, the lower part made generally of a scarlet and black stuff—a manufacture of the country—and the upper part of yellow satin, with a satin vest of some bright colour, and covered with gold or silver, open in front and turned back. The hair plaited in two braids behind, and the plaits turned up and fastened together by a diamond ring; long ear-rings, and all sorts of chains and medals and tinkling things worn round the neck. A long, ranged along the street wall and fill the air with their whining. He will only work if the labour be short and the pay immediate: he will always drink and gamble and steal when he can; he is the ready instrument for any crime, and his dagger is equally prompt to avenge another man's quarrel or his own. It is hard to conceive a more fearful type of the corruption of our human nature. To ourselves the wild savage, in his unbridled lust and cruelty, is a less repulsive object than this heartless denizen of a so called civilized community.

It is impossible to describe the condition of the leperos without being suspected of exaggeration. This great mass of vagabonds lead a life of infamy and crime utterly uncontrolled by any law. At times, when their excesses become intolerable, they are suddenly repressed with but little regard to the forms of justice; but in most cases it is quite useless to apply to the police, who are either their accomplices or fear the vengeance of their associates. In 1845, an address was presented to the municipality about certain thieves who exercised their calling in mid-day—the complaint being not so much of the crime itself as of the time chosen for its performance. Assassination is terribly common and causes but little remark. It is fearful to think of the low estimate at which human life is held; a dying lepero will confess a murder with less compunction than the neglect of some superstitious observance. The prevalent immorality, and the passionate jealousy of the Mexicans, most frequently prompt them thus to avenge any fancied wrong, and an assassin is easily hired for a few dollars. Rarely is there a drinking bout in the pulque-shops which does not end in a combat with daggers; and in the majority of cases the bystanders will calmly look on whilst one of the combatants is slain, without interfering to save him. It is quite sickening to dwell on this topic. There are only two ways by which men can be governed: they must either be held in control by a strong established authority, or they must learn, through the influence of the gospel, to govern themselves. In Mexico political freedom has relaxed the bonds of a despotic rule, and the people being without the leaven of truth have fallen into a state of anarchy even more intolerable.

Perhaps a single illustration may serve to convey an impression of the state of things. Madame Calderon mentions that one evening a number of gentlemen were chatting on the balcony of their house, when they observed a movement amongst the people below. A small knot of persons had been laughing and talking together, with occasional disputes and blows. Suddenly a man darted out of the crowd and tried to climb a neighbouring wall, but whilst doing so he was pursued and stabbed in the back. As he fell, the wife of his murderer rushed up and plunged her knife several times into his heart, and then calmly wiped it and restored it to its sheath: the bystanders smiling all the while. Some soldiers coming up at the moment, the assassins were captured red-handed. But this lady, who viewed Mexico in the most favourable light, adds, "No sensation was excited by this, which is an every day occurrence."

It detracts greatly, too, from the poetry with which our fancy would surround the picturesque street-life of Mexico, to learn that the city is "the headquarters of dirt." Men, women and children, revel in undisturbed uncleanliness. The graceful reboso, thrown over the head and falling in folds down the shoulders, is a comely covering to the untidy long hair of the women, and encourages the neglect which it so well conceals. Indolence, the prevalent vice of the country, causes even the wealthier class to receive morning callers in most offensive dishabille; this they deem a privilege which they are loth to surrender; and improvement in this respect has been greatly retarded by repeated convulsions that have overturned society and ruined so many. Indeed, the wealth of which we have spoken is rapidly vanishing, and the massive silver ornaments are passing through the mint to supply their once wealthy owners with the commonest necessaries of daily life.

Smoking is one of the most prevalent habits of Mexico, and no doubt contributes to enhance the natural indolence of the people. Men, women and children, all indulge in the pernicious practice, but of late years it has been discontinued by ladies *in public*. Their presence is not, however, any check to its enjoyment by the male portion of the population, and places of general assembly are enveloped in a cloud. In the theatre every division is wreathed in smoke, not excepting the box of the prompter.

The Spaniards have imported their bull-fights into Mexico, and they are among the principal amusements of the people. All the rabble of leperos and all the fashion of the city assemble to the sight, which is only worthy the brutality of the former. It is quite unnecessary to give any description of the well known conflict, which has been surrounded with a halo of poetry that has had the effect of falsely concealing its repulsive features, but except the personal bravery of the matadors, it does not present a single redeeming quality. It has not even the recommendation so necessary to English ideas of fair play to the goaded animal: however high his courage he is doomed when he enters the ring, and being hemmed in is attacked by a succession of foes until he falls a victim to their strokes.

There are few truer indications of the condition of a people than the character of their amusements, and those of the Mexican populace are not calculated to win our good opinion. Besides the bull-fight, gambling and cock-fighting are favourite recreations. Not far from Mexico is the village of San Augustin de las Cueras, and for the three days of its fête all the city resorts thither and abandons itself to these sports. Mingled in strange confusion the noble and the lepero throng the cock-pits. The president of the state is not ashamed to lend his example to the support of the proceedings or to stake his money with the dirtiest of the crowd; and even well dressed women sanction, by their presence, the cruel sport. At evening the gaming tables are surrounded by an excited mob, fortunes are made and lost, and all the debauchery and despair attendant upon such events ensue. Who would work when a turn of luck may produce more profit than months of labour? It is but fair to add that the fête is conducted with much outward decorum.

Dancing and singing are favourite amusements with the Indians. The dance is graceful but monotonous, and the songs reach the same level of common sense as the negro melodies which have been so popular at home. One would have thought that all sentiment must be choked in addressing a fair one as "My well lined sweet syrup;" but Mexican tenderness survives the shock. The most popular of their dances is called the Palomo, (the Dove,) and it is accompanied by its appropriate song; a translation of which lies before us, but it is really too absurd for insertion.

There are but few distinctive features in the country towns of Mexico; the houses are constructed on the same plan as those described above, but even in the capitals of the smaller states they rarely present any items of comfort. In the neighbourhood of the silver mines immense churches and the palaces of former proprietors testify to the wealth once produced by the mines; but they are now abandoned to decay. On the northern frontier of Mexico progress is checked by the insecurity of the country, for so bitter is the hostility of the Indians that none dare venture beyond the walls of the frontier towns unarmed. All commercial transactions with the United States and the southern provinces are carried on by traders bristling to the teeth with weapons, and the flocks that are turned out to pasture are watched by shepherds with loaded guns, and even at times have been seen feeding under the shelter of artillery.

From an early period after the conquest large tracts in Mexico were assigned to the Spaniards, and these immense estates, termed *haciendas*, are distributed over the country. Many of these are leagues in extent and include large plantations of sugar, indigo, and maize, and vast pasture grounds through which cattle roam by thousands. To the better class of *haciendas* there are attached large and roomy dwellings, with all the necessary buildings for the manufacture of the farm produce: the whole enclosed by a strong wall and shut in by gates strongly barred at night to keep out the Indians. In the days of Mexican prosperity, under the viceroys, these country houses were favourite places of resort. Open house was kept in the true Spanish style of hospitality. The tables groaned beneath the abundance of dishes which were placed upon them. The dishes were then carried round, and a portion of everything placed on the plate of each guest, who consumed it with spoon and fork, table knives being far from common. Pyramids of beautiful flowers adorned the feast, and pulque and ardent spirits were supplied with a too liberal hand.

In strange contrast with the activity of the early settlers, a blight of almost inconceivable indolence and indifference seems to have fallen on most of the country proprietors. Their forefathers used to cut down the trees on their land that the Indians might not idle away their time beneath the shade, but the present generation abandon themselves to the most listless apathy. You may visit a large and splendid estate, on which the proprietor resides, and find it totally abandoned to the feeding of cattle; without the slightest agricultural improvement, not even a plantation of plantains and bananas. In country places bread is unknown, the inhabitants subsisting on tortillas, with oranges and the fruit of coyol palm. M. Froebel visited a *hacienda* where "the host had several thousand cows on the savannas around his habitation, but he had neither milk nor butter. He ordered a cow to be killed the day after our arrival; but as meat will scarcely remain fresh a day in that climate, especially during the rainy season, the eatable parts of the animal were cut into slices to be dried in the air during the intervals between the showers that fell throughout the day. The vultures carried away the best part of it before our eyes, and what remained and was brought to us for dinner the next two or three days was of a *haut goût*, rather too strong for our taste. We tried to supply our table by shooting game, but the cook always ate the breast and left us the bones; and as we were guests of the house we could not complain of this impudence, which seems to be the general fashion."

You arrive at a *hacienda* on your day's journey and inquire for the master of the house; there he lies half asleep in a hammock that swings under a neighbouring tree. He rises to receive your letters of introduction (if you have any) clad in nothing but a loose white shirt that hardly comes down to his knees. The women are at work among the corn or baking tortillas in the kitchen: at either occupation they have the same garb, a loose petticoat that extends from the waist to the knees; all other garments are supplied by a necklace with a large cross hanging from it. Children run about without a vestige of clothing, and if a frock be thrown over them on account of a stranger's presence, in a few minutes they are to be seen wearing it folded on their heads or under their arms. These are not the manners of poor Indian serfs, but of the dons, the country gentlemen and their families.

Evening comes and all the household, guests and servants, gather together in the piazza. Most likely the skin of an ox is brought in, and all sit down to shell the corn that is thrown upon it, and when the process is over some pigs will be introduced to pick up the grains that have fallen as the corn was cleared away. If your host be in a hospitable and cheerful mood a supply of pulque will stimulate the party to tell stories in turn.

After supper all retire to bed. If only a passing stranger you must be content with an ox-hide swung with strings from a frame in the wall of the open piazza. Should there be several occupants of the apartment the ropes will have to be left loose in order to accommodate the number, and your bed will form a deep sack in which you will find yourself curiously doubled up, your heels as high as your head, and your body sinking down in the middle. If you are treated as an intimate friend you will fare yet more strangely. The bed room will be hung round with hammocks occupied by the host and different members of the household, who, as they retire to rest, will light their cigars and smoke till they fall asleep. Frequently during the night you will be aroused by the clicking of flint and steel, as one or another of your associates strikes a light to while away the hours of darkness or lull himself to sleep by the cigar, his constant companion by night and day, at home or abroad, in sorrow or in joy.

With the need for breakfast the work of the women begins. Eternal tortillas serve for every meal throughout the day; they are the bread of Spanish America. At one end of the kitchen stands a griddle, resting on three stones, with a fire burning beneath. The woman goes to a large earthen jar, containing Indian corn steeped in lime-water to remove the husk, and taking a handful works it between a stone plate and stone roller into a thick paste. When sufficiently bruised it is patted flat with the hands and placed on the griddle to bake; when done enough the tortilla is made. The same operation is repeated for every meal. It must be something like living on hot coarse biscuit.

One of the most stirring events at a *hacienda* is the occasion of the Herraderos or bull marking. The thousands of cattle which roam over a large estate are driven down to the *plaza de toros* to be branded with the initials of the owner's name. From far and wide neighbours and Indians assemble to the spectacle, and occupy every spot that commands a good view of the scene, whilst a platform is commonly erected for the master of the *hacienda* and his friends. If it be in the neighbourhood of some large town the most celebrated matadors are invited, and a band of music is commonly added. All come in their smartest costume, and it is regarded as quite a gala day. The scene is a most exciting one. The men who are to be employed in marking the bulls ride about in all the display of deerskin pantaloons, embroidered jackets, and silver buttons. A thousand bulls rend the air with their loud bellowings. They are driven into an enclosure, and from thence, some three or four at a time, are sent on into the *plaza de toros:* then the struggle begins. They stand for a moment eyeing their opponents: some paw the ground and dash fiercely at the horsemen, often wounding them at the first onset; others turn and fly panic-stricken, but all at last share the same fate. The horseman throws his lasso round the bull's thick, shaggy neck, brings him to ground with a jerk; other herdsmen tie the creature's legs, and a man with a hot iron brands the letters on his hide. Some take the burning with stoical indifference, others dash their heads against the ground with helpless rage, and then, on being released, rush off like mad things to rejoin the herd.

The boldness of the actors in these scenes contrasts strongly with the general cowardice of the Mexican character. They receive most severe wounds, yet, unless disabled from riding, fearlessly start off on a new venture, whilst those who are quite unable to cope with the bulls from their wounds or their youth often beg for permission to share in the sport. Much of this is doubtless due to the excitement of the spectacle, and to the fact that so many are looking on to smile approval on the most daring. The Herraderos is a time of general holiday, and feasting and dancing add to its fatigues, which last for several days in succession. As if the branding did not exhaust their thirst for adventure, a bull-fight is commonly added to the catalogue of amusements.

There is another kind of sport called *coléa de toros*, or bull tailing, to which the country farmers are much addicted. A number of animals are collected into a large corral, around which assemble the horsemen exciting and maddening them with cries and blows. When all is ready, one is driven out, and dashes at full speed along the open plain, with all the horsemen in pursuit, the sport being to seize the bull by the tail and throw him down. As the poor goaded creature hears the uproar behind, he redoubles his speed, and as he varies his course it requires a first-rate seat to avoid an accident in the crowd of horsemen. As they tear along in a cloud of dust the bull alone is visible some yards ahead, and when one of the horsemen takes a decided lead, the women shout their vivas and wave their rebosos. At last some one, swifter and stronger than the rest, seizes the bull by the tail, and, wheeling his horse with a sudden plunge on one side, upsets the huge animal, and leaves him rolling and bellowing with fright and pain. Cruel as is this sport, it exhibits the splendid riding of the Mexicans, which is very different from the stiff and stilted fashion of park-riding in the capital. To pursue a bull at full gallop, wheeling with every change of his career, and then suddenly to stop without previously relaxing your speed, in order to lay hold of his tail and jerk him over, requires a strength and a seat in the saddle of no common excellence.

Another country amusement is yet more cruel, and has no redeeming features,—it is called El Gallo. A cock, whose neck has been well greased, is tied alive to a tree, and the horsemen race up to it and try to pluck it so as to break the string. But when one has secured it he is followed by the rest, who endeavour to wrest it from him, and the bird is pulled to pieces in the struggle. The mangled limbs are presented by the horsemen as love tokens to the ladies

This leads us to speak of the most revolting characteristic of Mexican amusements, the duels and bloodshed by which they are commonly accompanied. Such brutal sports as those above described have an inevitable tendency to dull the better feelings of the heart. The deceitfulness of sin, and the subtlety of Satan, are nowhere perhaps more strikingly manifested than in the depraved tastes which are excited under the name of pleasure. All sense of right and wrong becomes perverted when men miscall vengeance by the name of honour, and when the sight of a combat with swords is deemed the fittest spectacle for women, who are ready to reward with their smiles the successful combatant. At a village fête in New Spain a small platform is generally erected upon which the maidens alone dance with great dexterity and grace. Dressed in all their finery they whirl rapidly round without spilling a drop from a glass of water placed upon their heads.

At such seasons the aspirant to a young girl's affections will spring forward and present her with his hat, which she receives without ceasing to dance; and should any rival be disposed to press his claims he will make a similar offering, the etiquette of the country prescribing that the maiden should show no outward signs of preference, but accept any such mark of politeness. The rivalry of the two suitors is commonly settled by an appeal to arms, and the poor girl has frequently to watch the combat in which the man she loves is vanquished, perhaps killed, and has then to hand the guerdon of victory to the conqueror. Such habits harden the hearts of any people, and render the country folk of Central America a strange mixture of cowardice and ferocity.

It is in their pleasures as much as in their serious occupations that the real character of a people may be discerned. In our own country the true bent of a man's taste and feelings is not to be gathered so truly from the labour by which his livelihood is gained as from the pursuits to which he resorts in his leisure moments. The first is often dictated by necessity, the latter arises from his own free choice. What shall we then think of the national character in which such amusements are rife as those we have been describing: where no kind of excitement is so welcome as that which involves the shedding of human blood, and where in the idle moments of pastime, and inflamed by wine and a false code of honour, men engage in deadly strife on the slightest cause.

Of course in such a state of things family feuds are being constantly aroused. Injuries received in fair fight are avenged by stealthy assassination, and the prevailing habit of wearing arms combined with the fiery tempers of those hot regions have their tendency to multiply deeds of blood. As justice so rarely intervenes that no one thinks of applying to her for aid in such matters, it becomes a point of honour that the nearest of kin to the slain should avenge his murder. Until this has been done he can take part in no fray, lest he should fall without having fulfilled his duty to his kinsman; and at a village festival men have been heard to lament their hard fate that they were restrained by such ties from taking their part in some sanguinary quarrel. Of course the avenger becomes in turn obnoxious to the wrath of his victim's family, and so the circle of crime and hatred goes on widening and extending its baneful influence. Painful as it is to dwell upon such a picture, it is well that by thus learning *the facts* that are passing in other lands we should see in them a confirmation of the truths revealed to us in the Bible. The heart of man is "deceitful above all things and desperately wicked," and only by the knowledge of salvation brought home to it by the Holy Ghost, is that heart converted and sanctified, and the evil truly remedied. Civilisation and good laws may restrain the passions and check outward violence, but beneath this restraint the evil lurks and will burst out terribly at times. The grace of God can cleanse the thoughts and constrain men to live not unto themselves but unto Him who died for them and rose again.

All accounts present us with strange pictures of travelling in Mexico. On the northern border a considerable trade was lately carried on between the American States and the town of Chihuahua. Large caravans of wagons, each dragged by five pairs of mules, and accompanied by a large body of muleteers, wagon drivers and others, traverse the vast unpeopled plains that separate Missouri from the Mexican city. The route over which they pass has no well formed roads, no places of accommodation for travellers, and no bazaars from which anything needful can be obtained; so that provision for the whole party, supplies of clothing and every kind of article which may be required by the way, even to spare wheels and axletrees, has to be added to the merchandise, and swells the bulk of the caravan. Where the path is firm, and lack of water or any other cause renders it necessary to press forward, from seventy to eighty miles can be traversed in twenty-four hours, but where the mud is deep the journey becomes painfully tedious. M. Froebel mentions that on one occasion it occupied a fortnight to get twenty-six wagons over a distance of twelve English miles.

A curious scene is presented at the frontier town from which the caravan starts on its journey across the prairies. A number of men are lounging about waiting for employment, like seamen on shore. Hundreds of mules are driven up in herds, and when the required number has been selected they are turned into an enclosure formed by the wagons, which are tied together by ropes at the wheels, one space only being left open for the entrance. Men are stationed with long whips to prevent the mules from creeping under or leaping over the ropes. When all are in the corral, as the enclosure is termed, the muleteers proceed to harness their cattle, most of them being perfectly wild things that have never been broken: and a famous struggle begins.

"The reader may picture to himself two or three hundred wild mules with ten or fifteen men among them, each endeavouring to fling the lasso over the heads of the animals one after another, to force the bit into their mouths, and to lead each to its place before the wagon to which it is to be harnessed. In a caravan of twenty to thirty wagons this first attempt occupies the greater part of the day, leaving no time to get the wagons in motion. The mules well know the lasso, and strive to escape it if possible. They crowd together closely, first on one side and then on the other of the corral, their heads turned to the centre, and hidden as much as possible: others thrust their heads under the wagons or between the wheels to prevent the lasso reaching their necks; while again others are more cunning: they stand stock still as if they were actually holding their necks patiently for the noose, but the expression of their eye fixedly watching the man with the lasso betrays their cunning. The man now whirls the cord in serpentine coils round and round over his head; the noose flies hissing with the precision of an arrow to its mark, whilst the animal stands as if rooted to the spot, but by making a small side motion of its head the lasso misses.

All these stratagems are, however, useless. Whilst the drove rush from side to side of the corral, one mule after another feels the lasso twisted round its neck. Then it tears away rapidly after its companions, dragging with it the man who holds the cord. A second and a third now come to his aid. The hard breathing of the half-strangled mules is heard amidst all the uproar and confusion of the scene. At length the men succeed in drawing the end of the cord between the spokes of a wheel, and the animal is gradually brought nearer and nearer to this point. As soon as it is close to the wheel, the cord is drawn round its body, and again put between the spokes so that the whole body is now brought into a noose. Thereupon the men endeavour to force the bit between its teeth, and just as they seem to have accomplished this, the animal in despair makes a last effort; it throws itself upon the ground, frees its legs from the cord by rolling over, jumps up, and with the noose still tightly drawn round its neck disappears in the thickest of the drove. The chase now begins anew until the animal has a second noose around its neck : half-strangled it is flung on the ground and mastered by forcible means, until the bit is in its mouth and the cord with a second noose fixed round its nostril. Upon this it is let out of the corral, and now begins the attempt to attach and harness it to the wagon ; and considering that in this manner ten mules are put to every carriage, and that this operation goes on at the same time in different parts of the corral, the reader may form an idea of the confusion of the whole scene. When trying to harness them, the animals entangle themselves in the harness, fling themselves on the ground and trample upon and kick one another. Sometimes they break loose and run off with part of the harness, when the Mexicans follow in pursuit mounted on the swiftest horses in the caravan. The mule, with the draught chains clattering at his heels, gallops madly on until the noose is again round its neck, when it is brought in and harnessed anew."

We have not space to quote at its full length M. Froebel's amusing description of the desert journey. When all is ready to start a fresh scene of confusion follows. Some of the mules refuse to stir, others pull in different directions from their companions in the same team, others again tear madly along dragging the wagons with such speed over the rough path as threatens to knock them to pieces. Broken harness has then to be mended, and many other vexatious delays occur. After a day or two things settle into their places, and the journey becomes so monotonous that any excitement would be gladly welcomed.

The caravans are subjected to many perils on their march. Throughout the whole district the native Indian tribes are hostile to Mexicans and Americans alike, and a constant watch has to be maintained or the traders would fall a prey to these cunning foes. When it is plain that the numbers and vigilance of the travellers make it dangerous to attack them openly, the Indians follow them stealthily, carry off everything they can lay their hands on, and try to drive away the mules when unharnessed at the close of the day. To prevent the loss of their mules advantage is taken by the drivers of the well-known fondness which the mule has for the horse. Every caravan is accompanied by a mare with a bell round her neck, called the bell mare, or the mother mare, and the whole drove of mules follow her closely. At night the bell mare is carefully tethered near to the corral, and it is in vain that the Indians endeavour to entice the mules from her; but if they succeed in carrying off the mare herself, they get possession of the whole drove.

Notwithstanding the hardships endured by the way, the necessity for keeping watch in turn through the night, and the necessary absence of most of the advantages of social life, there seems to be a peculiar charm in these expeditions. The discomfort, of course, is greatly augmented in bad weather. A blanket spread on the ground, with a saddle for a pillow, is not a pleasant couch. If you seek refuge under the wagons you probably find yourself lying in a puddle:

whilst the odour of the skins that are stretched over the wagons makes a bed inside them far less tolerable. But in fine weather, the sense of independence, the waving vegetation stretching for leagues all round, the clear dry air, all exert their influence over the mind. And as the caravan winds along its path, marked often by a tall line of sunflowers, the traveller anticipates with regret a return to the restraints of social and civilized life.

In almost all parts of Mexico alike travelling is rendered dangerous from the insecurity of the roads. The ancient hostility between the native Indians and the Europeans or their descendants, seems to have been aggravated rather than allayed by the lapse of years; and the disorganized condition of the country since the period of the revolution has further tended to increase the evil. Even between Vera Cruz and the capital the public diligences could not travel unaccompanied by an escort of soldiers, and their presence often adds but little to the confidence of the passengers, as they would generally be the first to fly from banditti if they were not acting in concert with them. Robbers armed to the teeth have long infested all the highways, and so great is the cowardice of the Mexicans that a single highwayman has been known to plunder a whole party of men well provided with weapons. The country has been now for many years at war either with the Americans on its northern frontier, or torn asunder by civil conflict; and the dissolute soldiery frequently take to the road, and thus supply themselves with booty, their pay being often much in arrears.

It would be difficult to exaggerate the result of this state of things. The common question put by any one you may meet on the road is, "Que novedad hay?"

(Is there anything new?) always having reference to the doings of the robbers. All along the journey from the coast to Mexico the road is marked by wooden crosses, each of which denotes the place where some unfortunate traveller has been murdered. With the nervous excitement so commonly seen in timid people, the conversation in the diligence is usually enlivened by minute particulars of some deed of more than ordinary cruelty, or the driver will every now and then put in his head to inform the passengers that they are approaching a specially dangerous spot.—" Now we are in a very bad place: look to your arms."

The Mexicans very rarely think of resisting, and the passengers have been known to protest in a body when a stranger joined them fully prepared for defence. "One fine morning," says Mr. Ruxton, "I took my seat in the diligencia with a formidable battery of a double-barrelled rifle, a ditto carbine, two brace of pistols, and a blunderbuss. Blank were the faces of my four fellow passengers when I entered thus equipped. They protested, they besought; every one's life would be sacrificed were one of the party to resist. 'Gentlemen,' I said, 'here are arms for you all; better for you to fight than to be killed like a rat.' No; they washed their hands of it; would have nothing to do with gun or pistol. 'Vaya; no es el costumbre' (it is not the custom)." As may be supposed the robbers occasionally catch a Tartar. They stopped the diligence with two English naval officers inside, and ordered the passengers to get out and fall on their faces; a couple of shots through the head was so satisfying a reply that the diligence proceeded without further molestation.

The dangers from the Indians by no means exhaust the discomforts of travelling in Mexico. In the remoter districts the roads are rendered almost impassable in bad weather, and every kind of misery is experienced in striving to force one's way through a muddy path where the mules stick fast beneath their burden. The annals of our army in the Crimean campaign, and the accounts which have reached us of Australian adventure, will have made the minds of most of our readers familiar with the distress which may be thus occasioned. To traverse a muddy road, through a thick forest, where the roots of trees project above the ground across the path; to be rolled over by the mule striking against such an obstacle, with the double chance of being brained against a tree or buried in the mud; or to be under your mule with the consciousness that he is kicking furiously in his efforts to rise again, are not pleasant incidents in a day's journey. Besides, on the narrow mountain tracks, which in many places are the only roads, it is not uncommon to meet, and be stopped by, a long line of mules, and should any accident befall one of the drove, all those behind must wait until matters have been set straight again. Add to this that when, after so miserable a day, the resting-place has at last been reached, it is by no means unusual to find that all forethought for the evening meal has been exercised in vain, and that in the transit the supplies have become mixed in confusion, and are quite spoiled. Even after a long march it is impossible to drink tea which has become mixed with oil, or eat bread and meat which are plentifully sprinkled with gunpowder.

The inns are quite in keeping with the roads. The building generally surrounds a courtyard appropriated to the horses and mules, and contains a number of rooms filthily dirty and without windows or furniture. The courtyard itself, save in the dry season, is deep in mud; and the house is utterly unprovided with any refreshment for travellers. In more remote places the venta or meson, as the inn is termed, is often entirely deserted, and travellers on arriving have to tear down the hoarding with which the entrance to the courtyard has been blocked up to prevent animals from straying into it.

The notion that it is his business and his interest to be civil and obliging never seems to enter into the head of the keeper of a venta. On entering you shout for the landlord, who appears with the key of the granary, and serves out the fodder required for the mules: the traveller is shown into a room with a clay floor, a raised platform of stone in one corner for a bed, and perhaps, as a special luxury, a small deal table. The luggage from the mule's back is put down in your room, and the saddles and harness in that of your muleteer. In answer to demands for meat, eggs, chocolate, or any other ordinary article of food, you will probably be told, "We have none." You may very likely forage through the whole village with little better success. Tortillas and frijoles will probably alone reward your exertions.

In a meson at which the diligence stops you may, perhaps, fare a little better. The conversation with the landlord may take some such form as this. Traveller.—"What is there to eat?" Landlord.—"Ah! my lord, there is nothing here." Traveller.—"Goodness! what a country have we come to." Landlord —"It is true, my lord, it is a very poor country." Traveller.—"But what are we to do, we are dying with hunger?" Landlord.—"Well, if your worships like it, they can have a fowl and frijoles, red peppers and tortillas."* This is a fortunate issue; but you must not venture to ask for too much. An Englishman had the audacity to ask for some water to wash in, and was accommodated with a small quantity in an earthenware saucer: but when he requested a towel, and endeavoured to explain his wishes by using several Spanish words, the indignation of the host could no longer be restrained. "Oh, what a madman is this,—towel, napkin, handkerchief—what on earth does he want? Yes, I see the fellow is half-witted, he wants water, towels, everything." On reading the different stories told of Mexican landlords we are tempted to ask what *is* their business. It is not their business, they say, to supply provisions, nor to furnish you with the means of making yourself comfortable; nor to give any information as to other travellers, or the state of the road; nor, in short, to do anything which a guest is likely to want. We should like to hear their duties defined by themselves.

It is expected that any traveller who may arrive shall be able to eat poached eggs and beans, without the aid of plate, knife, fork, or spoon. The eggs are taken up on a tortilla, and the beans fished out of the dish by the aid of the same instrument. Chocolate is served in a small hickory cup with a rounded bottom, so that like an egg it cannot stand on the table, and you must wind your pocket handkerchief into folds and set the cup in it as a support.

There is another discomfort attending upon a sojourn at the venta of a country town. No sooner is the arrival of a stranger noised abroad, than the courtyard swarms with persons from every shop in the place who come to press their wares upon him. Every kind

* Ruxton, p. 63.

of article for home use or for the road, which the place contains; saddles, bridles, clothing, fruit in every variety, pulque and colinche, are all pressed upon you by the traders who clamour for your custom. Beggars in great number and washerwomen generally swell the throng. When these have taken themselves off, a more respectable body will gather round the door simply to stare at the traveller: indeed this inquisitive curiosity in the Mexicans is most annoying. They will even enter the room, (if they think you are disposed to suffer them,) and pry closely into the baggage, or hang around you to peer over what you are doing.

It is not difficult to convey a generally accurate conception of the country towns of Mexico. Almost without exception they bear the marks of decline, and are inhabited by a population evidently inferior to that which they once contained. Few of these towns are without many deserted houses, and large buildings now unoccupied speak of a prosperity which has passed away. In many instances this is due to the failure of the mines; in others it is the result of civil war or of earthquakes; whilst in others again the insecurity of the country has induced all to depart, save those whom necessity obliged to remain. The unrivalled salubrity of Chihuahua, and its favourable situation for trade, have not been able to counterbalance the effect of these baneful influences. The natural fertility of the country fails to keep down the price of the very simplest provisions. There are but few producers, and customers are scarcer still.

We have already alluded to the insecurity of the country in speaking of the dangers of travelling, but it is not easy to estimate it truly without incurring a suspicion of exaggeration. In the various mining and cattle stations scattered over the country, at a distance from any town, the inhabitants pass the life of those who are holding the territory against a foe. There is hardly a homestead which has not its mournful story of sudden raids of the Indians in which some of the family have been carried off or slain. Sometimes children are stolen and brought up by the natives, so that they have acquired a love for Indian life, and when recovered by their friends have been unable to conform to the habits of civilized life, and have escaped to rejoin the Indian tribe. Smoking ruins, *haciendas* once flourishing now deserted, occasionally a whole family swept away—such are the miseries with which the traveller meets on his journey. As an instance of the height to which the evil has risen, it may be mentioned that at Chihuahua, the great emporium of trade with the United States, it is not safe to take a short walk, even by day, beyond the walls unarmed, and that flocks driven out to pasture are guarded with artillery: whilst so precarious is the life of the shepherds, "that merchants refuse to give the most respectable of them credit, because they may at any moment be murdered by the Indians."

The government, which is powerless to repress these evils, is yet too suspicious of its own subjects to allow them to associate together for mutual defence. Attempts to recover property which had been carried off by soldiers have been reprimanded as meddling with the province of the military powers. Any of the Anglo-Saxon races would demand of their rulers that they should afford them adequate protection, or else would organize a committee for their own safety, as has been done in cases of emergency in California and Australia. But the Spanish American races seem totally devoid of any such energy of character.

We must, however, bring this sketch of the social condition of Mexico to a close. It is impossible to conclude it without a painful feeling of disappointment that a country possessed of such natural advantages, and with all the material elements of prosperity, should yet remain in so sad a plight. To what are we to attribute such a result? Why have not the cultivation of her fertile fields, and the working of her rich mines, ensured to Mexico the same benefits which our own island home has derived from its agricultural and commercial activity? What is it that can have paralyzed the well being of a people on whom with so lavish kindness the gifts of God are strewn? Is there any explanation possible of so terrible an issue? It is not answer enough to attribute the result to the indolence and apathy of the Mexicans; we must search deeper still for the causes of that indolence and apathy.

We believe that it admits of a truthful explanation. The misery of Mexico is due to the intolerance of the Romish priesthood, which has kept the people in gross ignorance and withheld from them the word of life. Fearful of any intellectual movement, lest it should weaken their influence over the popular mind, the Mexican clergy have allowed their flocks to grow up in a state almost as barbarous as that of their Aztec forefathers. A blind and superstitious adherence to the ceremonies of the Romish church, united in many instances with a secret adhesion to their pagan idols, has been accepted as the most desirable frame of mind for the native community; and if the Creoles have had a larger share of mere creature comforts they have remained at nearly the same intellectual level. Without any ennobling or self-denying thought, without any of the stimulus either to sacrifice of self or to exertion of mind, which a knowledge of the Bible is calculated to produce, without any conception of those higher objects for which man was placed upon the earth, no wonder if the Mexicans have sunk to so degraded a condition. Mere material prosperity has never ennobled a nation, nor has intellectual activity and acuteness, without the influence of divine truth,— of this India and China are conspicuous examples. But of all the nations of the earth, perhaps Mexico stands out as the most striking illustration of the powerlessness of mere physical advantages to enrich a country where virtue and religion are unknown.

But whilst we ponder over so mournful a picture, should we not also be led to meditate on our own responsibility in the possession of an open Bible and a pure creed? Who hath made us to differ? and what have we that we have not received? If this precious privilege be ours we must one day answer for the manner in which we have used it. As we look back to the time when the Bible was first made known through the land, we may say, "the Lord hath done great things for us, whereof we are glad:" but when we look into our own hearts, can we praise God that we have found pardon and peace through the blood of his Son? All the superior benefits we enjoy as Englishmen are as nothing compared with those treasures which Jesus purchased for us with his own blood, and which he is ever ready to bestow on all that seek them at his hand. We have a highly elaborated condition of society, we have much active practical benevolence, we have a polished intercourse with our fellow countrymen, and countless elements of civilisation, all which tend to make our earthly life more pleasant and to alleviate many of its ills; but there is danger that amidst such outward improvement we should forget that the heart of man remains unchanged, and that it needs as really and as thoroughly to be converted by the Holy Spirit as does the heart of the most uncivilized and uncouth savage. In spite of the many distinctions between different nations of the earth, all men are divided into two great classes, the saved and the lost. May it be ours, as we have the means, not to rest satisfied until we have received the grace by which we are made " heirs of God, and joint heirs with Christ."

CHAPTER IX.

NATURAL PRODUCTIONS OF MEXICO.

Beauty of Mexican scenery—Banana—Its productiveness—Its preparation and use—Cassava—Maize—Maguey—Pulque—Its preparation—Chocolate—Friar Gage's account of its preparation—Plantations of cocoa—Fruits—Tunas—Pineapples—Columnar cacti—Coyol palm—Flowers—Orchids—Bird-beaked oncidium—Fourcroya longæva—Cochineal—Its cultivation—Locusts—Their destructiveness—Arab account of them—Tortoises—Turtles and their eggs—Alligators—Aboma—Golden-tree snake—Rhinophryne—Axolotl—Buffaloes—Their herds and hunting—Prairie marmot—Their villages and associates—Jaguar—Cougar—Prong-horned antelope—Virginian opossum—Racoon—Black vultures—Their greed and fierceness—Owlets—Quails—Maternal instinct—Parrots: chocollitos—Mocking bird—Curious effects of its song—Humming-birds: Flame-bearer; Sabre-wing; Ruby-throat—The God of nature—Conclusion.

It would require many volumes fully to describe the natural productions of Mexico, as they comprise the choicest gifts conferred on almost every region of the globe. In no country has the munificent hand of the Creator dispersed more lavishly everything that is pleasant to the eye and good for food. Mexico itself is the land of flowers, of stately trees and waving palms and ferns, of clustering vines and blooming cacti. Its shores are laden with the rich vegetation of the tropics; its table-lands, at certain elevations, are smiling in an atmosphere of eternal spring, that nourishes alike many of the fruits of the temperate and tropical zones, and its wide-spreading plains are clothed with forests of oak and pine or carpeted with fields of corn and maize. When the country was first discovered by the Spaniards they found all the choicest productions of the western hemisphere gathered within its boundaries; and since their entrance the kindly soil has welcomed the introduction of almost every European species which ministers to the wants of man. It is hardly an exaggeration to say that in Mexico the most useful and delicious natural productions of the entire globe may now be gathered.

The beauty of Mexican scenery is wonderfully diversified by this variety of vegetation. On the banks of rivers and in every shaded spot beneath the tropical zone a dense mass of foliage meets the eye—it is a sea of intense green. Groves of plantain and cocoa-nut trees, alternate with feathery palms and columnar cacti. Beautiful parasites, such as the vanilla, wave in festoons from the tallest trees and dip their long tendrils down into the water as if to drink and carry life to the trunks that bear them. Huge aloes and prickly pears present an almost impenetrable wall. Magnificent orchids jut out abruptly from the branches of living trees or fasten upon the dead trunks that lie scattered in the forests. Whilst the maguey, the tall bending reeds of the sugar cane, and a multitude of other plants, with their fruits and flowers, diversify the landscape. The woods resound with the loud chatter of birds of gaudy plumage: cardinals, catbirds, macaws, and parrots, flit from tree to tree, or swing upon the boughs. Beautiful little humming birds dart to and fro, or hang poised on murmuring wings at the mouth of some favourite flower. Monkeys with noisy chatter and sudden shrieks chase one another in the branches, or sit demurely watching the passing traveller. Every pool swarms with water-fowl—ducks, cranes and bitterns. The very air seems alive with insects, and at eventide clouds of fire-flies glitter in the twilight. There is, we must admit, a reverse to so fair a picture. Poisonous serpents lurk amidst the long grasses of the forest. Swarms of mosquitoes attack every inch of unprotected skin and irritate the unhappy sufferer almost to madness. And, worse than all, amidst the luxuriant vegetation the deadly malaria takes its rise, whose virulence is so terrible that it decimates the population and has given to Vera Cruz the ill-omened title of "City of the Dead."

From the description we have already given of the character of the Mexicans, our readers will be prepared to learn that full advantage is not taken of these great natural blessings. Jalisco probably enjoys the best situation in point of soil, climate, and communication with the coast, but it is described by Mr. Ruxton as a district "where all tropical productions *might* be cultivated and are not." Yet the list of fruits which are offered for sale in its markets is sufficiently tempting. It comprises oranges, lemons, grapes, chirimoyas, bananas, platanos, plantains, camotes, granaditas, mamayes, tunas, pears, and apples. Cotton, cochineal, and vanilla, as well as every variety of cereal can be raised ; yet most of these species are abandoned to the spontaneous production of nature, and little or no labour is bestowed upon them. To gather such fruits as grow of themselves, to cultivate very imperfectly a small patch of maize or plantains, and to starve when this ill-tended crop fails him, is the habit of the Mexican Indian. How largely his indolence has been fostered by the fertility of his native soil will be seen as we proceed to speak of some individual products.

Foremost amongst the plants which are used for food in Mexico we must place the banana and the plantain. They are as much the staple food of the native population as rice is in India and China. Humboldt questions whether any other kind of plant upon the earth's surface produces so considerable an amount of nourishment as the banana. It is propagated by suckers; and eight or nine months after the sucker is planted the banana begins to come to maturity. The fruit may be gathered in the tenth or eleventh month. When the stem is cut after gathering the fruit, there is generally found among the numerous shoots a scion which has already attained two-thirds of the height of the parent tree, and which bears fruit three months later. So that in a plantation of bananas, it is only necessary to cut down the stems of the ripe fruit, and to dig once or twice a-year about the roots in order to obtain an excellent crop. In the course of a year a plot of ground of a thousand square yards will produce four thousand pounds weight of bananas; whereas it would only have yielded about thirty pounds of corn, or ninety pounds of potatoes. Or as corn contains more nutriment than the banana, the comparative productiveness of the two crops will be more truly estimated from the fact that a piece of ground which, if planted with corn would support two persons, will maintain fifty if planted with bananas. Nothing astonishes Europeans more than the extreme smallness of the extent of cultivated land about huts which contain a numerous family of natives.

The fruit of the banana is consumed in a variety of forms. It is sometimes roasted, sometimes eaten raw.

It is also dried, like figs, in the sun. In this latter form it is very popular with the natives, but Europeans find it hard and indigestible. A sort of farina is also made from it by cutting the green fruit into slices and drying it in the sun, and when it has thus become friable it is reduced to a powder. So productive a plant has had a tendency to encourage indolent habits. In a climate where very little clothing is required, where the heat contributes to enervate the frame, and where nature demands but little sustenance beyond that supplied by vegetable products, the ordinary stimulants to exertion are wanting. With his little plot of ground and his rude hut, the Indian of Mexico was perfectly content, and the Spanish government, which desired to carry off the profits of his increased energy, was frequently urged to arouse the people to further exertions by the destruction of the banana plantations. In many districts of Mexico one man without any fatiguing labour could support an entire family by working two days only in the week.

The same district in which the banana is cultivated produces the jatropha or cassava, from the root of which manioc or tapioca is obtained. There are two species of cassava, the sweet and the bitter. The juice of the latter is poisonous until it has been boiled, when it may be used with impunity. The cultivation of manioc requires more care than that of the banana, and implies a higher degree of civilisation among the people who make use of it. Humboldt remarks that a New Zealander would not have had the patience to wait for so tardy a crop.

It is amusing to read Friar Gage's account of the cassava:—"It hath," he writes, "near forty kinds of leaves, which serve for many uses. For when they be tender they make of them conserves, paper, flax, mantles, mats, shoes, girdles, and cordage. On these leaves grow certain prickles, so strong and sharp that they use them instead of saws. From the root of this tree cometh a juice like unto syrup, which being sodden will become sugar. You may also make of it wine and vinegar. The Indians often become drunk with it. The rind roasted healeth hurts and sores, and from the top boughs issueth a gum which is an excellent antidote against poison."

Superior in importance, at least in Mexico, to any of the plants just described is the culture of maize or Indian corn. At the period of the Spanish conquest this plant was cultivated from the south of Chili as far north as Pennsylvania, and it is still so widely sown throughout Spanish America that when the crop fails a general famine is the result. The maize is too well known in Europe to require any elaborate description; but its fruitfulness in Mexico far surpasses that at which it arrives in the old world. Most of the domestic animals in Mexico are fed upon Indian corn. Fowls, dogs, and mules, all suffer alike when there is a scarcity, and the most terrible results have ensued on its failure in such districts as Guanaxuato, where, at one time, more than 14,000 mules were employed in working the silver mines. No plant varies so much as does the maize in the return which it yields to the husbandman. In some cases it produces fortyfold, in others it rises to three hundred. In warm and damp regions two and even three crops may be raised in a year; the indolent Mexican, however, is generally content with one. Maize is served up to table in a great variety of shapes. The grain is boiled in water or parched, and the flour is made into a nutritious bread, termed tortillas, or employed in the manufacture of a kind of gruel, sweetened with honey or sugar, and called "atolli," of which no less than sixteen varieties are to be met with in the recipe books of Mexican housewives.

The principal injury to the maize crop in Mexico is inflicted by the langosta—a species of locust, which at times descends upon the corn fields in such a swarm that the widest breadth of land which has been sown is entirely stripped in the course of a few hours. The langosta makes a periodical visitation to many districts, but does not generally alight upon the fields which are planted high up upon the mountain sides, and by sowing his seed above the range usually taken by the destroying insect the Indian frequently contrives to escape his ravages.

Any enumeration of the commoner articles of food would be very incomplete which failed to make mention of *pulque*—the national liquor of Mexico. "The maguey (American aloe), *Agava Americana*," says Mr. Ruxton, "is cultivated over an extent of country embracing fifty thousand square miles. In the city of Mexico, alone, the consumption of pulque amounts to the enormous quantity of eleven millions of gallons per annum, and a considerable revenue is derived by the government from its sale. The plant attains maturity in a period varying from eight to fourteen years, when it flowers; and it is during the stage of inflorescence only that the saccharine juice is extracted. The central stem, which encloses the incipient flower, is then cut off near the bottom, and a cavity or basin is discovered, over which the surrounding leaves are drawn close and tied. Into this reservoir the juice distils, which otherwise would have risen to support and nourish the flower. It is removed three or four times during the twenty-four hours, yielding a quantity of liquor varying from a quart to a gallon and a half.

"The juice is extracted by means of a syphon made of a species of gourd, called *acojote*, one end of which is placed in the liquor, the other in the mouth of a person who, by suction, draws up the fluid into the pipe and deposits it in the bowls he has with him for the purpose. It is then placed in earthen jars, and a little old pulque, called the *madre de pulque* (mother of pulque), is added, when it soon ferments, and is immediately ready for use. The fermentation occupies two or three days, and when it ceases the pulque is in fine order. Old pulque has a slightly unpleasant odour, which heathens have likened to the smell of putrid meat; but when fresh it is brisk and sparkling, and the most cooling, refreshing, and delicious drink that ever was invented for thirsty mortal."

No less characteristic is the consumption of chocolate in Mexico. Old Gage waxes quite eloquent as he describes the virtues of this article of food and the various methods in which it was served up two centuries ago:—"The tree which doth bear the cacao is so delicate, and the earth where it doth grow is so extreme hot, that to keep the tree from being consumed by the sun they first plant other trees, which they call *madres del cacao* (mothers of the cacao), and when they are grown up to a good height, fit to shade the cacao trees, then they plant the cacaotals. The fruit doth not grow naked: but many of them are in one great husk, and therein besides every grain is closed up in a white juicy skin, which the women also love to suck off from the cacao, finding it cool, and in the mouth dissolving into water. There are two sorts of cacao, the one is common, which is of a dark colour, inclining towards red, being round and peaked off at the ends. The other is broader, and bigger, and flatter: this is white and is more drying; and this especially more than the other *causeth watchfulness and driveth away sleep*, and, therefore, is not so useful as the ordinary.

"As for the rest of the materials which make up this chocolatical confection there is notable variety. For some put into it black pepper, which is not well approved of by the physicians, because it is so hot and dry; but commonly, instead of this, they put into it long red pepper, called chile, which, though it be hot in the mouth is yet cool and moist in its operation. It is further compounded with white sugar, cinnamon, clove, aniseed, almonds, hazel nuts, orange-flower water, some musk, and as much of achiotte (whatever that may be) as will make it look the colour of a red brick. But how much of each of these may be applied to such a quantity of cacao the several dispositions of men's bodies must be their rule. The ordinary receipt of Antonio Colmenero was this:—To every hundred cacaos two pods of chile, one handful of aniseed and orejuales, and two of the flowers called bainilla (vanilla?) six roses of alexandora, beat to powder, two drachms of cinnamon, of almonds and hazel nuts of each one dozen, of white sugar half a pound, of achiotte enough to give it the colour."

After this elaborate description of a dainty then unknown in England, Friar Gage enters upon the medicinal qualities of some of the above-named ingredients, and descends to particulars which we cannot transfer to these pages. Nor will the greater fastidiousness of modern taste cause our readers the loss of much valuable knowledge; for the worthy friar accounts for the effects produced by the intermixture of hot and cold materials in a way that seems hardly intelligible to himself, and which sounds to us like arrant nonsense. "Now for the making and compounding of this drink I shall set down here the method. The cacao and other ingredients, having first been all of them dried, must be beaten in a mortar of stone. When it is well beaten or incorporated, then with a spoon is taken up some of the paste, which will be almost liquid, and is made into tablets; or without a spoon put into boxes, and when it is cold it will be hard." Then follow further learned discussions on some particles of the chocolate which "do pinguefie and make fat," when it is boiled in water, and which fat is removed. But the strangest paragraph to our modern notions is one in which Gage suggests that we should trade with the Spaniards for it, "not slighting it so much as we and the Hollanders have often done upon the Indian seas; of whom I have heard the Spaniards say, that when we have taken a good prize, a ship laden with cacao, in anger and wrath we have hurled overboard this good commodity, not regarding the worth of it."

The tree which produces the cacao nut is known to botanists by the generic name of theobroma, a Greek word which signifies "food for a god." It seldom rises to a greater height than twenty feet, and has large, oblong and pointed leaves, not unlike those of the hickory. The flowers are small and of a pale red colour, and as these fall off large pods are gradually formed, measuring from four to five inches in length, and turning to a reddish colour as they ripen. Some of the pods will contain as many as fifty nuts. Besides the plantains mentioned in Gage's description as the mothers of the cacao, it is customary to plant an erytheina, or coral tree, by the side of each cacao tree, and as the erytheina grows very rapidly, it after a time affords all the requisite protection from the sun's rays, and the plantain is then cut down. "The coral tree attains to a height of sixty feet, and at the end of March or the beginning of April throws out a multitude of flowers of a bright crimson colour. At this season an extensive plain covered with cacao plantations is a magnificent object. Viewed from a height the far-stretching forests of erytheina present the appearance of being clothed in flames."

Mr. Squier, to whose pages we are indebted for some of these particulars with respect to the cacao tree, furnishes us with further information as to its commercial importance. Before the conquest the nuts were not only extensively used as food, but were also employed as money; and, at the present day, they are found necessary as a medium of exchange for small purchases in all the principal towns of Central America. Two hundred nuts are estimated as equivalent to a dollar.

"The cacao tree is so delicate and so sensitive to exposure that great care is requisite to preserve it during the earlier years of its growth. It commences to bear in seven or eight years, and continues productive for from thirty to fifty years. Capital and time are therefore requisite to start an estate, but once established it is easily enlarged by annual additions. One man it is calculated is able to take care of a thousand trees and harvest their crop. As a consequence cacao estates are more valuable than those of sugar, cotton, indigo, or cochineal. A good plantation, with fair attention, will yield an annual average product of twenty ounces of nuts per tree, which, for one thousand trees, equals twelve hundred pounds. At the usual market price this would give three hundred dollars per annum for each thousand trees and each labourer. An estate is valued at a dollar per tree." *

In speaking of the plants used for food we must not omit to mention the various kinds of beans, which, under the general name of *frijoles*, are universally employed at the tables of the Mexicans. You can hardly sit down to a meal in Mexico, whatever may be its character, without having *frijoles* and *tortillas* placed before you.

Let us turn for a moment to the fruits, the number of which is almost endless. Limes, lemons, oranges, apples, pears, grapes, citrons, tamarinds, tunas or prickly pears, guavas, pines, mangoes, chirimoyas, granaditas, mamays, papayas, zapotes, apricots, jocotes, and many others, are all to be met with in the different parts of Mexico. One of the most widely spread is the tuna, or prickly pear, and around almost every village, and sometimes for a considerable distance along the road side, there are orchards of this fruit, and women pile up large quantities under the trees with the prickles removed ready for eating. The quantity of tunas which a Mexican muleteer will consume is something astounding, a pile of the fruit disappearing with incredible rapidity under their attacks. The fruit is full of juice, very nourishing and wholesome, and particularly grateful after a hot and dusty journey across the table-land. As the traveller rides along he can frequently pluck a delicious tuna hanging over his path, and thus refresh himself without stopping. Gage tell us that in his day the Spaniards used to jest with strangers by

* Squier's Central America.

taking half-a-dozen prickles of the tuna and rubbing them in a napkin, "wherewith a man wiping his mouth to drink, those little prickles stick in his lips, so that they seem to sew them up together, and make him for a while to falter in his speech, till with much rubbing and washing they come off."

Pine apples are common enough in Mexico, and are made into a very delicious preserve. The raw fruit is not so popular, as from its very cold and juicy nature it is thought to be productive of diarrhœa. To correct any such injurious tendency the Mexican housewives cut the pine apple into slices and soak it for half-an-hour in salt and water. The slices are then placed in fresh water, and so served up for desert.

Besides the vegetable products already mentioned there are certain trees and shrubs which contribute to give its special character to Mexican scenery, and which, therefore, must not be passed over in silence. One of the most striking of these is the columnar cactus, or organo, (so called from its resemblance to the pipes of an organ,) which is used as a hedge to enclose the gardens and fields of the Indian villages. The hedge of organo may be called a living vegetable wall, and its only fault is that it requires attention or it will grow too high: as the columns frequently reach to fifteen or twenty feet. A fence of this cactus is formed with very little trouble. Old plants are split up into stumps of a certain length, and these are planted side by side, care being taken not to put them upside down. Instead of remaining a fence of dead timber the plants soon strike root and form a living hedge, through which pigs and poultry cannot force their way.

Another very beautiful feature in the forest of

Mexico is the cocoyol or coyol palm, whose leaves, varying from fifteen to twenty feet in length, bend like gigantic plumes almost to the earth in curves of exquisite grace. "This palm produces a flower nearly a yard in length, golden in colour, which bursts from a pod of richest brown, and is followed by a cluster of nuts, each of the size of a grape shot, from sixty to a hundred in number. The shell is thick, hard, black, and capable of being finely carved and polished. It is frequently worked into rings and other ornaments by the Indians. The kernel resembles wax, but is harder, and rich in oil. It is extracted by crushing the nuts and placing them in vases of water, whence it is skimmed as it rises to the surface."

Frequent reference has been made in the former part of this volume to the flowers with which Mexico abounds, and which were so largely used by the Mexicans before the Spanish conquest. In strange contrast with the terrible human sacrifices offered by the Aztecs were the garlands worn by the officiating priests, and with which their trembling victims were not unfrequently decorated. The native Indians still retain the same passionate fondness for flowers. The laziest of them will cultivate a few bright blossoms around his hut, or, at least, will select a site for his dwelling where flowers spring up abundantly from the soil. We cannot then omit a passing notice of the strange and beautiful tribe of orchids, which gives a special character to much of the tropical vegetation of Mexico, as well as to a large part of the more temperate regions of the table-land.

We have lately become familiar with many of the orchids in this country, and their strange habits, their unusual forms, often at once grotesque and beautiful, their extreme brilliancy of colour, and the great rarity of many of the choicer specimens, invest them with a peculiar interest. Every one now-a-days pays a visit to some of the large flower shows held in town and country, and there beholds some of this noble family of plants, strangely perched upon some fragment of bark or some branch of a tree, and setting all our preconceived notions at defiance by thrusting out its flowers in the direction in which any other plant would strike its roots. Although the orchids are often termed parasites, yet the epithet is not correctly to be applied to them, since they do not draw their sustenance from the trees on which they grow. You may cut off the branch on which a large orchid has established itself and the flower will continue to flourish in entire indifference as to whether its supporter lives or dies.

We wish it were possible for us to convey by our description any adequate idea of the beauty of these flowers. At one time, growing upon the branch of a living tree, at another, springing from the bark of some prostrate giant, they everywhere meet the eye of the traveller through the forests of Mexico. From a knot of bulbous roots there sprout long graceful leaves, often exceeding two feet in length, amidst which bloom the most gorgeous flowers; now rising on an upright stem, as in the family of the epidendra, and now again bending gracefully downwards, as in the long and straggling garlands of the oncidia.

In no quarter of the world do the orchids assume such grotesque and marvellous shapes as in Mexico. There is a strange fellow, called the *Oncidium Ornithorhyncum*, or bird-beaked oncidium, which resembles a swan: the flower itself forming the body, and its stalk the arched, graceful neck of the bird. This exquisite orchid is found in Mechoacan, and throws out groups of beautiful pink flowers of the shape we have mentioned, flowing down from the plant on fine thin stems. It is difficult to conceive a more elegant plant. The blossoms have the scent of fresh hay.

In complete contrast with the bird-beaked oncidium is the *Cyrtochilum Bictoniense*, which has a long spear-like stem adorned with purple or rose-coloured blooms. A very strange and magnificent plant was found in a dark ravine near Jalapa. From the bottom of its bulbs issue flower-stems from one to two feet in length, (its leaves often exceed this size,) and out of these sprout globose yellow flowers. This is named *Barker's Peristeria*. Amongst the more striking examples of the Mexican orchids we may also name the *Epidendrum Aurantiacum*, with its erect masses of golden orange blossoms; the *Lælia Autumnale*, which has large, handsome, and fragrant flowers, and is commonly known as "the Flower of the Saints" in Mexico; and last, but not least curious, the *Mor Pardina*, so called from its strange likeness to a leopard.

Among the more exceptional vegetable productions of the country is one found upon Mount Tanga, in Oaxaca, the *Fourcroya Longæva*. It is a species of gigantic yacca, and belongs to the family of amaryllidacea. Its stem rises fifty feet in height, and above this its flower-spike springs up some forty feet more, the entire length of which is clothed with flowers in as close array as the fox-gloves that abound in our English woods and hedges.

The transition is easy from plants to insects, as a very close relation exists between the vegetable world and two of the most important insects of Mexico. The first of these is the cochineal (*coccus cacti*) one of the most valuable products of the country. When the Spaniards arrived they found the dye obtained from the cochineal already in use among the people, and as an indigenous product of the country it demands a full description at our hands.

The cochineal reaches its perfection only when fed upon certain varieties of the cactus, the *nopal* of the ancient Mexicans. This insect is chiefly cultivated in Oaxaca, where some of the plantations contain fifty or sixty thousand nopals, planted in lines, and all kept down to a level height of four feet, that the insects may be more readily gathered from them.

" The cultivators prefer the more prickly varieties of the plant as affording protection to the cochineal from other insects ; to prevent which from depositing their eggs in the flower or fruit both are carefully cut off. The greatest quantity, however, of cochineal employed in commerce is produced in small nopaleries belonging to Indians of extreme poverty, called nopaleros. They plant their nopaleries in cleared ground, on the slopes of mountains or ravines, two or three leagues distant from their villages; and when properly cleaned, the plants are in a condition to maintain the cochineal in the third year. As a stock the proprietor, in April or May, purchases branches or joints of the tuna de castilla, laden with small cochineal insects recently hatched. These branches, which may be bought in the market of Oaxaca for about half-a-crown the hundred, are kept for twenty days in the interior of their huts, and then exposed to the open air under a shed, where, from their succulency, they continue to live for many months. In August and September the mother cochineal insects, now big with young, are placed in nests made of a species of tillandsia, called taxtle, which are distributed upon the nopals. In about four months the first gathering, yielding twelve for one, may be made, which in the course of the year is succeeded by two more profitable harvests. In colder climates the seeding (semilla) as it is termed, is not placed upon the nopals until October or even December, when it is necessary to shelter the young insects by covering the nopals with rush mats, and the harvests are proportionably later and unproductive. In the immediate vicinity of the town of Oaxaca the nopaleros feed their cochineal insects in the plains from October to April, and at the beginning of the remaining months, during which it rains in the plains, transport them to their plantations of nopals in the neighbouring mountains, where the weather is more favourable."*

The greatest attention is necessary when the insects first begin to deposit their young upon the nopals. The nests or boxes in which the mother insects have been placed are pinned to the leaves of the cactus, and in a few hours, if the weather be favourable, the leaf will be covered with the young insects. The nest must then be removed to another leaf and so on until the whole plantation is swarming with the little creatures. Care must also be taken that too many of the young ones do not fasten upon a single leaf, as in that case they will not come to perfection owing to lack of sufficient nourishment, and the crop will be much deteriorated in value. The seeding cannot be performed successfully during a high wind, and should an unexpected shower come on, or even a heavy dew, it will wash the young from the leaves and destroy an entire crop in a few minutes.

* Kirby and Spence's Entomology.

The most valuable cochineal in the market consists of the dead bodies of the mother insects, gathered after they have done breeding, this is known in the trade as "black cochineal;" the "silver cochineal" is composed of the younger insects.

"If the young escapes injury during the first ten days after it attaches itself to the leaf of the nopal it has a fair chance of reaching perfection. At the end of about twenty days it undergoes its first *muda*, or transformation, and about a month thereafter its second change, with each change slightly shifting its position on the leaf. At the period of the first *muda* the male and female insects are about the same number, but fifteen days before the second change the male grub passes into a chrysalis, with a downy covering. He next spins a fine thread, and letting go his hold on the leaf hangs therefrom for fifteen days more. He then breaks his shell and emerges in the form of a very small fly. As soon as the impregnation is effected he drops from the leaf and dies. The insects remaining are all females, which reach maturity in about ninety days, and then commence to breed. It is left upon the leaf long enough to produce a sufficient quantity of young insects for the second crop, which attach themselves to the same leaves and repeat the changes already described." *

The insect is liable to injury during the operation of gathering it from the leaf, and it is commonly brushed off with a squirrel's tail or just touched with a pointed piece of cane. For hours together the patient Indian women sit beside the same plant, and were not their labour so very cheaply procured it is questionable whether any crop could be raised which

* Squier.

should give a profit on the cost of its production. The insects when collected are killed by throwing them into boiling water or placing them in the ovens of vapour baths.

Whilst the cochineal is so great a source of profit to the Mexican, nothing can be more destructive than the locust of which we have already spoken. Some conception may be formed of the myriads in which this terrible insect at times appears from the statement of Mr. Squier, that he once rode through a column of locusts which was fully ten miles in width. When present in such masses they darken the air as they swarm together in clouds, and in their passage they destroy every green thing before them. A whole forest will become brown with the multitudes that settle upon the trees, and appear as though it had been seared with fire, and the air will be filled with them as thickly as with the falling flakes in a snow storm.

"Their course," writes Mr. Squier, "is always from south to north. They make their first appearance as *saltones* of diminutive size, with red bodies and wingless, when they swarm over the ground like ants. At this time vast numbers of them are killed by the natives, who dig long trenches two or three feet deep and drive the *saltones* into them. Unable to leap out, the trench soon becomes half filled with the young insects, when the earth is shovelled back and they are thus buried and destroyed. They are often driven in this way into the rivers and drowned. Various expedients are resorted to by the owners of plantations to prevent passing columns from alighting. Sulphur is burned in the fields, guns are fired, drums beaten, and every mode of making a noise put in requisition for the purpose. In this mode detached plantations are often saved; but when the columns once alight no device can avail to rescue them from speedy desolation. In a single hour the largest maize fields are stripped of their leaves, and only the stems are left to indicate that they once existed."

The plains of Mexico are not the only region of the world which is liable to the incursions of the locust; their deadly invasions are equally dreaded by the inhabitants of every country which they are wont to visit. So terrible does this insect, which resembles a grasshopper in form, appear in the eyes of the Arabs, that they assert that it has the head of a horse, the eyes of an elephant, the horns of a stag, the chest of a lion, the belly of a scorpion, the neck of a bull, the wings of an eagle, the thighs of a camel, the legs of an ostrich, and the tail of a serpent. This long list of members is intended, we presume, metaphorically to delineate the invincible nature of the plague which they occasion. The same thought is expressed more pithily in the fabled address of the locust to Mahomet. "We are the army of the great God; we produce ninety-nine eggs; if the hundred were completed we should consume the whole earth, and all that is in it."

The other insect plagues of Mexico are the same as those which trouble everywhere the inhabitants of tropical regions. Mosquitoes swarm in the neighbourhood of every piece of water; horrible little fleas, called *chignes*, bury themselves beneath the skin and produce painful ulcers if they be not speedily extracted; and bugs swarm in all the cabins of the natives, as well as in the inns to which the traveller betakes himself.

There is no lack of reptiles in Mexico, and foremost

in importance amongst them are the family of tortoises and turtles. The delicacy of the flesh of turtle was unknown in England two centuries ago, and we doubt not that the aldermen of that period envied the experience of Father Gage as they read his description of so novel a dainty. "We fed," he writes, "for the first week almost upon nothing but tortoise, which seemed likewise to us, that had never before seen it, one of the sea monsters, the shell being so hard as to bear any cart wheel, and in some above two yards broad. When first they were opened we were amazed to see the number of eggs that were in them,—a thousand being the least that we judged to be in some of them. Our Spaniards made with them an excellent broth, with all kinds of spices. The meat seemed rather flesh than sea-fish, which being corned with salt, and hung up two or three days in the air, tasted like veal. Thus our hens, our sheep, our powdered beef, and gammons of bacon, were some days slighted, while with greedy stomachs we fell hard to our sea-veal."

In the different regions of tropical America a great variety of tortoises are found. The whole tribe is remarkable for its tenacity of life. The most severe wounds are frequently endured, and the turtle, when let go, seems to walk off as calmly as if it were uninjured. In the instance of the snapping turtle cases have been recorded in which, when the head was severed from the body, the mouth violently closed upon a stick which was inserted in its jaws; and the heart when taken out was still throbbing, contracting, and expanding, and continued beating until noon of the following day.

The habits of these creatures have been carefully watched and accurately described by Audubon, from whose account we borrow the following vivid portrait of the turtle's behaviour when laying her eggs.

"On nearing the shore, and mostly on fine calm moonlight nights, the turtle raises her head above the water, being still distant thirty or forty yards from the beach, looks around and attentively examines the objects on shore. Should she observe nothing likely to disturb her intended operations, she emits a loud hissing sound, by which such of her enemies as are unaccustomed to it are startled and apt to remove to another place, although unseen by her.

"Should she hear any more noise, or perceive any indication of danger, she instantly sinks and goes off to a distance; but should everything be quiet, she advances slowly towards the beach, crawls over it, her head raised to the full stretch of her neck, and when she has reached a place fitted for her purpose she gazes all around in silence. Finding all well, she proceeds to form a hole in the sand, which she effects by removing it from under her body with her hind flappers, scooping it out with so much dexterity that the sides seldom, if ever, fall in. The sand is raised alternately with each flapper, as with a ladle, until it has accumulated behind her, when, supporting herself with her head and fore-part on the ground, she with a spring from each flapper sends the sand around her, scattering it to the distance of several feet.

"In this manner the hole is dug to the depth of eighteen inches, or sometimes more than two feet. This labour I have seen performed in the short space of nine minutes. The eggs are then deposited one by one in regular layers to the number of one hundred and fifty, or sometimes nearly two hundred. The whole time spent in this operation may be about twenty minutes. She now scrapes the loose sand back over the eggs, and so levels and smooths the surface that few persons on seeing the spot would imagine that anything had been done to it. This accomplished to her mind, she retreats to the water with all possible despatch, leaving the hatching of the eggs to the heat of the sand.

"When a turtle, a loggerhead for example, is in the act of depositing her eggs she will not move, although one should go up to her, or even seat himself on her back: but the moment it is finished off she starts, nor would it be possible for one, unless he were as strong as Hercules, to turn her over and secure her."

Despite all these precautions, however, the turtles are watched at the period of egg-laying, and immense quantities of the eggs are dug up and consumed for a variety of purposes. They form a very delicious food, and even the eggs of those species whose flesh is disagreeable are excellent in flavour. Great numbers are broken up into large vessels, that the oil which they contain may be extracted from them. Indeed from its cradle in the sand to the last day of its existence the turtle is exposed to the assaults of innumerable foes.

The rivers of Mexico abound in crocodiles and alligators, whose huge forms may often be seen lying like logs upon the surface of the water. Few objects in nature are more strangely repulsive than is the appearance of these creatures as they bask in the hot sand, or crawl over one another with an awkward, lazy gait. The alligator will rarely assail a man unless attacked, but when once his fury is aroused nothing can quench it as long as a spark of life remains. Possessing the same tenacity of life with which so many reptiles are endued, a combat with an enraged alligator is a fearful spectacle. Every part of the creature's body may be pierced with wounds before the life can be driven out of it, and all the while the alligator writhes and struggles, snapping its huge jaws with a violence that would crunch a bone in two. Happily for its assailants the reptile cannot move its head with much facility; but let them beware of coming within reach of its tremendous tail, which it lashes from side to side. It can strike a blow with it that would fell an ox. It should be added that the alligator would rather avoid such mortal combat, and only acts in this fashion when no way of escape is left open to it. At night the alligator bellows so loudly as to drown the roar of the wild animals in the forests that skirt the rivers' banks.

A number of lizards, some of them very beautiful, are met with in Mexico; but the different species have not been delineated with scientific accuracy, nor could we undertake in these pages to present a complete list of the different individuals. We must pass over the tynanas, the scorpions, and other unpleasant looking creatures, and can only notice one or two specimens of the snake tribe before we proceed to the animals and birds.

The most celebrated of the snakes of Mexico is the ringed boa, or aboma, which in ancient times was worshipped by the Mexicans, and was propitiated with human sacrifices. In colour this creature is generally of "a rich chocolate-brown, with five dark streaks on the top and sides of the head, a series of large and rather dark rings along the back, and two rows of dark spots on the sides." The mode in which this serpent destroys its prey is not by twisting itself in spiral folds around its victim, but by winding itself, fold over fold, on the same part of the body so as to increase its power of crushing at a single point, and thus to squeeze its prey to death. A violent blow on the tail or chopping it off is the best mode of disabling the monster.

It is not difficult to conceive the superstitious terror with which this powerful snake was regarded by the Mexicans. They had abundant and painful experience of its deadly power, and they might readily be persuaded that some mighty spirit dwelt within its beautiful but terrible form. The Aztec priests were accustomed to charm the abomas, and would handle them with impunity, and even permit them to wind around their bodies; whilst the wondering natives looked on with astonishment and reverence at men who possessed such supernatural powers.

An exquisite member of the family of snakes is the golden tree snake (*Dryiophis Acuminata*). " It is a most lovely species, and of a singular length, looking more like the thong of a gig whip than a living reptile. It lives in trees, and its colours are wonderfully soft and delicate. The general tint is grey, tinged with yellow, and having a golden reflection in certain lights, and being decidedly irridescent in others. The body is profusely covered with minute dottings of black."*

There are many quite harmless individuals of the snake tribe in Mexico, which the natives treat as pets and cherish in their huts. In return for such kindness these reptiles keep the dwellings clear from rats and other destructive vermin.

There are two very singular species of *Batrachia*, or frogs, found in Mexico. The first of these is known

* Wood's Natural History.

as the rhinophryne, (*Rhinophrynus Dorsalis,*) and is a slate-gray coloured frog with a row of yellow spots down the back and scattered on its sides. Its legs are much thicker than in the ordinary frog, and the feet are half-webbed. But the chief peculiarity is in the head, which is rounded and merged into the body, and if cut off could hardly be recognised as belonging to a frog at all. The other creature is the *Axolotl*, whose history and character has furnished abundant occasion of discussion to naturalists. It is supposed to be the tadpole of some large batrachan, but its change into its adult form has not yet been recorded. The axolotl is met with in the lakes near the capital, and is frequently served up to table.

The most important of Mexican, and indeed of North American, quadrupeds is the buffalo. These roam by thousands over the open country, and wander in herds almost as large about the wide domains of a *hacienda*. They are commonly gregarious, but at times a male will separate from the rest and live apart with the chosen object of his affections. When a large number are gathered together their bellowing may be heard, on a calm day, at a distance of at least ten miles. Tremendous battles occasionally take place amongst them. On such occasions they paw the ground in a circle, sometimes ten feet in diameter, lash themselves into a terrible fury, and then rush at one another full tilt with a violence which might almost crack a skull of iron. Strange to say such encounters have never been known to end fatally—the hump so greatly strengthens the spine, and the shaggy hair about the head to some degree weakens the force of the blow. When a large herd is crossing a river the calves will get upon the backs of the old folks and so be ferried over.

As the caravans cross the prairies that lie between Mexico and the United States they come upon buffaloes in incredible numbers. Sometimes for several days in succession they journey incessantly through them, and on taking the teams to water in the evening it is difficult to prevent their becoming intermingled with them. All night long their bellowing is heard around the camp, accompanied by the howling of innumerable wolves, which always follow close upon their heels, and pounce upon any calves that may fall out of the ranks or upon any sick or aged bulls. M. Froebel mentions that on one occasion the herds formed a close line at least eight miles in length, and he estimates that this herd, which surrounded his party for a week while travelling, must have consisted of millions of animals "Further on," he adds, "after passing through this herd, we found the grass of the prairie cropped closely off, to the great inconvenience of our draught animals. The buffaloes had journeyed along, grazing as they went, and for hundreds of miles further south the carcasses of these beasts lay scattered on the plain in such abundance that not a spot was free from the traces of their bones.

"During our journey through the buffalo herd we were of course never in want of flesh meat. In half-an-hour or less an animal could be procured. During the greatest abundance the flesh of cows and of young calves was alone deemed good enough, and of many slain animals we ate only the tongues and the marrow bones. The liver also of young animals is delicious, and the marrow from the leg bones is one of the greatest delicacies. If the reader desire a characteristic picture of good living in the prairie, let him imagine a troop of travellers seated round a fire of buffalo dung, upon which a buffalo marrow bone is being roasted. When it is believed to be sufficiently done, the bone is split open with a hatchet and the marrow is taken out in a lump. In contrast to these delicacies of the wilderness must be placed the flesh of an old bull, which is almost uneatable and obstinately resists all attempts to convert it into anything more digestible than a hank of cord.

"Buffalo hunting was pursued on a small scale by our party. If meat was wanted a man rode forth into the midst of the herd with a six-barrelled revolver. The great mass of buffaloes is divided into herds, and these again into bands, each under the guidance of a single bull. The connection of the whole mass is never quite broken up, though the single bands rove about always following their leader independently in a straight line. The hunter selects one of the animals from a troop and pursues it. Now this part of the herd is set in commotion. All the different troops near immediately begin running in all directions over the plain, always following their leader in a straight line, and leaving their beaten tracks only when compelled to do so. The issue of the chase depends on the horse and the skill of the rider. The horse is kept on the left side of the buffalo, and the huntsman approaches the animal before firing so near as almost to touch its shoulder with his pistol. None but a very unskilful huntsman ever expends his six charges without bringing down the animal. I have never seen resistance on the part of the buffalo, nor any combined defence of an attacked troop. I also observed that the whole herd never took any other notice of an enemy in the midst of them than that the nearest bands moved aside."

The district in which the buffalo is found is also inhabited by a sociable little creature, the prairie marmot, or prairie dog, as it is commonly, but very incorrectly, termed. Nothing can be more barren than the sites which these creatures select for their dwellings. They choose a bare spot with a clayey soil beneath a hard surface, and on this they raise innumerable little cones, each with a mouth, the crater of a small volcano, that forms the entrance to the marmot's abode. These mounds are generally clustered together into what is called a prairie dog village, and they extend in some places over many square miles. They destroy every vestige of vegetation about them, and in consequence the draught cattle of caravans are subjected to serious inconvenience from want of fodder.

The sociable propensities of the prairie marmot are not satisfied by this association with his own species, but he shares his dwelling with others. Poverty makes strange bedfellows; but probably no more curious combination was ever effected than that which is witnessed in a marmot village, whose other inhabitants are rattlesnakes and owls. M. Froebel admits that he had always deemed the notion to be fabulous until he saw it with his own eyes; and he assures us that it is invariably the case—the three friends are always associated together.

"On approaching a marmot village, the real builders of the dwellings are seen everywhere popping their heads curiously but cautiously out of their holes, or sitting upon mounds of earth near the opening, and those who are away from the burrows immediately run home. Suddenly a whistling call is heard, and the animals have all at once disappeared; at the same time little owlets, grey-brown, sprinkled with yellowish white, with soft noiseless plumage, are seen fluttering about from one hole to another. Many fly in to their four-footed companions, whilst others alight at the entrance and sit with a demure look as if keeping watch over the dwellings. The little bird, whose body is not larger than a turtle-dove's, can see perfectly well in broad daylight. It was not till afterwards that I convinced myself of the presence of the third fellow-tenant, nor do I know for a fact whether the rattlesnake is as regular an inhabitant of these marmot holes as the owl. I have frequently seen rattlesnakes basking in the sun before these entrances, and coming out of or going into the holes. The manner in which the snake rewards the hospitality shown to it interested me particularly: it takes upon itself the task of freeing its kind host from a too numerous progeny. Whether it does the same for the owlets, or whether these turn their special attention to the young rattlesnakes, I am unable to say."

The jaguar is the fiercest of all American animals. Equally beautiful and ferocious: his skin is much prized by huntsmen, but it needs no small caution in attacking him, as he does not hesitate when provoked or when excited by hunger to fly at a man. The cougar, the ocelot, and the American black bear, are all much inferior to him in strength and courage, indeed he is equal in fierceness to the dreaded tiger of Bengal. This creature abounds in the tangled forests of Mexico and Central America, and emerging from thence he will assail the cattle or wild horses of the ranchero with the coolest audacity.

The great American naturalist, Mr. Audubon, gives some interesting particulars relating to the jaguar. His practice is to lurk near the watering places frequented by cattle, "When lying in wait at such a spot, this savage beast exhibits great patience and perseverance, remaining for hours crouched down, with head depressed and still as death. But when some luckless animal approaches, its eyes seem to dilate, its hair bristles up, its tail is gently waved backwards and forwards, and all its powerful limbs appear to quiver with excitement. The unsuspecting creature draws near to the dangerous spot; suddenly, with a tremendous leap, the jaguar pounces on him and fastens upon his neck with his terrible teeth, whilst his formidable claws are struck deep into his back and flanks. The poor victim writhes and plunges with pain and fright, and makes violent efforts to shake off his foe, but in a few minutes he is unable longer to struggle and yields with a last despairing cry to his fate. The jaguar begins to devour him while yet alive, and growls and roars over his prey until his hunger is appeased. When he has finished his meal, he sometimes covers the remains of the carcass with sticks, grass, weeds or earth, if not disturbed, so as to conceal it from other predaceous animals and vultures, until he is ready for another banquet. On one occasion a small party of rangers came across one while feeding on a mustang or wild horse. The animal was surrounded by eight or ten hungry wolves, which dared not interfere or approach too near 'the presence.' The rangers gave chase to the jaguar, on which the wolves set up a cry like a pack of hounds and joined in the hunt, which ended before they had gone many yards, the jaguar being shot down as he ran, upon which the wolves went back to the carcass of the horse and finished it.

"The jaguar has been known to follow a man for a

long time. Colonel Hays, whilst alone on a scouting expedition, was followed by one of these animals for a considerable distance. The colonel, who was aware that his footsteps were scented by the animal, having observed him on his trail a little in his rear, had proceeded a good way and thought that the jaguar had left, when, having entered a thicker part of the wood, he heard a stick crack, and being in an Indian country whirled round expecting to face a Wakoe Indian; but instead of a red-skin he saw the jaguar, about half crouched, looking right in his eye, and gently waving his tail. The colonel, although he wished not to discharge his gun, being in the neighbourhood of Indians who might hear the report, now thought it high time to shoot, so he fired and killed him." *

The cougar or puma is also abundant in the more savage regions of the country. This creature is commonly called the lion by the inhabitants of Spanish America; but in courage and ferocity it is very inferior to the African king of the forest. It is only when greatly pressed by hunger that it ventures to meet the face of man. The cougar and the tiger cat, or ocelot, are among the most graceful of the wild animals of North America.

Mexico possesses two species of the deer tribe. The prong-horned antelope is a stately and elegant creature, which wanders in large herds over the Sierra Nevada. Occasionally, when they perceive the huntsman or passing traveller, they will pause in their rapid course, and gaze at him, with their beautiful heads raised proudly erect and their bright large eyes turned full upon him. Then, suddenly seized with the conviction that he is no friend of theirs, they will dash off like

* Audubon's Quadrupeds of North America.

lightning and are lost in the distance. Sometimes the huntsman takes advantage of their curiosity, and by waving his handkerchief, himself remaining quite still, will draw the inquisitive creatures within the range of his rifle, and then send a bullet through the fattest before it has time to fly. Another stratagem is occasionally employed by the Indians. They throw themselves on their backs and kick up their heels in the air with a piece of rag tied to them, when the wondering creatures come up to see what so strange a sight can mean and receive an arrow in their flanks by way of explanation.

The prong-horned antelope roams in large herds of a thousand or more together. Travellers who strike upon their trail frequently mistake it for that of a flock of sheep, and indulge in visions of mutton for the following day, which are of course doomed to disappointment. These vast herds are occasionally seized by an unaccountable panic. The idea seems to lay hold of them that they are in a dangerous position, and off they scamper, not unfrequently in their headlong fright rushing into the very peril they hoped to avoid. On such occasions they have been known to tear down from their inaccessible retreats amongst the mountains into the midst of a caravan that was traversing the valley.

The Virginian or common American deer is also an inhabitant of Mexico, abounding throughout the northern districts. Its dappled coat reminds one of the English fallow deer. The Indians frequently trap the does by imitating the bleat of the fawns, or they light a large fire by night and its blaze attracts them. Large numbers fall a prey to these two simple devices.

Few animals excited more astonishment on its first

discovery than the Virginian opossum, which is also a denizen of Mexico. The strange marsupialia of the Australian continent were still unknown, and hardly any other creature could be compared with this incongruous animal, which, with the head and ears of a pig, was found sometimes hanging on the limb of a tree and occasionally swinging like a monkey by the tail. Around that prehensile appendage a dozen sharp-nosed, sleek-headed young, entwine their own tails and sit upon the mother's back.

"The astonished traveller approaches this extraordinary compound of an animal and touches it cautiously with his stick. Instantly it seems to be struck with some mortal disease: its eyes close, it falls to the ground, ceases to move, and appears to be dead! He turns it on its back and perceives on its stomach a strange, apparently artificial, opening. He puts his fingers into the extraordinary pocket, and lo! another brood of a dozen or more young, scarcely larger than a pea, are hanging in clusters on the teats. In pulling the creature about, in great amazement, he suddenly receives a gripe on the hand—the twinkling of the half-closed eye, and the breathing of the creature evince that it is not dead, and he adds a new term to the vocabulary of his language that of 'playing 'possum.'"

The opossum walks along with a slow, heavy gait. When pursued it does not greatly increase its speed, but takes refuge in a tree, and only as a last resource feigns to be dead. The cunning creature is endowed with an extraordinary number and variety of teeth which enable it to consume every kind of food. Nothing seems to come amiss to it in the way of provision: corn, fruit, birds' eggs, insects, young rabbits, and mice, all find their way into its maw.

This very heterogeneous diet is assimilated into most agreeable flesh ; and the fondness of the negroes for hunting " de 'possum " is stimulated by the hope of a savoury dish not unlike roast pork.

Equally well-known to the slaves on the cotton plantations is another Mexican animal, the racoon. This creature seems to unite something of the bear with the nature of the squirrel, and on account of the formation of its feet it was placed by Linnæus in the ursine family. It has a stout body, a round head with a long tapering nose, bald and movable snout, ears wide, low, and erect, and a long tail marked with alternate bars of black and brown hair. A number of these tails sewn together side by side form the hearth-rugs and mats now so much used in England. The racoon is a frequent pet in Mexico, as it is easily tamed, and causes much amusement by its cunning and pretty ways.

Like the opossum, the racoon is omnivorous, and a great epicure he is withal. Birds' eggs he deems a special delicacy, but he is yet more fond of the eggs of the soft-shelled turtle. His bright eye stealthily watches the mother as she seeks out some retired spot in which to deposit them, and no amount of sand heaped over them can save them from his claws. In confinement the fellow will eat sugar, honey, chesnuts, fish, poultry, in short, almost anything, and he becomes almost frantic when the first two are placed just beyond his reach. No one on the farm knows better where to find the ripest Indian corn, or selects with better judgment the very choicest samples. In the early harvest season he commits sad havoc on the crops, and he, therefore, finds a deadly foe in the planter. He is also an admirable fisherman: and there is a Mexican variety which is called, from its diet, the crab-eating racoon. At low water this creature visits the banks or shore, and drags out oysters and shell-fish from their dwellings and devours them. It is said that occasionally a sturdy bivalve closes on the paw of the racoon, and holds him fast, and he thus falls a victim to the returning tide.

The racoon loves to hide in a hollow tree lying in a well-shaded swamp. Sometimes he drives out other creatures from their nests and appropriates the dwelling as his own. It is a favourite habit with him to roll anything that is offered him under his fore paws. If a mug be given to one, he will place one paw inside it and try to make the other on the outside join its fellow. He is much fiercer than the opossum when hunted down. The one submits without a struggle to his fate, the other fights fiercely with the dogs. His greatest enemy is man. The negroes hunt them with their dogs, sell their skins to the hatter, and put the body into the pot to furnish a delicious meal.

We must notice some of the more remarkable birds of Mexico. Of these a great variety might be named: the lakes of the American continent abound with water birds of the duck tribe and many varieties of waders; the woods are resonant not only with the song of warblers but with the harsh notes of thousands of parrots, macaws, and toucans, whose brilliant plumage hardly compensates, in the estimation of the human inhabitants, for the lack of melody in their notes; humming birds dart through the air, or hang poised at the mouth of the flowers with their murmuring wings; and fierce birds of prey, with greedy gullets and strong wing, wheel across the broad plains or perform the office of scavengers in the streets of the city.

To begin with the latter. Every stranger on arriving at Vera Cruz remarks the number of black vultures—zopilotes as they are called by the people. They are like large carrion crows, and have black feathers, with gray heads, beaks, and feet. Their appearance is far from agreeable as they congregate upon the roofs or fly down to feed upon any carrion that may be lying in the road; but they are useful and are consequently protected by law. These birds afford a curious instance of how long a common error once promulgated will be maintained without an appeal to facts. They were reported to have almost incredible powers of smell, and were thought to be guided by this sense to their prey. From some cause Audubon was induced to question this statement, and he contrived a number of experiments for the purpose of testing its truth. Having procured the skin of a horse, he had it carefully stuffed with clean straw and placed in a conspicuous position. A number of zopilotes at once attacked it, and although they of course failed to find any palatable morsel, yet they hovered about it for some time as being loth to leave so likely-looking a prey. The same birds passed by a dead hog, which had been slightly covered over with bushes, although the putrid body emitted a poisonous odour. These and other experiments eventually proved that it is by his piercing keenness of sight and not by his sense of smell that the black vulture is guided.

Nothing can exceed the rapacity of a flock of these vultures. They fly in troops, wheeling in circles and interlacing the flight of one another, so that twenty of them will cover an area of two miles. Nothing escapes their vision. When prey is seen, down swoops the fortunate observer, and by his rapid flight attracts his nearest companion, who follows him, and then in succession come the whole pack. If the object discovered be a buffalo, lately dead, or some creature whose hide is too tough for their beaks, they hover around it, taking occasional tugs at some more tender spot until they obtain an entrance to the carcass. Then follows a scene of most disgusting voracity; they fall to work like famished cannibals, quarrelling among themselves, driving the weakest from a share in the booty, tearing the flesh from one another's bills, wrestling, snorting to clear their nostrils, hissing at a furious rate, gorging themselves until they are quite stupified, or until the bones are cleared.

Occasionally after such a feast the gluttonous bird is unable to rise from the ground: but he is not therefore an easy prey. A farmer once ran up to one in this condition and seized it in his arms, when the filthy creature disgorged over him such a torrent of filth that he speedily relinquished his hold. Such is the strength of wing of these birds that when hungry they will swoop down upon and carry off lambs but newly born. After a feast they may be seen basking in the trees, spreading out their wings to the breeze to air or cool themselves. Repulsive as they are, these birds are of immense value in so hot a climate and with so indolent a people, as the carrion which they consume would speedily breed pestilential fevers under that burning sun.

No bird is commoner in the fields of Mexico and the Southern Republics than the quail and the Mexican partridge. They are worthy of a passing notice for their peculiar fidelity to their young. When the brood is hatched, the mother leads them forth in search of food, guiding them by her cry, and at times gathering them beneath her wings like a hen. But should a stranger suddenly approach, the parent bird utters a peculiar note of warning as a signal for her little ones to disperse, and then exerts all her artifices to attract and concentrate attention upon herself. Throwing herself in the path, she pretends to be wounded, fluttering along and beating the ground as if with an injured wing, until she has succeeded in misleading the pursuer to a distance that may secure the safety of her progeny, when she disappears to gather them once more around her. Not seldom her own life is the forfeit of her affection. It is impossible to read of this loving maternal instinct without being reminded of Him who would have so sheltered Jerusalem, and of whose people it is said, "He shall cover thee with his feathers, and under his wings shalt thou trust: his truth shall be thy shield and buckler."

Amongst the individuals of the parrot tribe there is a small green species called "chocollitos," which are great favourites with the inhabitants. They soon become very tame and will assemble round the dinner table, which in fine weather is commonly placed in the open air, receiving any sweets offered them and contending for the largest pieces. "They are in general of an amiable disposition," says M. Froebel. "This temperament was shown in a touching manner by a sad catastrophe that carried away one of the little creatures. Being forsaken by his mate, when he understood the whole extent of his misfortune, and after he had made the last unsuccessful attempt to bring back his faithless companion, the unhappy creature, heartbroken by his wrongs, took his lonely seat on the perch on which he had passed happier nights closely pressed to the side of his partner, refused to eat and drink, and one morning was found dead on the floor below."

M. Froebel relates a curious story of the fate that befell some others of the chocollitos. A tame deer was kept in the court-yard, and at dinner time was occasionally furnished with pieces of meat. In this way it is supposed he acquired a taste for animal food; for one day he was seen to seize one of the little birds, and before rescue was possible he devoured it alive. From this time forward the deer turned savage, feeding on parrots, ducks and chickens, until he had to be destroyed.

Of the songsters of this vast region none can rival the mocking bird either in beauty of melody or variety of note. Its plumage is tame compared with many of the denizens of the tropics, but its elegance and lithesomeness betoken the intelligence that belongs to this extraordinary bird. It would be difficult to find a winged creature with so diversified a domicile as the mocking bird. Though naturally shy he will build his nest near to human dwellings, in a cedar or holly bush, in a solitary thorn, or in a dense wood. Berries and a variety of winged insects afford him food. Every neighbour who lives near his home supplies him with a lesson for imitation. By day and night equally he trills his song, and when he is surrounded by a whole chorus of songsters his voice rises higher and higher above them all, until they are subdued to a jealous silence; and then, as though proud of his victory, the little bird will take his station on the top of a low thorn, and pour forth his sounding medley with redoubled energy.

The mocking bird may be reared in confinement, and is fed on Indian corn, finely chopped meat, with fruit and berries. If he seems dull or indisposed a few spiders thrown to him are found to remove the symptoms of disease. Unlike the nightingale he loses little of his energy in a domesticated state. " When he commences his career of song," says Wilson, "it is impossible to stand by uninterested. He whistles for the dog; Cæsar starts up, wags his tail, and runs to meet his master. He squeaks out like a hurt chicken; and the hen hurries about with hanging wing and bristled feathers, to protect its injured brood. The barking of the dog, the mewing of the cat, the creaking of a passing wheel-barrow, follow with great truth and rapidity. He repeats the tune taught him by his master, though of considerable length, fully and faithfully. He runs over the quiverings of the canary, and the clear whistlings of the Virginia nightingale or red-bird, with such superior execution and effect, that the mortified songsters feel their own inferiority, and become altogether silent; while he seems to triumph in their defeat by redoubling his exertions. In short there seems hardly any limit to his imitative powers."

It may be supposed that curious results sometimes follow on the exercise of these peculiar talents. The woodlark fancies that it hears the cry of its mate, and rushes wildly about to find her: the smaller birds dive in terror into the thicket to avoid an imaginary bald eagle, whose scream they hear close to them: and the sportsman sets off ardently in the pursuit of game which is perhaps not within miles of him, deceived by the imitation of its cry. Nothing can be more incongruous than the occasional effect of this bird's excessive fondness for variety. The beautiful song of the thrush is suddenly interspersed with the crowing of cocks or screaming of swallows, and then instead of returning to the original melody diverges to the plaintive notes of the robin, or the shrill reiteration of the whip-poor-will.

Love for his young renders the mocking bird full of courage. "Neither cat, dog, animal nor man, can approach the nest without being attacked." No sooner does a cat make its appearance than it is assailed until it beats a retreat. But its special enmity is reserved for the black snake, the most insidious foe of its young: on perceiving its approach the bird darts at it, aiming with its beak at the snake's head, which is the most vulnerable part, and despite all the reptile's pretended powers of fascination it rarely escapes without being killed, unless it is very large, and even then it is generally glad to escape from the fury of this noble bird.

The ravines, termed "barrancas," which are common in the volcanic regions abound in owls, a family of king-fishers remarkable for the brilliancy of their plumage, and a very beautiful creature called, from its haunts, the guarda-barranca, it is of a light greenish-blue, with two long feathers in its tail; several specimens of this bird are to be seen at the British Museum. There is also no want of large game. Cassowaries of different kinds, as big as a small turkey, and very delicate for the table, are to be met with in abundance. Froebel shot a small kind of eagle, "or rather harpy, carrying one of the large green parrots, called lora, in its claws. It was a bird of the proudest appearance, of the most ferocious valour, and of an incredible tenacity of life. With the exception of the long feathers of the wing and tail, which were of a dark bluish-grey, the whole bird was of the purest white. Its head was large and broad like that of an owl, with long feathers in the neck, which gave the bird a most savage aspect. Its eyes were very large, with yellow iris; and the indomitable courage in their expression only died away with the extinction of life."

But the pride of all the winged inhabitants of Mexico and Central America are the humming-birds. The broad savannas, the fields, the orchards, the gardens, and the deepest recesses of the forest are all enlivened by the presence of these beauteous little creatures, of whom more than forty varieties have been discovered in this portion of the continent. Even the mountainous districts in which the veins of metal are worked are not without some members of this family. Gould remarks, that where the precious ores abound the humming-birds are unusually brilliant and glittering. Of their lustrous colour it is impossible to give any adequate description, they must be seen to be appreciated, and even the beautifully preserved specimens that have been exhibited in this country convey but a faint impression of their dazzling appearance, as they sparkle beneath the rays of a tropical sun. Many of their names have been suggested by their resemblance to the brightest and gaudiest things of earth. The flame-bearers, the caciques, the tyrian-tail, the coquettes, the sabre-wings, the satellites, blue-breast, purple-throat, ruby-throat, star-throat, the azure-crowns, the garnet, the sparkling-tail, and the violet-ear, are titles which indicate the varied characteristics of these extraordinary birds. There is a peculiar metallic lustre on their feathers, the colours of which, in many instances, are blended together in strong contrast, so that the living creature in motion seems to be powdered with the dust of precious stones. But we must proceed to speak of one or two individuals more particularly.

There is the rufous flame-bearer (*Selasphorous Rufus*), a bird of exquisite beauty with a gorgeous ruff gleaming like a magic carbuncle. With all the energy of joyous life it darts from flower to flower, poising itself in the air as it extracts the drop of honey, or carries off a minute insect from the petals. Like all its race, this flame-bearer is very quarrelsome. When the female is sitting should any one approach its nest it will dart out angrily, burning like a coal of brilliant fire, and uttering a most peculiar reverberating bleat. So sharp is the cry that the stranger will search on the ground for its author, never dreaming that it proceeds from the little bird: which will mount high into the air, and then descend rapidly with more noise than it would seem possible that so small a creature could produce.

Another strictly Mexican species is D. Latter's sabre-wing, notable for the superb dark-blue markings on its back. It is the boldest of the humming-birds, and will drive away every bird that ventures to enter its territory. All day long it may be seen near to one favourite shrub, sucking the blossoms one by one, (the Mexicans call it *Suce-fleurs-royal*), and never leaving the same tree, which it permits no one else to approach. It is only seen during two months in the year, when it frequents the forests of Jalapa.

The vicinity of Vera Paz is haunted by the Princess Helena's Coquette, which exhibits, perhaps, a more extraordinary combination than can be found in any other species. Picture to yourself a fairy elf with wide spread wings, a broad crest of green, its throat surrounded by a frill of darker feathers, and these again guarded by a collar, rufous gold in colour, and pointed with sharp spikes, behind which spreads out a tail of a golden orange hue; its beak pointed like a needle, and three long, black feathers as fine as hair springing from and hanging down on each side of its head; a most comical creature, as beautiful as strange.

We will conclude our notice of the humming-birds with an extract from Audubon on the ruby-throat, (*Trochilus Colubris*), which admirably describes the mode of breeding and general habits of the whole family. "No sooner has the returning sun again introduced the vernal season, and caused millions of plants to expand their leaves and blossoms to his genial beams, than the little humming-bird is seen advancing on fairy wings, carefully visiting every open flower-cup, and, like a curious florist, removing from each the injurious insects which would otherwise ere long cause their beauteous petals to droop and decay. Poised in the air, it is observed peeping cautiously and with sparkling eye into their innermost recesses, while the ethereal motion of its pinions, so rapid and so light, appear to fan and cool the flower without injuring its fragile texture, and produce a delightful murmuring sound well adapted for lulling the insects to repose. This then is the moment for the humming-bird to secure them. Its long delicate bill enters the cup of the flower, and the protruded double-tubed tongue, delicately sensitive, and imbued with a glutinous saliva, touches each insect in succession, and draws it from its lurking-place to be instantly swallowed. All this is done in a moment, and the bird as it leaves the flower sips so small a portion of its liquid honey that the theft, we may suppose, is looked on with grateful feeling by the flower, which is thus kindly relieved from the attacks of her destroyers.

"I wish it were in my power to impart to you, kind reader, the pleasures which I have felt whilst watching the movements and viewing the manifestation of feelings displayed by a single pair of these most favourite little creatures, when engaged in the demonstration of their love to each other: how the male swells his plumage and throat, and dancing on the wing whirls round the delicate female: how quickly he dives towards a flower and returns with a loaded bill, which he offers to her, to whom alone he feels desirous of being united: how full of ecstasy he seems to be when his caresses are kindly received: how his little wings fan her as they fan the flowers, and he transfers to her bill the insect and the honey which he has procured with a view to please her: how after their union the courage and care of the male are redoubled: how he even dares to attack the tyrant flycatcher, hurries the blue-bird and the martin to their boxes, and how on sounding pinions he returns joyously to the side of his lovely mate. Reader, all these proofs of his sincerity, fidelity, and courage, with which the male assures his mate of the care he will take of her while sitting on the nest may be seen, but cannot be portrayed.

"Where," adds Audubon, "is the person who, on seeing this lovely creature moving on humming winglets through the air, suspended as if by magic in it, flitting from one flower to another with motions as graceful as they are light and airy, pursuing its course over our extensive continent, and yielding new delights wherever it is seen;—where is the person, I ask of you, kind reader, who on observing this glittering fragment of the rainbow, would not pause, admire, and instantly turn his mind with reverence toward the Almighty Creator, the wonders of whose hand we at every step discover, and of whose sublime conceptions we everywhere observe the manifestations in his admirable system of creation?"

As we read of these most striking natural productions of Mexico, we may join with the psalmist and exclaim, "O Lord, how manifold are thy works! in wisdom hast thou made them all; the earth is full of thy riches," Each living creature, down to the meanest, is found to fulfil its own designed part in the economy of God, and those who, like the zopilote, are most repulsive to our notions have yet a value and use in their appointed offices.

> "These are thy glorious works, Parent of good,
> Almighty, thine this universal frame,
> Thus wondrous fair; thyself how wondrous then!
> Unspeakable, who sitt'st above these heavens
> To us invisible, or dimly seen
> In these thy lowest works; yet these declare
> Thy goodness beyond thought and power divine."

As the poet hints, this is the right use of the study of nature, that it should lead us to seek after the God who made it. We ought to "rise from nature up to nature's God." Sun, moon, and stars, in their courses, and nature in its order, teach that there is a God; but the Bible alone teaches that there is a Mediator between God and men, a Saviour through whom all that believe are justified. As we read the accounts of his works, we may learn that God is wise and good; but as we feel our own sinfulness, we must go to the Scriptures and learn that he is Love. Nature tells us that there is a God, but it does not bring us near to him, it does not enlighten us as to the mode in which we may find acceptance with him. Most perilous is it to be content with the knowledge of God revealed in his works without studying the revelation he has given us in his word. There only we learn that he has appointed a way by which we may be reconciled to him, and that his surpassing love has devised a salvation such as man's heart could never have conceived. Oh let it be our concern that this free salvation be made our own, and that we are safe in an unreserved reliance on his promise—"Him that cometh to me I will in no wise cast out." Yielding to this gracious invitation we may look beyond the grave for a world whose glories "eye hath seen, nor ear heard, neither have entered into the heart of man the things which God hath prepared for them that love him."

INDEX.

ABOMA, the, 308.
Acapulco, port of, 6, 8.
Acehedo, 123.
Acojote, 291.
Acolhuans, the, 30.
Agava Americana, 290.
Aguilar, Geronimo de, 66.
Alaman, Don Lucas, 173.
Alameda, the, 17, 255.
Alasanza, 121.
Alcabala, the, 228.
Alderete, 102.
Allende, 146.
Alligators, 307, *et seq.*
Alvarado, 3; left in charge of Mexico, 88; violence of, its results, 89; 101.
Alvarado, Alonzo, 118, *et seq.*
Alvarado, Gonzales, 118, *et seq.*
"Alvarado's Leap," 94.
Alvarez, Gen., 186.
American aloe, 290.
American deer, 317.
Amusements, 259, *et seq.*; country, 265, *et seq.*
Anahuac, plateau, 4.
Andrade, Juan, 172.
Angostura, Gorge of, 185.
Antelope, the prong-horned, 316, *et seq.*
Apaches, the, 26, 137.
Apodaca, 158; designs of, 161.
Arredondo, 159.
Athens of Anahuac, 32.
Audiencia, the, 117, *et seq.*
Audubon, quoted, 305, *et seq.*; 314, *et seq.*; 321, 329, *et seq.*
Augustine I., 165.
Avios, 220.
Axolotl, the, 310.
Ayuntamiento, the, 136.
Aztecs, the, 40, *et seq.*; government and laws, 41, *et seq.*; taxes, 43; means of communication, army, 44; literature, picture-writing, 45; religious system, 52, *et seq.*; rise against the Spaniards, 80, *et seq.*; defeated, 101, *et seq.*; victory of, 103; siege and capture of their city, 104, *et seq.* (*See* Mexico).
Azunza, 141.

BANANA, the, 287.
Banco de Avio, the, 173.
Barker's Peristeria, 299.
Barradas, Gen., 178.
Barragan, Gen. Miguel, 171.
Barrancas, 326.
Bataller, 145.
Batrachia, the, 309, *et seq.*
Baudin, Admiral, 183.
Beggars, 242, 256.
Berenguer de Marquina, 141.
Birdbeaked oncidium, 298.
Birds, 320.
Birth of a child, mode of informing of, 245.
Boa, the ringed, 308.
Bolanos mine, discovery of, 131.
Bonaparte, Joseph, 144.
Branciforte, 140.
Bravo, Don Leonardo, death of, 153.
Bravo, flight of, 156, 165; vice-president, 169.
Bravos, the two, 151.
Brigantines, thirteen, transport of, across the mountains, 97.
Buffalo, the, 310, *et seq.*
Bula de Cruzada, 228.
Bula de Defuntos, 229.
Bull-fights, 259.

Bull-marking, 265.
Bulls, papal, taxes on, 228.
Bustamente, 170; administration of, 172; resigns office, 175; re-elected president, 182; unpopular, 184, 221.

CACAO, the, 291, *et seq.*
Cactus, the, 296.
Calderon, bridge of, 149;
Calderon, Madame, quoted, 243, *et seq.*; 252, 258.
California, Lower, 27, 185.
Calleja, his cruelty, 148, 151.
Callers, 243.
Camanches, 26.
Camino de Oaxaca, 177.
Caravans, 270.
Casa-Mata, act of, 166.
Cassava, the, 288.
Cassowary, the, 326.
Catalina Xuarez, 62.
Catorce, mines of, 24, 217.
Cayman, lake, 8.
Cempoalla, the march to, 75.
Cempoallans, the, 85.
Centralists, the, 168, 170.
Cervantes, 63.
Chalco, lake, 17; town, 30, 99.
Chapala, lake, 8.
Chapoltepec, 101.
Chevalier, M., 231.
Chiahuitzlan, 77.
Chiapas, state of, 10.
Chichemecs, the, 30.
Chihuahua, 26, 137; its salubrity, 279.
Chilpanzingo, congress of, 150, 153.
Chinampas, 17.
Chocolate, 291.
Chocollitos, the, 323, *et seq.*
Cholula, city of, 14; march to, 81; massacre of, 83.
Cholulans, their repulse, 40, 82.
Churches, 194; interior of, 203.
Clergy, the Romish, 192.
Coccus cacti, 299.

Cochineal, the, 299, *et seq.*
Cock, the, (el Gallo,) 267.
Cock-fights, 260.
Cocoyol, the, 297.
Coffre de Perote, the, 6.
Cohahuila, lake, 8; state of, 26.
Coléa de toros, 266.
Colhuacan, 30.
Colima, 5, 22.
Commerce, restrictive system of, 224, *et seq.*; result of their removal, 230.
Comonfort, Gen., 186.
Concepsion, Villa de, 237.
Concha, Gen., 154.
Convents and monasteries, 196.
Coquette, Princess Helena's, 328.
Coral tree, the, 294.
Cordilleras, the, 6, 16, 216.
Cordova, treaty of, 164.
Cortez, 3; derivation of his title, Marquis del Valle de Oaxaca, 12; his early history, 61; dispute with Velasquez, reconcilement, and advancement, 62, *et seq.*; character, 64, *et seq.*; daring disobedience, 65; voyage of discovery, 66, *et seq.*; insists on seeing Montezuma, 69; contests of his adherents with those of Velasquez, 72; revolt against the authority of Velasquez, 73; his double dealing, 77; daring stroke of policy, 78, *et seq.*; treatment of Montezuma, 87, *et seq.*; defeats Narvaez, 88; his disastrous retreat, 92, *et seq.*; proceeds against neighbouring towns, 96, *et seq.*; narrow escape of, 99, 103; detects a conspiracy, 100; estimate of, 108; recall, etc., and death, 112.
Cortez, Don Martin, 119.
Cos, Gen., 180.

Costumes, 253, *et seq.*
Cougar, the, 316.
Country sports, 265, *et seq.*
Country towns, 279.
Coyol palm, the, 297.
Cozumel, 65, *et seq.*
Cries, street, 251.
Criullas, Marquis of, 133.
Creoles, the, 145, 234.
Crocodiles, 307.
Cuautla de Amilpas, 151.
Cuernavaca, 99.
Cuitimba, river of, 19, 21.
Customs of Society, 242, *et seq.*
Cyrtochilum Bictoniense, 299.

DANCING and singing, 260.
De Croix, 133.
De la Serna, 127.
Deer, the, 317.
Del Fuerte, 7.
Diaz, Bernal, quoted, 49, 87, 102.
Diego and the Virgin, 208.
Drake, 122.
Dryiophis Acuminata, 309.
Duero, Andres de, 63.
Durango, city of, 26; insurrection in state of, 125.

ECHAVARI, 165.
Education, 249.
El Gallo, or the Cock, 267.
Elizondo, 149.
Epidendrum Aurantiacum, 299.
Erytheina, 294.
Escalante, 79, 85.
Escálona, Duke of, 128.
Etiquette, 244, *et seq.*
European politics, influence of, on Mexican affairs, 134.
Every day life in Mexico, 240.

FANNING's volunteers, 182.
Farias, Gomez, 179; his pronunciamiento, 184.
Farmers, 180.
Federal Constitution, the, 167.
Federalists, the, 168, 170, 183.
Ferdinand VII., 142.

Festivals of the Romish Church, 205.
Fête day, a, 254.
Flamebearer, the, 328.
Floating gardens, 17.
Flores, Don Manuel, 137.
"Flower of the Saints," 299.
Flowers, 297, *et seq.*
Fonseca, opposition of, 111.
Fourcroya Longæva, 299.
Fremont, 185.
French, the, and Mexico, 183.
Fresnillo, 4, 25.
Frijoles, 295.
Froebel, M., quoted, 235, 262, 311, 313, 323, *et seq.*, 326.
Frogs, the, 309, *et seq.*
Fruits, 295, *et seq.*

GAGE, Friar, quoted, 13, 125, 192; account of the cassava, 288; on the virtues of chocolate, 291, *et seq.*; 295, 305.
Galeana, 151.
Galvez, Don José, 133; Bernardo de, daughter of, 136.
Gapuchinos, 146.
Garcia Guerra, 124.
Gelves, Marquis, 127.
Gigedo, Count Revilla, 130, *et seq.*
Gigedo II., 137; character and rule of, 138., *et seq.*
Golden tree snake, 309.
Gould, quoted, 327.
Grijalva, 60, 62.
Guadalupe, cathedral of our Lady of, 208.
Guadalaxura, 22, 149,
Guanaxuato, 24, 146, 160, 221, 289.
Guatemozin, 99.
Gulf stream, the, 2.
Guarantees, the three, 162, *et seq.*
Guarda-Barranca, the, 326.
Guerrero, 163, 165; administration, 171, 174.

Guillermo, Don, 235.
Guzman, Nunez de, 112.

HACIENDAS, 261, *et seq.*
Hays, Colonel, 316.
Helps, quoted, 64.
Herraderos, 265.
Herrera, President, 185.
Hidalgo, Miguel, a leader of the insurrection, 146, *et seq.;* death of, 149.
Houses, 241, *et seq.*
Houston, Gen., 182.
Huitzilopotchli, the god, 53.
Humboldt, quoted, 18, 141; his estimate of the clergy of Mexico, 193, 222, 287, *et seq.*
Humming birds, the, 327.

IGUALA, plan of, 163, *et seq.*
Indian corn, cultivation of, and uses, 289, *et seq.*
Indians, undying hostility of, to the Spaniards, 115, 149; number in Mexico, 234; dangers from, to travellers, 274.
Inns, 276.
Insects, 299.
Insecurity of the country, 280.
Iturbide, 154; character, &c., of, 161, 167; plans of, 162, *et seq.*; president, 164; proclaimed emperor, 165; close of his career, 166.
Iturrigaray, 141.
Ixtlilxochitl, 96.
Iztaccihuatl, 5.
Iztapalapan, 97.

JACAL, the mountain, 6.
Jaguar, the, 314, *et seq.*
Jalapa, its products, 12, 185.
Jalisco, 22; Indians of, revolt, 113, 180; its natural productions, 286.
Jamaica captured, 129.
Jaral, Marquis of, 159.

Jatropha, the, 285.
Jesuits, the, 133.
Jorullo, its origin alluded to, 5; described by Humboldt, 18.
Juarez, 186.

KEARNEY, Gen., 185.
Kirby and Spence, quoted, 300.

LABORDE, career of, 222.
La Canada, mines of, 222.
La Esperanza, vein of, 223.
La Garza, 166.
La Xuage, church of, 206.
Lælia Autumnale, 299.
Langosta, the, 290, 303.
Lares, Amador de, 63.
Las Casas, quoted, 62, 67.
Las Cruces, 147.
Latter's D., sabre wing, 328.
Law Courts, 232, *et seq.*
Leonidas, 147.
Leperos, the, 191; quarter of, 241, *et seq.;* described, 256.
Lina, 160.
Lizards, 308.
Llanos, 154.
Locust, the, 290, 303.
Lorenzano, Archbishop, 135.
Los Remedios, first of, 160.

Madre de pulque, 291.
Madres del cacao, 291.
Magarino, 93.
Magdalena, port of, 27.
Maguey, the, 290, *et seq.*
Maize, cultivation and uses of, 289.
Manchester of Mexico, 13.
Mango de Claro, hacienda of, 176.
Manioc, 288.
Marina, Donna, 68.
Market, 253.
Matrimony, patroness, 210.
Marmot, the, 313.
Mayer, quoted, 12, 14, 114, 117, 136, 150, 234.

INDEX. 337

Matamoros, 151, 154.
Matamoros, 185.
Maxtla, 32.
Mayo, the, 23.
Mechoacan, 18, 299.
Mendoza, 112; made governor of Peru, 116.
Mesia, 127.
Meson, a, 277.
Mestizos, the, 234.
Mexia, 183.
Mexico, and the Mexicans—physical geography, 1, et seq.; political divisions, 10, et seq.; state and valley, 14; the capital, 16; central provinces, 23; history and character of its inhabitants, 28, et seq.; at its origin, 41; agriculture and working in precious metals, 47; merchants; domestic and social life, 48; religious system, 52, et seq.; its conquerors and conquest, 59, et seq.; siege of the city, 101; under Spanish viceroys, 110, et seq.; insurrection in, 128; auto-da-fe in, 129; development of its resources, 130; famine, 131; increase of luxury and magnificence in the capital, 135; improvidence of the people, 136; intestine strife, 145, et seq.; its constitution, how formed, 180; the people haughty and incapable, 184; war against Texas, 185; and America, 185; the unsatisfactory issue of republican government in, 186; religion, etc., 189, et seq.; the clergy, 192; the churches, 194; convents and monasteries, 196; want of enterprize on the part of the people, 230; civil condition,

232; population, and classes, 234; characteristic features of, 235, et seq.; social condition, 240, et seq.; domestic life, 247, et seq.; education, 249; streets and street cries, 251, et seq.; habits and amusements, 259, et seq.; disorganized state of the country, and its effects, 274, et seq.; misery of, due to Romish priesthood, 281; its natural productions, 284, et seq.
Mexitli, teocalli of, 17, 41.
Mina, Xavier, expedition of, 158, et seq.; death of, 160.
Mines, their produce in early ages, 218; mining adventures, 220, et seq.; future prospects, 224.
Mint, established at Mexico, 113.
Miramon, 186.
Mocking bird, the, 324, et seq.
Moctezuma, the, 7.
Montagno, 170.
Montejo, 71.
Monterey, viceroy, 26; Count of, 123; 185.
Montezuma, 38, 40; mode of life described, 49, et seq.; embassy of, to Cortez, 69, 80, et seq.; his reply to the demand of Cortez, 70, et seq; plot of, 82; fall of, 87, et seq.; death of, 91.
Mor Pardina, 299.
Morelia, 21.
Morelos, 151, et seq.
Munoz, 120, et seq.

NAHUATLACS, 30.
Narvaez, 88, 94.
Negrete, 167.
New Leon. (See Nuevo.)
New Mexico, 185.
New Spain, 60, 122.
Nezahualcoyotl, his romantic

Z

history, 32, *et seq.*; specimen of his muse, 34; his wealth, 35; his character, 36, *et seq.*; specimen of poetry, 58.
Nezahualpilli, birth of, 38; death, 39.
Nopal, the, 300.
Nuevo Leon, 25; mine of, 132, 137, 160.
Nunez, Vasco, 60.

OAXACA, 12, 180, 299.
Obregon, 221.
Ocelot, the, 316.
O'Donoju, 163.
Olid, 101.
Olmedo, Father, 91.
Oncidium Ornithorhyncum, 298.
Opossum, the Virginian, 318.
Orchids, the, 298.
Organo, the, 296.
Orizaba, peak of, 5, 153.
Otero, 222.
Otomies, the, 31, 123.
Our Lady de los Remedios, 14, 147, 207; legend of, 209.
Our Lady of Guadalupe, 207.
Ovando, 61.
Owlets, 313.
Oaxaca, 153.
Oyamel, the, 6.

PALMAR, 152.
Palomo, the, 261.
Panuco, the, 7.
Papal Bulls, taxes on, 228.
Paredes, Gen., 185.
Parents and children, relation of, 248.
Parras, lake, 8.
Parrot tribe, 323.
Partridge, the, 322.
Pascuaro, lake, 8.
Pasco, 17, 255.
Pedraza, 170, 175.
Penance, public, 211.
Peonage, 235.
Peralta, Gaston de, 119.

Peru, 116.
Pestilence, terrible, 121.
Philip II., 17.
Picaluga, 174.
Pine apples, 296.
Pizarro, 116.
Plaza de toros, 265.
Plaza mayor, the, 17.
Popocateptl, 5.
Population, 234.
Prairie dog, 313, *et seq.*
Prescott, quoted, 29, 34, 44, *et seq.*, 58, 87, 99.
Prickly pear, 295
Princess Helena's Coquette, 328.
Prisons, 233.
Processions, religious, 202.
Provincias internas, 9.
Puebla, natural advantages of the state, 13, 180.
Pueblana peasant, costume of the, 254.
Pulque, 290.
Puma, the, 316.
Pyramid of Cholula, 14, 82.

QUADRUPEDS, 310, *et seq.*
Quail, the, 322.
Quauhpopoca, 87.
Quebradillas, mine of, 223.
Queretaro, 20, 23.
Quetzalcoatl, temple of, 14, 82; the god, 53.

RACOON, the, 319, *et seq.*
Rancheros, 176.
Rayon, 149.
Regla, Count de, 221.
Remedios, Virgin de los, 14, 147, 207; legend of, 209.
Repartimientos, 113, 123.
Reptiles, 304, *et seq.*
Rescatadors, 220.
Rhinophryne, the, 310.
Rhinophrynus Dorsalis, 310.
Rio Balsas, 7.
Rio Grande del Norte, 7.

Robbers, 274, et seq.
Robinson, quoted, 157, 180.
Romanism, the creed of Mexico, 168; as it is in Mexico, 191, et seq.; festivals, 205; intolerance of the priesthood, 281.
Ruby-throat, the, 329.
Rufous flamebearer, 328.
Ruxton, quoted, 22, 24, et seq., 206, 239, 275, 278, 286.

SABRE-WING, 328.
Sacrifices, human, 54, et seq.
"Sad night," the, 94.
Saltillo, 149.
San Augustin de las Cucoas, 260.
San Christobal, 15, 98, 155.
San Domingo, convent of, 177.
Sandoval, 97, 101, 114.
San Juan de Ulua, 114; garrison of, 171.
San Luis Potosi, 24, 185.
San Pedro, 19, 21.
San Lorenzo, 124.
San Jacinto, battle, 182.
San Xavier, ravine of, 222.
Santander, the, 7.
Santa Anna, 165, 170, 175; principal facts of his career, 178, et seq.; elected president, 179; capture of, 182; declares for Bustamente, 184; meets Gen. Taylor, 185; decline of his popularity, 186.
Santa Clara, convent, 23.
Santa Fé; fall of, 129.
Santa Ines, 21.
Santa Lucia, 210.
Santa Theresa, order of, 212.
Santiago, the, 7.
Scavengers of the streets, 320.
Scenery, its beauty and diversity, 285, et seq.
Scott Gen., 185.
Selasphorous Rufus, 328
Servants, 246.
Sierra Altamira, 4.

Sierra Madre, 4.
Silver mines, 216, et seq.; produce in early ages, 218; extraordinary results of, 221; future prospects of, 224.
Sinaloa, state of, 22.
Smoking, 259.
Sombrerete, 25.
Sombrero, 159.
Sonora, state, 22.
Soto la Marina, 158, 167.
Spaniards, conquest of Mexico by the, 59, et seq.; rule by viceroys, 110, et seq.
Squier, quoted, 294, et seq., 302, et seq.
Street cries, 251.
Streets of Mexico, 253, 256.
Suce-fleurs-royal, 328.

TABASCO, 7, 10; Rio de, 67.
Tabascans, the, defeat of and submission, 67, et seq.
Tacubaya, 18.
Tacuba, 98.
Tamaulipas, 7, 11.
Tamora, 128..
Tampico, 7, 11, 178.
Tanga, mount, 299.
Tapioca, 288.
Tasco, 222.
Taylor, Gen., 185.
Tehuacan, 153.
Tenochtitlan, 41.
Tepanecs, the, 32.
Teran, Gen., 156.
Terceros, 221.
Teuhtlile, 69.
Texas, 137, 180, et seq.; seek to enter American Union, 185.
Tezcatlepoca, feast of, 55.
Tezcuco, lake, 15, 96; city, 18, 31, 98.
Theobroma, 293.
Thompson, Waddy, 206.
Tiger cat, the, 316.
Tlascala, 30, (meaning of the

name,) 39; bishop of, 128.
Tlascalans, the, 39; united to the Spaniards, 80, 94, *et seq.*
Toltecs, the, 29.
Toluca, 5; plan of, 180.
Torquemada, 113.
Torres, 159.
Tortillas, how made, 264, 295.
Tortoises, 305, *et seq.*
Totonacs, the, defend their deities, 78.
Towns, the, 261, *et seq.*, 279, *et seq.*
Trade, 224, *et seq.* (See Commerce).
Travelling, 270, *et seq.*; discomforts of, 273, *et seq.*
Trochilus Colubris, 329.
Truck system, 231.
Truxillo, 147.
Tula, the, 15; city, 29.
Tumba, 18.
Tuna, the, 295.
Turtle, the, 305, *et seq.*
Tuxtla, 4.

UNITED States and Mexico, 185.
Urrea, Gen., 184.
Usumasinta, the, 7.
Utrecht, peace of, 225.

"VAGABOND Life in Mexico," quoted, 217, 242.
Valderrama, 117.
Valenciana, Count of, 221.
Valenciana vein, 221.
Valladolid, 154.
Valle, Marquis del, 118; acquitted, 120.
Velasco, 116; death of, 117.
Velasco, governor of New Spain, 122.
Velasquez, 60, *et seq.*; contest between his adherents and those of Cortez, 72; sends troops to arrest Cortez, 88; opposition of, 111.
Venegas, 146, 152.
Venta, 278.
Vera Cruz, 9; state and port of, 11; the city founded, 73, 77; capture of the fort, 183.
Vera Paz, 116, 328.
Veta de la Biscaina, 221.
Veta Madre, 24, 216.
Victoria, Guadalupe, 151, 153; fidelity of the Indians, 156, *et seq.*, 163, 165; declared president, 169.
Villafana, 101.
Virginia deer, the, 317.
Virginian opossum, 318, *et seq.*
Volcanoes, 4.
Vultures, 321, *et seq.*

WHEELBARROW not to be found in Mexico, 231.
Wilson, quoted, 325.
Wood's "Natural History," quoted, 309.

XALTOCAN, fall of, 98.
Xochimilco, 16, 30, 99.
Xolotl, 30; his death and burial, 31.
Xuarez, Catalina, 62.

YAGUI, the, 7, 23.
Yucatan, discovery of, 62, *et seq.*, 180.

ZACATECAS, 25, 180, 223.
Zahuapan, lake, 97.
Zavala, 170.
Zitacuaro, 150.
Zoloc, 101.
Zopilote, the, 321, *et seq.*
Zumpango, 15.
Zuniga, 128.

PUBLICATIONS

OF THE

RELIGIOUS TRACT SOCIETY.

ARCTIC DISCOVERY AND ADVENTURE. Royal 18mo. With a Map. 3s. 6d., cloth boards.

BRAZIL: its History, Natural Productions, Habits and customs of the Natives, &c. Map and numerous Engravings. Fcp. 8vo., 4s., cloth boards.

OUR HOME ISLANDS. By the Rev. THOMAS MILNER, M.A., F.R.G.S. Royal 18mo. Each 2s. 6d., cloth boards.

 I.—THEIR NATURAL FEATURES.
 II.—THEIR PRODUCTIVE INDUSTRY.
 III.—THEIR PUBLIC WORKS.
 Each Volume is complete in itself.

INDIA: an Historical Sketch. By the Rev. GEORGE TREVOR, M.A., Canon of York, late Chaplain of the Madras Establishment. With a Map. Royal 18mo., 3s., cloth boards.

INDIA: its Natives and Missions. By the Rev. G. TREVOR, M.A. Cloth boards, 3s.

THE OTTOMAN EMPIRE. The Sultans, the Territory, and the People. Royal 18mo. With a Map. 2s. 6d., cloth boards.

JAPAN OPENED. Compiled chiefly from the Narrative of the American Expedition to Japan. Engravings. Royal 18mo. 3s., cloth boards.

RUSSIA, ANCIENT AND MODERN. By the Rev. GEORGE TREVOR, M.A., Canon of York; Author of "India," &c. Royal 18mo. With Two Maps, 4s., cloth boards.

THE SPANISH PENINSULA. A Sketch of its Past History, Present Condition, and Future Prospects. Royal 18mo. With Maps, 3s., cloth boards.

EDUCATIONAL WORKS.

THE HISTORY OF ENGLAND; from the Invasions of Julius Cæsar to the Year 1852. By THOMAS MILNER, A.M., F.R.G.S. 12mo. With Two Maps. 5s., cloth boards.

THE ELEMENTS OF ENGLISH HISTORY. By J. C. CURTIS, B.A.. 1s., limp cloth.

THE HISTORY OF GREECE: from the Earliest Times to A.D. 1833. By Professor STOWELL, D.D. 12mo. With a Map. 2s. 6d., cloth boards.

THE HISTORY OF ROME: from the Earliest Times to the Fall of the Empire. By THOMAS MILNER, A.M., F.R.G.S. 12mo. With Three Maps. 3s., cloth boards.

A UNIVERSAL GEOGRAPHY, in Four Parts: Historical, Mathematical, Physical, and Political. By THOMAS MILNER, A.M., F.R.G.S. Illustrated by Ten Coloured Maps. 12mo. 5s., cloth boards.

THE BIBLE HANDBOOK: an Introduction to the Study of Sacred Scripture. By JOSEPH ANGUS, D.D , Member of the Royal Asiatic Society. 12mo. edition. With a Map. 5s., cloth boards; 7s. half-bound. 8vo. Edition, with Engravings. 10s., cloth boards.

PALEY'S HORÆ PAULINÆ. With Notes and a Supplementary Treatise, entitled HORÆ APOSTOLICÆ. By the Rev. T. R. BIRKS, A.M. With a Map. 12mo. 3s., cloth boards.

PALEY'S EVIDENCES OF CHRISTIANITY. With Introduction, Notes, and Supplement. By the Rev. T. R. BIRKS, A.M. 12mo. 3s., cloth boards.

THE ANALOGY OF RELIGION to the Constitution and Course of Nature. Also FIFTEEN SERMONS. By JOSEPH BUTLER, LL.D. With a Life of the Author, a copious ANALYSIS, Notes, and Indexes. By JOSEPH ANGUS, D.D. 3s. 6d., cloth boards.

THE ELEMENTS OF MORAL SCIENCE. By FRANCIS WAYLAND, D.D., late President of Brown University. With Notes and Analysis. By JOSEPH ANGUS, D.D. Author of "The Bible Handbook," &c. 12mo. 3s., cloth.

PUBLICATIONS OF

THE BOOK OF PSALMS. According to the Authorized Version: arranged in Parallelisms. With a Preface and Explanatory Notes. 3s., extra cloth boards; 3s. 6d. with curtain flaps to cover edges.

MEMOIR OF AN INDIAN CHAPLAIN, the Rev. CHARLES CHURCH, M.A., of the Madras Establishment of the East India Company. By the Rev. JAMES HOUGH, A.M. Fcap. 8vo., 2s., cloth boards.

MEMOIRS OF THE LIFE AND LABOURS of the Rev. SAMUEL MARSDEN, of Paramatta, and of his early connexion with the Mission to New Zealand and Tahiti. Edited by the Rev. J. B. MARSDEN, M.A. Portrait. Royal 18mo. 3s., cloth boards; 3s. 6d. cloth boards, gilt edges.

THE CHRISTIAN CHAPLET: a Wreath of Prose, Poetry, and Art. Fcap. 8vo. Eight beautiful Coloured Engravings. Elegantly bound, gilt edges, 4s.

THE CORONAL: or, Prose, Poetry, and Art. A Book for all Seasons, at Home and Abroad. With Eight beautiful Engravings in Oil Colours. Fcap. 8vo. 4s., elegantly bound, gilt edges.

THE CHRISTIAN WREATH OF PROSE, POETRY, and ART. With Eight Coloured Engravings. Fcap. 8vo. 4s., extra boards, gilt edges.

FLOWERS FROM MANY LANDS. A Christian Companion for Hours of Recreation. In Prose and Verse. With superior Engravings of Flowers in Oil Colours. 4s., elegantly bound.

THE CHRISTIAN GARLAND. A Companion for Leisure Hours. Coloured Engravings. Fcap. 8vo. 4s., extra boards, gilt.

THE ROSE BUD. A Christian Gift to the Young. Fine Wood and Coloured Engravings. Royal 16mo. 4s., extra boards, gilt edges.

THE ROCK OF AGES: or, Scripture Testimony to the Eternal Godhead of the Father, and of the Son, and of the Holy Ghost. By EDWARD H. BICKERSTETH, M.A., Incumbent of Christ Church, Hampstead. A New and Revised Edition. 4s., cloth boards.

THE RELIGIOUS TRACT SOCIETY.

MEMOIR OF OLD HUMPHREY. With Gleanings from his Portfolio, in Prose and Verse. 18mo. Portrait. A new edition. 2s., cloth boards.

THE LIFE OF AMELIA OPIE. By Miss BRIGHTWELL. With Portrait. Fcap. 8vo. 2s. 6d., cloth boards.

THE NEW BIBLICAL ATLAS AND SCRIPTURE GAZETTEER. Containing Twelve superior Maps and Plans, together with Descriptive Letterpress. Super-royal 8vo. 2s. 6d., plain; 4s., outlines coloured; 6s. 6d. on imperial drawing paper, full coloured, and bound in boards.

A HARMONY OF THE FOUR GOSPELS; in the Authorized Version. Following the Harmony of the Gospels in Greek. By EDWARD ROBINSON, D.D., LL.D. Two Maps. Royal 12mo. 3s., boards.

A BIBLICAL CYCLOPÆDIA; or, Dictionary of Eastern Antiquities, Geography, Natural History, &c. Edited by JOHN EADIE, D.D., LL.D. With Maps and Pictorial Illustrations. 8vo. 7s. 6d., cloth boards; 9s. 6d., half-bound; 11s. 6d., calf.

THE LAND OF PROMISE; or, a Topographical Description of the Principal Places in Palestine. 12mo. Map and numerous Engravings. By JOHN KITTO, D.D., F.S.A. 5s., extra cloth boards.

THE HEAVENS AND THE EARTH. By the Rev. T. MILNER, M.A. With Engravings. Royal 18mo. 2s. 6d., cloth boards; 3s. extra boards, gilt.

A HISTORY OF THE VAUDOIS CHURCH, AND OF THE VAUDOIS OF PIEDMONT. By ANTOINE MONASTIER, formerly Pastor in the Canton de Vaude. 12mo. Frontispiece. 4s., cloth boards.

THE ATONEMENT; being Four Discourses by CHARLES LORD BISHOP OF GLOUCESTER AND BRISTOL, Dr. CHALMERS, W. ARCHER BUTLER, M.A., and ROBERT HALL, M.A. Fcap. 8vo. 1s. 6d., cloth boards.

REGENERATION; being Five Discourses by DANIEL WILSON (Bishop of Calcutta), DANIEL DE SUPERVILLE, Dr. GEORGE PAYNE, Dr. JOHN CAIRD, and R. H. SEELEY. Fcap. 8vo. 2s. cloth boards.

www.ingramcontent.com/pod-product-compliance
Lightning Source LLC
Chambersburg PA
CBHW031849220426
43663CB00006B/558